THE HONOR DRESS OF THE MOVEMENT

A CULTURAL HISTORY OF HITLER'S BROWN SHIRT UNIFORM, 1920–1933

The Honor Dress of the Movement

TORSTEN HOMBERGER

UNIVERSITY OF MASSACHUSETTS PRESS AMHERST AND BOSTON

Printed in the United States of America

ISBN 978-1-62534-605-6 (paper); 604-9 (hardcover)

Designed by Deste Roosa
Set in Sabon LT Pro, Futura PT, and Potsdam
Printed and bound by Books International, Inc.

Cover design by Derek Thornton / Notch Design
Cover photo: *Nazi Germany, German Nazi activist Horst Wessel marching at the head of his storm troopers in Nuremberg, 1929*. Colored photo. Courtesy INTERFOTO / Personalities, Alamy.com.

Library of Congress Cataloging-in-Publication Data
Names: Homberger, Torsten, 1976– author.
Title: The honor dress of the movement : a cultural history of Hitler's brown shirt uniform, 1920–1933 / Torsten Homberger.
Other titles: Cultural history of Hitler's brown shirt uniform, 1920–1933
Description: Amherst : University of Massachusetts Press, 2021. | Includes bibliographical references and index.
Identifiers: LCCN 2021017185 (print) | LCCN 2021017186 (ebook) | ISBN 9781625346049 (hardcover) | ISBN 9781625346056 (paperback) | ISBN 9781613768808 (ebook) | ISBN 9781613768815 (ebook)
Subjects: LCSH: Nationalsozialistische Deutsche Arbeiter-Partei. Sturmabteilung—Uniforms. | Nationalsozialistische Deutsche Arbeiter-Partei. Sturmabteilung—History. | Paramilitary forces—Germany—History. | Germany—History—1918–1933.
Classification: LCC DD253.7 .H66 2021 (print) | LCC DD253.7 (ebook) | DDC 324.243/0238—dc23
LC record available at https://lccn.loc.gov/2021017185
LC ebook record available at https://lccn.loc.gov/2021017186

British Library Cataloguing-in-Publication Data
A catalog record for this book is available from the British Library.

A portion of chapter two was previously published in an earlier form as "Nazi Dress: Hitler's Stormtroopers and Appearance Management, 1921–1933," (coauthored with Linda Arthur-Bradley) in *Critical Studies in Men's Fashion* 2, nos. 2 & 3 (2015): 183–97.

FOR MY FAMILY.
ESPECIALLY MY LATE GRANDFATHER,
WHO MADE THIS PROJECT POSSIBLE,
AND MY WONDERFUL WIFE,
WHOSE ENCOURAGEMENT ALLOWED ME TO FINISH IT.

CONTENTS

Acknowledgments ix

Introduction
HITLER AND HIS STORMTROOPERS 1

Chapter One
THE MILITARIZATION OF POLITICAL CULTURE IN WEIMAR GERMANY, 1918–1933 15

Chapter Two
FROM A TROPICAL TUNIC TO THE BROWN SHIRT 31

Chapter Three
THE BROWN GARMENT OF HONOR, MATERIAL CULTURE, AND SOCIAL CONTROL 56

Chapter Four
ASSEMBLING THE TROOPERS—THE LOGISTICS OF MILITARIZATION 76

Chapter Five
THE PROFESSIONALIZATION OF A CIVIL WAR ARMY 95

Chapter Six
CLASSLESS HEROES—THE CENTRALITY OF THE BROWN SHIRT IN MYTHIC NAZI FILM AND LITERATURE 107

Chapter Seven
HAMBURG, 1921–1933, A CASE STUDY 131

Conclusion
WEIMAR CULTURE AND THE END OF WEIMAR DEMOCRACY 181

Notes 185

Index 205

ACKNOWLEDGMENTS

This book did not start out in its current form. It began as a doctoral dissertation and changed considerably through numerous conversations, collaborations, and advice over the years that contributed considerably to my understanding. All mistakes and misunderstandings in this book, however, are my own.

I am grateful to the archivists in Berlin, Koblenz, and Hamburg who provided access to valuable primary sources. I am especially indebted to an archivist in Berlin, who I unfortunately only know by last name. Herr Schneidereit allowed me access to source material that had been reserved by another researcher. Since that researcher did not visit the archive during my stay, Herr Schneidereit made the decision to grant me access the material. To this day, I very much appreciate his kindness.

I am also thankful to the educators and historians who read the manuscript, in whole or in parts, and who offered valuable criticism and encouragement, including Raymond Sun, Jesse Spohnholz, Linda Arthur Bradley, Andrew Wackerfuss, Timothy Brown, Bruce Campbell, Geoffrey Giles, Eleanor Hancock, and Pamela Swett. I am especially grateful to Daniel Siemens, who could have covered the material in his own book yet allowed a junior scholar to pursue this part of SA history, and to Eve Rosenhaft and Peter Fritzsche, who provided invaluable input during the final review stages of peer review.

THE HONOR DRESS OF THE MOVEMENT

Introduction

HITLER AND HIS STORMTROOPERS

In a back room of the German Historical Museum archive in Berlin, locked in a small fire-safe vault, is a collection of original Nazi uniforms. The archive, in fact, houses a remarkable collection of artifacts that are not frequently on display. Closed to the public, its contents are tightly guarded by curators. To earn approval to view such historical relics, a researcher must devote months to a chain of email communication and letters of recommendation that establish credentials. To weed out all but the most serious, this is followed by personal visits and on-site interviews before a researcher gets final approval to enter the vault. After such a drawn-out process, the museum staff open the doors only for short, supervised research visits.

Those lucky enough to make it inside the vault see that it contains a few shirts and breeches hanging neatly on hangers, a typical brown coffee-can-shaped cap with a brown visor, and a brown leather belt with shoulder strap, among other Nazi artifacts. One set of shirt and breeches is made of the same cotton material and is matching in hue. The keen researcher's eye also catches a high-end pair of riding breeches made out of sturdier corduroy material. The corduroy does not quite match the hue of the thinner cotton. It is darker and more vibrant. The exposure to light faded the cotton faster than the corduroy. The brown fabric of the matching shirt and riding pants looks faded and worn. These textiles, while carefully preserved, are old and have a musty odor. When taken off their hangers and laid out, one recognizes that shirt and breeches were tailored for a tight fit. This was the uniform of a fit, athletic man. The riding pants themselves are blemished. The stains, most likely sweat stains, on the lower thigh, are still present where the breeches were tucked into a pair of high boots.

Today, this single old uniform set looks wrinkled, tainted, and lifeless. It is nothing but a rather unassuming artifact studied by historians in the back rooms of archives. Nevertheless, in the later years of the Weimar Republic from 1926 to 1933, these shirts and breeches gave life to fascist symbolism and established an effervescent fascist style. Scores of young men marching in disciplined columns for Hitler's National Socialist German Worker's Party (Nationalsozialistische

Deutsche Arbeiterpartei, or NSDAP), or Nazi Party, wore bright, new, clean, and pressed uniforms of just this type.

In fact, by January 1933, the brown-clad columns of Hitler's Stormtroopers (Sturmabteilung, or SA), the paramilitary arm of the Nazi Party, had acquired potent cultural meaning. Wearing their trademark Brown Shirts, the men of the SA became the living symbol of the brown Nazi movement in Weimar Germany. Those who study the end of the Weimar Republic agree that in 1932, the SA helped carry Hitler to power in the last democratic elections of the Weimar Republic. By then, the SA had about four hundred thousand men, which was more than the combined number of regular German military and police forces.[1] This book seeks to disclose the background, the development, and the use of the brown uniform by the Stormtroopers in the service of Hitler and his movement. The history of the SA uniform informs an extended analysis of Weimar politics. Its use tells us a great deal about the connections among fashion, consumerism, and fascist utilization of culture. This is highly relevant as the rise of fascism is noticeable once again.

This book started with an apparent contradiction in the scholarly consensus on the SA. The relevant scholarship suggests that the SA provoked violence. They provoked their opponents into attacking SA men, afterward claiming that they were merely defending themselves, despite triggering the initial confrontation. This tactic, according to Peter Longerich, demonstrated the incompetence of the state to maintain order and thus paved the way for a Nazi takeover in the name of stability.[2] Yet, following this line of argumentation, violence seemed contradictory since large sections of Weimar society desired order—not chaos. For the traditionally liberal city of Hamburg especially, this situation seems paradoxical given the Nazis' electoral performance prior to Adolf Hitler's consolidation of power.[3] This contradiction, however, can be explained by framing the analytical focus on positive image construction within the context of violence and the Nazi rise to power. The SA also acted disciplined when in public, which made the right impression on conservatives and other potential supporters. Longerich views this dual character of violence and discipline as simply the adaptability of the SA in different locations.[4] Thomas Balistier develops this argument further. The SA, according to Balistier, epitomized a contradiction between violent indiscipline and orderly discipline. Indeed, they made violence attractive. This argument about duality is promising. Yet Balistier upholds it by relatively weak evidence in the form of a discussion of sensual aesthetics based on body posture, literary criticism of song lyrics, and psychoanalysis.[5]

This brief discussion of the seeming contradiction in the relevant scholarship on the SA brings the significance and context of this book into its appropriate framework. This book will provide cultural historical evidence as to how the SA constructed their positive dual image, which led to Nazi successes in the polls by the early 1930s. The key to reconciling the dichotomy between violence and discipline, or order and disorder, is the uniform of the SA. The uniform embodied SA duality. In essence, it served two functions. First, it had a signal function that triggered violence among other politicized groups with incompatible ideology, such as the communists. During clash violence with opponents, the uniform made the men look intimidating and provided hidden protection. The second function of the uniform also relates to appearance and impressions. They made the men look neat and athletic to potential supporters. A Hamburg case study confirms that this was effective. Despite rising SA violence, Hamburg's bourgeois press reflected the belief that the SA represented order and discipline, while the leftist paramilitaries represented public disorder and criminality. This book thus demonstrates how fascists combined material culture and politics during the Weimar era in image-construction processes. The uniform is an illuminating way to ascertain the duality of the SA, its broad appeal, and its distinctiveness regarding the other paramilitary groups.

This book is therefore not an organizational history of the SA, but rather a cultural history of the SA uniform. The current success of Daniel Siemens's comprehensive monograph on the SA validates the need for a more nuanced analysis of SA culture.[6] Siemens investigates the early history of the SA and its loss of power in 1934. He adds to the analysis of the SA by highlighting its uses and functions after 1934, as, for instance, in the German-occupied territories, and by showing how the SA contributed to the crimes of the Shoah. Siemens also adds an investigation into how the SA transformed into a mass political organization with a membership in the millions by briefly exploring SA subculture. This book's approach to this history aligns itself and exists in discourse with a growing body of literature based on nuanced cultural approaches.

One example of this cultural approach to SA history is Andrew Wackerfuss's monograph *Stormtrooper Families*.[7] Wackerfuss presents a history of the SA and its subculture, within the city of Hamburg.

His case study focuses on SA publications, the relationships between individual troopers and their leadership in the city, and the uses and function of violence. Wackerfuss's largest contribution adds a gendered component to the study of social networks and Stormtrooper subculture by exploring the history of gay men within the organization. His approach, however, reveals contradictions. The men of the SA were both rebels and defenders of traditional norms. They acted violently, yet ultimately about one-third of Hamburg's electorate voted for the Nazi Party, making it a mass party incorporating many elements of Hamburg's citizens. Between 1929 and 1933, the Protestant middle-class vote moved from the moderate parties to the Nazis. This inconsistency can also be viewed as an inherent contradiction in Weimar society. Weimar politics embraced fascist ideals, yet Weimar culture, even the subculture of the SA, was rather progressive.

Although slightly more dated, Irene Guenther's monograph on female fashion during the Third Reich indicates how these apparent contradictions can be explained through successful image construction.[8] During their rule, the Nazis failed in their attempts to construct a successful female image that not only complied with their ideology but also promoted German nationalism and established Germany as a leading fashion producer. Guenther maintains that females in Nazi Germany challenged a top-down image construction process from the bottom up, rendering it unsuccessful. Nazi ideology clashed with the daily lives of German women. Guenther's book demonstrates that Hitler did not formulate a coherent female fashion policy. This argument also reflects the notion that Nazi politics and policies were restrictive, whereas women used fashion and thus material culture to counter these restrictions.

This book's focus is not on women, but rather on effective male image-construction processes in a similar top-down manner by the Nazis during the Weimar period. Modeled on Guenther's approach using clothing, this method can resolve the contradictions laid out by Wackerfuss's subcultural methodology. Hitler, indeed, formulated coherent and detailed guidelines when it came to the dress of the SA. During the Weimar period, Nazi ideology and dress did not clash with but rather mirrored the preferences of some conservative sections of society. Thus, Nazi electoral gains do not need to be framed as an irreconcilable contradiction.

To explore the cultural history of the SA uniform, it is opportune to lean on the work of scholars who have combined the overarching methodological categories of modernity and changing aesthetics to highlight the connections between the materiality of Weimar culture and politics. These connections open inroads for the use of additional critical categories such as gender, uniforms, and men's fashion to explicate right-wing extremism in Weimar political culture.

Before the Industrial Revolution and the modernization of society, slenderness was viewed as a sign of vulnerability accompanying malnutrition. Modernity reversed this view. Medical discussions in the twentieth century, for instance, assessed opulence negatively. New cultural norms set by modern icons such as movie stars slowly changed the accepted norm to slender figures. During the twentieth century, these developments contributed to the growth of a specialized beauty industry. Modern visual media then encourages individual identification with the given norm and body modification.[9] Changing cultural norms were thus related to capitalism, consumerism, and mass media.

Symbolic and performative actions in Weimar political culture, as, for instance, rallies and marches, were therefore based on and measured against a highly defined cultural concept of beauty. The concepts of aesthetics, material culture, and political culture are closely related. An investigation into political marches, rallies, sports, and national festivals reveals that Weimar Germany indeed had a vibrant political culture in support of the democratic project. The political parties of the center-Left also fostered the development of mass consumption to strengthen capitalism and with it the liberal democratic system. The combination of political and cultural narratives demonstrates that parties across the entire political spectrum used consumerism for their own, oftentimes conflicting, ends.[10]

It is also important to recognize the connections between consumer culture and radical politics during the Weimar era. Not all political uses of culture and consumerism supported democracy. The development of modern consumer culture and the demise of liberal democracy in Germany occurred simultaneously. The communists despised consumerism. Nevertheless, the communists also used marketing and advertising to uphold communist subculture. The Nazis officially opposed modern consumerism, as their boycott of Jewish-owned department stores in April 1933 clearly showed. Just like the communists, however, the Nazis maintained an ambiguous relationship with consumerism. They, for instance, exploited the smoking habits of their SA troopers.[11]

This relationship resulted from the Nazi attitude toward modernity and from experiences in the First World War. Traditional family ties and gender roles seemed to erode in a modernizing world. In this situation, hypermasculinity became the hallmark of the ideal male.[12] The First World War furthermore strengthened this trend and introduced millions of European men to the functions and uses of uniforms. Heightened anxiety about international conflicts, hypernationalism, and association with values such as discipline, toughness, and masculinity before and after the outbreak of the First World War resulted in an exaggerated uniform fashion trend in civilian society.[13] The use of uniforms in industrialized societies entailed a form of social control when bureaucratic organizations became more important for the functioning of theses societies than earlier forms of associations, such as feudal or family relations. Police forces and armies thus stand for order and high aptitude.[14] The First World War thus allowed for a combination of gender ideals and material culture. The conflict put a mark on men's fashion during the 1920s and 1930s.[15] Military style became high male fashion during, and after, the First World War. The military uniform, specifically, became a sign of effectiveness and power and thus influenced male fashion.[16]

Ultimately, a cultural historical methodology is timely because it is informed by a fresh approach to the history of the Weimar Republic. The well-established paradigm that the politics of the Weimar Republic was backward looking, antidemocratic, and "bad," whereas Weimar culture was advanced, democratic, and "good," is dated because it obscures how interrelated both areas of the republic were.[17] The methodology of this book is in line with other historians whose work is aimed at broadening the concept of Weimar culture.

Anthony McElligott, for instance, analyzes the notion of authority to highlight continuities between the German Empire, the Weimar Republic, and the Nazi dictatorship. He maintains that the quasi rule of the military under Paul von Hindenburg and Erich Ludendorff from 1916 to 1918 caused a redefinition of state authority. It was this process, which continued throughout the Weimar period, that allowed Hitler to claim sole authority within Germany in 1933. McElligott views the Weimar era as an integral part of this development and points to the contested nature of authority. The Weimar state sought to establish its own authority through the creation and maintenance of democratic traditions, as, for instance, reoccurring republican festivals that combined democracy with authoritarianism. According to McElligott, Weimar politics was as experimental as Weimar culture and allowed for a "cultural authoritarianism" that ultimately paved the way for Hitler and the Nazis.[18] Weimar culture was thus more complex than previously assumed.

Like Anthony McElligott, Nadine Rossol highlights continuities between the culture of the Weimar Republic and Nazi culture. Rossol specifically analyzes festivities and political symbolism and argues that the Nazis did not create the aesthetic staging of mass events. Rather, from the mid-1920s onward, the republican Weimar government established political symbolism, aesthetics, and a festive culture that included mass spectacle based on marching uniformed masses and a strong sense of nationalism.[19] Rossol concludes that the Nazis then simply expanded the already established traditions when they themselves took over the state and rebranded political spectacle in the name of fascist ideals after 1933. Weimar culture, then, shaped the political culture of Nazism.

As McElligott and Rossol illustrate, the republican leadership embraced authoritarianism and nationalism. This book thus contributes to a reevaluation of Weimar political culture through a focus on Nazi culture. The Nazis developed their own aesthetics over the course of the Weimar years. The Nazis originated in, and were an integral part of, Weimar's political culture. A dual focus on festivities, like propaganda marches, as well as incidences of political violence not only widens our concept of Weimar culture but also historicizes the concept to put it into its proper historical context.[20]

Of course, this investigation also relies on the findings of scholars who have defined the role and the forms of political violence in Weimar Germany. The works of both Eve Rosenhaft and Dirk Schumann are crucial in defining this phenomenon. Dirk Schumann argues that after the unsuccessful and bloody attempt of German communists at a revolution in March 1924, in Saxony, "political violence took the form of smaller clashes during which the use of firearms and serious consequences tended to be rare." Violence oftentimes occurred when marching groups were attacked or heckled. In such scenarios, the police oftentimes became a third party. Brawls in the streets and in meeting halls were commonplace. This form of violence could occur spontaneously—for instance, when opposing political groups clashed during marches or while disseminating election material. It could also take the form of planned attacks on political opponents.[21] The actual violence, however, was marked by a rather short duration and a small number of participants.[22] Rosenhaft and Schumann apply the term *clash violence* for this form of a public, ritualized, and political violence. The term is used in this analysis as well.[23]

From 1924 onward, clash violence became a common occurrence in the streets of Weimar Germany, as spaces where mass politics was lived out.[24] It was the parties of the Right and their respective paramilitaries and veterans' organizations that kept the streets a contested space.[25] Their increasing attempts to appropriate the streets as places for political activism caused clash violence with the Marxists, who originally had claimed this public space as their own.[26] Frictions only heightened because the paramilitaries on the Right considered it their duty to eliminate Marxism without willingness to compromise.[27] In this situation, the Marxist parties reacted and established political paramilitaries of their own in order to defend themselves against rising violence from the Right.[28] Right-wing paramilitaries were therefore novel in giving bourgeois sections of society access to the streets as a political arena.[29] Clash violence, in turn, became a constant factor in Weimar politics because of the actions of the Right.[30] The radical parties on the Left and the Right, the communists and the Nazis, gained more and more members in their respective paramilitaries in the wake of the economic collapse of 1929 and were responsible for most occurrences of clash violence from that time on.[31] The drastic intensification of violence after 1930, however, can be attributed to the efforts of the Nazis to take over Marxist neighborhoods in the cities of Weimar Germany.[32]

Regarding this book's analysis, Rosenhaft's finding that the communists' party base simply reacted to the violence from the Nazis and that this violence was solely defensive and thus justified is of importance. Schuman agrees that it was the right-wing paramilitaries that caused the explosion of violence after 1930. He, nevertheless, makes the important distinction that Marxist rhetoric, with its constant emphasis on violence in propaganda, was also a reason for the explosion of violence.[33] The Marxists put the fear of revolution into bourgeois circles and thus were equally responsible for right-wing reactions. This book is a contribution to this ongoing historiographical debate on political violence in Weimar Germany. By focusing on SA tactics, the available documentary evidence demonstrates that the Nazis provoked violence, yet the violence was initiated in many instances by the communists. This distinction is important because the Nazis exploited this fact in the bourgeois press by arguing that they merely defended themselves as well as bourgeois norms and values. This book thus shows that material culture, in the form of the brown SA uniform, was central to fascist tactics.

It is important to note that the uniform of the SA developed under specific cultural circumstances. The influences of militarism on the political parties on the Right are crucial. The development of the brown uniform occurred within a political culture that harbored a general affinity for militaristic showmanship, including uniforms and flags that suggested strength and determination. The right-wing paramilitaries actively contributed to this militarization of politics through the adoption of disciplined marches and rallies by thousands of uniformed participants.[34]

One should also note that the dress of the fascists changed over time. This change reflected a change in purpose. The SA changed its function several times from 1920 to 1933. Its earliest form started as a troop protecting right-wing speakers in 1920. By 1921 it developed into a secret army in the service of antirepublican and conservative elites. After the failed attempt at a coup d'état in 1923, Hitler went to prison, and the Nazi movement largely stalled, pushing the remnants underground. After Hitler's return in December 1924, he changed tactics. He still wanted to abolish Weimar democracy, yet he now wanted to use his newly established reputation in conservative circles nationwide, gained after his public trial and after the publication of *Mein Kampf,* to come to power. In 1926 the purpose of the SA thus changed again. This time it became a public political propaganda and terror organization for Hitler's fascist movement.

Rather than taking power through violence alone, the SA actively participated in election campaigns. When violence against state authorities failed, Hitler changed tactics, deciding to work within the system to get access to the political power that he coveted. Although the SA still used violence, clash violence against political opponents was different from the violence in the failed coup attempt. The Nazis exploited clash violence for its propagandistic value. The ultimate goal became the dismantling of the republican system from within.

With this change in purpose and tactics came a visual transformation. The early SA, during the period from 1920 to 1924, did not have a formal uniform, but rather a general style of dress. They preferred army gray trench coats and ski caps. This style was similar to other paramilitaries and reflected a general affinity for militarism. It also represented the symbolic adoption of the gray color of the German military and thus the German state. The Nazis seeking power in the state through electoral processes, however, needed a paramilitary party uniform that, ideally, would appeal to broad sections of the German electorate and simultaneously make the SA stand out from the other paramilitaries. In 1926 Hitler officially adopted a khaki-colored shirt that was already in use with some Stormtrooper units. The first Brown Shirts, however, were developed and introduced by SA officers when Hitler was still in prison in 1924. After 1926 the shirt and the added components consisting of a brown ski cap, a brown tie, and matching breeches with sturdy footwear ultimately constituted a look that was attractive both to the young men in the SA and to large portions of German society. With the dramatic growth of the SA from 1930 to 1933, the sale of the shirt by the SA to the men in specialized SA brand stores allowed the Nazis to siphon revenue off the men and simultaneously establish a large and highly visible propaganda troop.

To explicate the history and function of the Brown Shirt uniform, this book is divided into three parts. The first part puts the history of the SA uniform into its proper historical context. The first chapter, "The Militarization of Political Culture in Weimar Germany, 1918–1933," outlines the different political uniforms during the Weimar years. From 1918 to 1933, politics represented a public spectacle in which all parties, veterans' organizations, and even religious groups occupied public spaces during uniformed parades and rallies. This chapter examines the uniforms of the most influential mass organizations during the Weimar years to show how their dress reflected their ideologies and to show the contrast the Nazis provided with their iconic Brown Shirts. By discussing German political uniforms in general, this chapter provides an essential background.

Chapter 2, "From a Tropical Tunic to the Brown Shirt," retraces the history of the brown Nazi uniform during the Weimar period. The way the Nazis dressed changed over time. A short description of Nazi dress development from its earliest roots in 1920 will show that the trademarked brown Nazi uniform, introduced in 1926, differed drastically from all other groups at that time. Nazi dress integrated features of youthfulness and hypermasculinity through a cut that was similar to contemporary sports and outdoor clothing styles. Simultaneously, the origin of the brown fabric with the colonial troops of the Imperial Army affiliated the SA with the lost empire. The Nazi uniform combined diverse cultural trends, including a general affinity for the military and uniforms as well as the popularity of sports and outdoor activities. By retracing the origins of Nazi dress, this chapter highlights the opportunistic character of Nazism. An SA officer with close connections to SA chief of staff Ernst Röhm introduced the typical cut of the Brown Shirt that Hitler unknowingly adopted in 1926. When Röhm fell out of favor with Hitler, so did the officer who first patented the Brown Shirt. Both men were gay and died by the hands of fellow Nazis in 1934. Hitler claimed that the SA leadership needed to be cleared of gay men. They did not die, however, because of their sexual orientation; they died because their leader no longer needed them. Yet because of this background, the Nazi leadership kept the origin of the uniform obscured.

The following three chapters on the Brown Shirts and material culture constitute the second part of this book. Chapter 3, "The Brown Garment of Honor, Material Culture, and Social Control," explicates how the Nazi image combined the features of aggressiveness and military-like discipline at a time when SA officers did not have the effective means to establish forced discipline among the men. This chapter shows that the Nazis, rather than falling back on voluntary discipline, used marketing techniques to establish a name brand. They then used the consumption of the name-brand Brown Shirt to achieve a certain level of uniformity and discipline among the troopers. Yet the German fascists did not only use capitalism to their advantage. They also appealed to the honor of the men by lending the garment a symbolic value, as in the military and police forces. They achieved this by enforcing strict regulations for when and how the Brown Shirt was to be worn. Furthermore, the Nazis revoked the privilege of wearing the official Brown Shirt as a penalty for undesired behavior. Thus, the tools for social control applied by the Nazis consisted of peer pressure and reward. This reward constituted the privilege to buy and then publicly wear the uniform as part of the movement. Finally, this chapter discusses the temporary prohibition of Nazi dress during the late Weimar years that highlights how and why SA uniforms became a vital factor in Nazi politics.

Chapter 4, "Assembling the Troopers—the Logistics of Militarization," demonstrates that the Nazis used mass rallies and marches to amplify the effects of visual propaganda based on the Brown Shirt. Early on, Hitler ordered that the SA must appear publicly as integrated units, rather than individuals in uniform. Nonetheless, the massing of thousands of uniformed men in specific locations was rather difficult to achieve. The Nazis used military expertise and middle-class resources to organize travel, food supplies, and lodgings as well as to overcome logistical challenges. This chapter shows that the Nazis did not rely solely on local SA units during contested election campaigns. The Nazis traveled long distances and impressed, or intimidated, with large groups of marching Brown Shirted SA. The annual party rallies, from 1926 until the outbreak of World War II, served as mass propaganda events, orchestrated from above. This chapter concludes with a description of the logistical efforts put into these mass rallies.

Chapter Five, "The Professionalization of a Civil War Army," is a discussion of the image changes introduced by the Nazis shortly before they came to power in 1933. Once in power, the Nazis introduced a business-suit jacket, a long woolen coat, and straight pants to be worn with shoes rather than boots. These changes made the SA look less radical and more like the professional military. These new elements represented a permanent change to the uniform. The brown outfit with cap, tie, Brown Shirt, riding breeches, and high boots became the *Traditionsanzug,* or traditional suit, and represented only part of an SA man's collection. The new uniform items were modeled after traditional military and business-suit models. Ultimately, the Nazis wanted to exude a sober and professional impression after they had taken power within the state.

The third and final part of this book is composed of two chapters. Chapter 6, "Classless Heroes—the Centrality of the Brown Shirt in Mythic Nazi Film and Literature," is a literary and film analysis. Once in power, the Nazis used all the resources of the German state to create propaganda films and literature about the Weimar era. In these films and books, the fascists created an idealized and mythic version of themselves during the Weimar period. To the German fascists, the uniform held an important meaning. The uniform made the men stand out and was a source of pride. Nazi film and literature constituted an important component of image construction because they combined the use and effects of the uniform with positive myths about the Nazis during the Weimar era. Chapter 7, "Hamburg, 1921–1933, a Case Study," explicates the history of the SA in Hamburg during the Weimar years. Contrary to the myths the Nazis created about themselves, this case study showcases how the public perceived the SA. Hamburg was not a traditional bastion of Nazi power. Hamburg, a liberal and independent city, serves as an ideal case study to show that even in a less than sympathetic environment, the Nazis used their image successfully to gain the trust of large sections of Hamburg's population. From 1926 onward, the Nazi presence in the city increased. Uniformed SA initially protected Nazi activists. During later city council election campaigns, SA men from surrounding areas flooded the streets during propaganda marches. This indeed caused political violence in proletarian neighborhoods. The bourgeois press, however, reflected the impressive appeal of the Nazis, as some conservative elites admired their disciplined and clean-cut image. This chapter demonstrates that the Hamburg Nazis found success by putting considerable effort into visual propaganda based on masses of uniformed SA. The Brown Shirted men made the right impression on bourgeois elites and triggered clash violence to be exploited for propagandistic purposes.

The concluding chapter, "Weimar Culture and the End of Weimar Democracy," demonstrates that Hitler, like all fascists, came to power by crafting an effective image for his movement. He combined preexisting popular cultural trends and modern elements into a uniform that amplified the effects of mass marches. Hitler merged a fashionable style with politics. Hitler did not try to convince voters solely through rhetoric or through violence alone. In fact, the rhetoric changed depending on the audience. Additionally, a focus on violence alone is misleading since it relates only half of the story. Therefore, the crucial impact of material culture in fascist politics, and in bringing about the end of Weimar democracy, cannot be underestimated. This conclusion is also not relegated to the past. It is of particular relevance in the first decades of the twenty-first century because modern fascists use image construction in similar ways.

This book is based on a broad range of sources. These sources include original uniforms housed and preserved in the German Historical Museum in Berlin (Deutsches Historisches Museum Berlin). Depictions of uniforms housed and preserved in the German Federal Archives for Visual Material in Koblenz (Bundesarchiv Bildarchiv Koblenz), however, are equally important primary sources. In addition, ample documentary evidence exists. From 1926 onward, so-called SA orders (SA Befehle, in acronym form SABE) explicitly document the establishment of Hitler's SA. They are currently compiled in the German Federal Archives for Documents (Bundesarchiv) in Berlin. These main archival files also include correspondence between regional SA offices and the central party headquarters in Munich. The Federal Archives also contain a large collection of files from the Hamburg SA. This book further draws on the records on the SA in the state archive of the city of Hamburg (Hamburger Staatsarchiv) and the archives of the Research Center for Historical Studies in the City of Hamburg (Forschungstelle für Zeitgeschichte in Hamburg). The files of the Hamburg SA and the unpublished memoirs of a former SA leader from Hamburg, Alfred Conn, constitute the essential evidence for the case study of the city of Hamburg. Hamburg's bourgeois and conservative newspapers *Hamburger Nachrichten* and *Hamburger Anzeiger*, as well as the communist *Hamburger Volkszeitung*, aid in a perception analysis. This case study also includes documentary evidence that is part of a collection of primary sources outlining the rise of Nazism in Hamburg put together by Werner Jochmann.[35]

Hitler came to power as part of a conservative coalition government in March 1933 and then dismantled democracy from the inside. Weimar voters could not foresee the extended crimes of the Nazis in power. Rather, Hitler convinced German voters that he was the right choice to lead Germany into a better future. A focus on Hitler's ideology alone is misleading because the rhetoric changed depending on the audience. A Nazi was many things to many different people. Hitler tried to persuade both farmers and workers with different and even contradictory messages. The uniform made a person a Nazi rather than ideology alone. Therefore, the crucial impact of material culture in fascist politics, and in bringing about the end of Weimar democracy, cannot be underestimated.

Chapter One

THE MILITARIZATION OF POLITICAL CULTURE IN WEIMAR GERMANY, 1918–1933

Hitler's SA developed in a unique political and cultural atmosphere in Germany after 1918. Some aspects of German political culture during the Weimar years were different from most other Western countries at the time. The actors on the political stage, the SA among them, acted in a manner that was comparatively more militarized. The roots of these differences lie in the radicalizing German war experience. The young radicals who participated in Weimar politics, however, were not all old enough to have served in the Great War. Among the generation born after 1900 especially, young German men seemed to have carried a degree of aggressiveness and radicalization into the political sphere that ultimately fostered an interwar militarization of politics. This generation felt redundant due to a stagnant economy and resulting lack of employment. The postwar economic crisis affected this generation especially severely, as many came of age in a time of increased competition for resources. These young men had also experienced a disruption of their formative years, during the war. Despite these challenges and a pervasive sense of futility, they were unable to prove themselves through actual participation in battle, which had traditionally been a primary means of attaining masculine honor.[1]

Thus, many members of this generation were radicalized by the war and its tumultuous aftermath on the home front. Many joined political parties with radical ideologies touting equally radical solutions to the problems of Weimar German society.[2] Yet this generation influenced by the war were not the only ones who joined radical parties. Veterans brutalized by the war claimed a more direct alienation from the unfulfilled promises of the German state and also joined these parties, contributing to a trend of broad societal militarization. Ultimately, both World War I veterans and the younger generation just coming of age accepted violence as a heroic and necessary part of political life. Some members of this cohort were therefore willing to take their respective ideologies to the extreme in order to effect change.

An especially extreme sample group exemplified how dangerous the consequences of this radicalization could become. Under the Nazi regime, some radicalized men became state-sanctioned murderers. The men inventing and implementing Heinrich Himmler's racist fantasies in the Reich Main Security Office, for instance, were largely members of this cohort. About 77 percent of the men working in this capacity belonged to the war-youth generation, especially those born after 1900. These young men represented the most extremist in ideology. This generation's nonparticipation in the war influenced their opinions insofar as they considered war a heroic endeavor, yet had not seen the horrifying realities of war firsthand. Military standards such as toughness and decisiveness, yet also callousness, became accepted, if not glorified, merits for males in civilian life.[3]

THE UNIFORMITY OF UNIFORMS

All political parties, not only the radical ones, changed because of the wartime experiences of their youthful members. A growing militarization of politics is illustrated by the prevalence of paramilitaries in Weimar politics. The largest paramilitaries besides the SA were the Stahlhelm Bund der Frontsoldaten (Steel Helmet League of Frontline Soldiers, representing the conservatives), the Reichsbanner Schwarz-Rot-Gold (Imperial Banner Black-Red-Gold, representing the social democrats, the German Democratic Party, and some of the Catholic Center Party), and the Roter Frontkämpferbund (Red Front-Fighters League, representing the communists).[4]

The youth generation and actual veterans of the Great War transferred their experiences and attitudes to the streets of the Weimar Republic via these political organizations. In fact, the preferred public venue for political activity was the street. The political propaganda march in the streets became a symbolic occupation of public space and represented another hallmark of the militarization of politics across the political spectrum.[5]

The general militarization of politics was reflected by the fact that all paramilitaries of the Weimar era adopted features of the regular military. Uniforms and symbols carried by marchers, for instance, were visual symbols of militarization. These symbols and identifiable uniforms, in turn, became essential components of political marches. The men marching for the Weimar paramilitaries cared deeply for aesthetic symbols. Symbols and symbolic actions were of utmost importance in an imagined political reality. They connected culture and politics. Uniforms, as a hallmark adopted from formal militaries, were an integral part of male fashion in the early twentieth century because they stood for strength and efficiency. The military origins of uniforms transferred these values to uniforms in general.[6] Therefore, uniforms and militaristic symbolism were important and ubiquitous in Weimar Germany. The SA, as the paramilitary of the Nazi Party, must be seen within the larger context of this multilayered militarization of Weimar politics. In order to explicate the visual differences of the SA to the other paramilitaries, the uniforms of each paramilitary need to be described in turn.

Because tailored uniforms were cost prohibitive to many, a generic uniform with only a cap, armband, or sash as a shared signifier was an option. This generic outfit was worn by different paramilitaries. Photographic evidence from the German National Archives in Koblenz shows that some members of the early SA, the Stahlhelm, and the Roter Frontkämpferbund at times wore a generic uniform of contemporary outdoors and sports clothing with these distinct, party-specific additions. This generic uniform consisted of Windbreakers, breeches, and matching shoes. The shoes varied but were similar to military models such as high riding boots, lace-up boots, or low boots with either leather gaiters or wool-wrap putties. Some of the men within all three paramilitaries also wore shoulder-strapped Sam Browne belts.[7] Each of these accessories had military roots.

Windbreakers were short, unlined, lightweight trench coats. Trench coats were first used by British officers in World War I. The British garment was influenced by colonial uniforms and was khaki colored, like all British officer uniforms in the Great War. Right before the outbreak of World War I, however, British officers wore expensive early forms of trench coats tailored according to military regulations. A fine tailor of each individual officer's choice produced a perfect fit. Originally, similar coats were also affiliated with Britain's upper classes because of its second background in leisure and sports clothing. During the war British clothing manufacturers combined both trends in the trench coat, which became a men's fashion staple in the war period and maintained its popularity after the war.[8]

A surviving Windbreaker, now in the holdings of the German Historical Museum in Berlin, belonged to a Reichsbanner man. The coat is made from a waterproof, heavy light-gray cotton material like the ones first patented in Britain, yet not in the typical khaki of the British military.[9] This specimen is double-breasted and features ten buttons organized in two columns, with five on each side. It has a relatively high, wide collar. It also has wide lapels and a storm flap, designed to protect the neck opening from leaking in rainwater. The Windbreaker also features a half belt at the back. The raglan sleeves, sleeves that extend in one piece to the collar, include straps around the wrists that end in two buttons that allow for a close buttoning at the wrists when adjusted to its tightest fitting. The straps and the half belt include the same brown buttons as the double-breasted front. The front of the coat features four pockets, each with button closures, and four smaller buttons of the same color as the larger ones. There are two nearly vertically angled slash skirt pockets, which are pockets that are suspended on the inside of the garment from slits on the outside that function as openings, with scalloped bottom flaps above the belt line. The coat flares out below the waist in a skirt effect and ends at the wearer's upper thigh. Two large pleated pockets with scalloped button flaps are located on the front of this skirt. The cut fits close at the waist.[10]

Windbreakers of this type functioned as the perfect jackets for Weimar paramilitaries. They served a practical purpose and made an especially masculine impression.[11] The men participating in the militarized political culture of the Weimar Republic dressed, in their view, like warriors. The adoption of a style of coat that was heavily influenced by British colonial army and elite-class sports backgrounds is interesting. The British had won the war and thus reinforced their masculinity. The men of the Weimar paramilitaries effectively mimicked the style of dress and visually claimed the same sense of power and elite masculinity for their outward image.

The trousers of choice for all paramilitaries of the Weimar era also originated in British bourgeois circles. They all wore breeches or riding pants. The name of the trousers reveals an even more noteworthy background. In England riding breeches are also called jodhpurs, after a city in the state of Rajastan in India. Polo-playing Rajastani elites first introduced their leg wear to British elite circles in the late nineteenth century. The breeches fitted tightly from below the knee to the ankle. They flared outward at the thighs and hips. These breeches became popular in Britain as bourgeois sports and leisure clothing during the early twentieth century. During the 1920s, the cut changed. The breeches curved out more on the thighs and fitted closer over the knees.[12]

The breeches of the Weimar paramilitaries show similarities to the shape and cut of British officers' breeches. Nevertheless, these breeches were not only worn in Britain and Germany but also part of a popular style of clothing worn by young men across the Western world. Breeches, for instance, also appear prominently in American mail-order catalogs from the mid-1920s. This style of breeches, in effect, was worn by soldiers, sportsmen, and workers across the West.[13]

To complete the generic paramilitary look, high riding, or alternatively lace-up, boots complemented the breeches well. These kinds of boots were expensive, though. Therefore, the breeches could also be worn with gaiters, wool-wrap putties, or simply low shoes with sturdy socks.[14] Gaiters were made of a protective sleeve covering the lower legs and ankles. They could be made from leather or some other sturdy material. They typically laced or buttoned closely to the calf. They were intended to give the wearer an extra waterproofing layer and provide protection from mud and vegetation. Wool-wrap putties, or leg wraps, served much the same purpose. They consisted of a long strip of cloth wrapped tightly, much like a bandage, from the ankle to the knee. According to British service regulations, the color of the putties was supposed to match the color of the service dress and be made from the same woolen material. Putties, like jodhpurs, originated in India. The British army adopted them because they were practical and an inexpensive variation of the gaiters.[15] Yet for Weimar paramilitaries, the military-like leg wear and footwear were not enough. In order to make the look even more militaristic, they opted to wear even more leather items based more directly on other military antecedents.

The Sam Browne belt was an accessory that every Weimar paramilitary used. The Sam Browne was a wide leather belt. It was wider than ordinary belts and worn over a jacket or military tunic. The belt was supported by a narrower shoulder strap that lay across the chest of the wearer, resting over the right shoulder. Of course, the belt had a military background as well. The English officer Sir Samuel James Browne served in the British army in India in the nineteenth century. He lost his left arm there in 1858. Originally, Browne invented the rigging to allow him to draw his sword with his right arm without the need to steady the scabbard of his saber with his (absent) left arm. The shoulder strap supported the scabbard and secured it closer to the left hip. The rigging, though originally only a practical aid, became a fashion trend that caught on. British officers started to wear a similar belt with a shoulder strap. During World War I, the Sam Browne belt came to signal an officer in the Allied armies. In the 1920s, '30s, and '40s, the belt became a military fashion item outside of Great Britain.[16]

Interestingly, the Nazis, just like British officers, showed a clear affinity for the militarized look that the Sam Browne belt lent its wearers. The uniforms of all Nazi organizations during the Third Reich included the belt (such as the Nazi Party, the SS, and even the Hitler Youth). The SA, however, started this trend during the earlier Weimar years. The French traveler Daniel Guerin, who visited Germany during the end of the Weimar period in 1932, noticed that the SA waxed their boots and shoulder straps to an exaggeratedly polished shine. He specifically noted that "especially boots, belts, shoulder straps, and holsters" made the men of the SA look particularly martial.[17]

Ultimately, all major Weimar paramilitaries, including the early SA, had obvious commonalities. They all acted belligerent in that they marched, wore uniforms, and carried symbols that represented their respective ideologies. Still, important details, as, for instance, the official uniform jacket of each paramilitary, as opposed to the generic trench coat, as well as their officially sanctioned caps, differed markedly. Furthermore, and most obviously discernible, symbols worn on the cockade of the caps, the belt buckles, and the flags were distinct among each group. A description of the color and cut of the official jackets, as opposed to the cheaper generic version, as well as a description of the caps and symbols of the major paramilitaries reveal important symbolic deviations.

STAHLHELM BUND DER FRONTSOLDATEN

The most influential paramilitary on the monarchist Right was the veterans' organization the Steel Helmet League of Front Soldiers (Stahlhelm Bund der Frontsoldaten). Former officer Franz Seldte, who had lost his left arm in the war, founded this organization on Christmas Day 1918 to foster camaraderie, provide economic support to former frontline soldiers, and put an end to the November Revolution. The Stahlhelm, as it was commonly called, was conceived of as an all-encompassing veterans' organization. Politics originally did not play a role. Membership was open to all men who had fulfilled the requirement of at least six months of service on the front line. This included supporters of the Social Democratic Party, liberals, and conservatives. The organization was aimed at providing support and giving voice to German veterans. It ostensibly stood above ideologies, party politics, and religion. The Stahlhelm used its uniforms like the military during the empire. Nevertheless, the aim of establishing a catchall veterans' organization was not successful. Ultimately, the

Stahlhelm attracted large groups of the political Right following the signing of the Treaty of Versailles and the resulting drastic downsizing of the German military. By the summer of 1922, the Stahlhelm had established five hundred locals in eighteen districts. With former Free Corps members filtering in, the Stahlhelm became increasingly antirepublican and politically active. By 1930 the Stahlhelm was the largest right-wing paramilitary force in Germany, with a membership of between four and five hundred thousand men.[18]

The official Stahlhelm cap, preserved in the holdings of the German Historical Museum, looks like a peaked cap styled in military fashion. Its crown is made from gray-green wool. The band of the cap is constructed from a darker bottle-green wool. The short visor consists of polished brown leather. Between the visor and the band, the cap also features a chinstrap of the same polished brown leather. The strap is attached to the sides of the hatband by two brown buttons. The front of the cap features two attached badges. The first is the round black, white, and red cockade of the Imperial Army located front and center on the band. It appeared as a white circle within a black circle with a red dot in the center. The second is a small badge located on the front of the crown right above the cockade. It has the shape of a German imperial steel helmet that bears the inscription "Der Stahlhelm." The cap has a saddle shape, where the crown at the front is lifted up. The cockade and the Stahlhelm badge are located at the band and the crown, respectively. The saddle-shape effect allows for the cockade on the band to be directly under the badge on the crown. On the sides and the back, the crown lays down over the band. This cap closely resembled the caps of imperial German officers.[19]

Stahlhelm jackets varied widely. Because its members had to provide their own uniforms in economically unstable times, the Stahlhelm shared a common style of attire, rather than a formal, standardized uniform, though for those with the means an official accoutrement was available. Some men wore their old Imperial Army uniforms with Stahlhelm badges, while others wore the generic Windbreaker. Official Stahlhelm uniform jackets were made from gray-green wool and, like the cap, closely resembled the uniforms of the Imperial Army. Some Stahlhelm jackets even included insignia of rank.[20]

The Stahlhelm uniform jacket in the holdings of the German Historical Museum in Berlin was tailored according to the specifications of the Stahlhelm and belonged to a member from Saxony. This particular specimen is made from gray-green wool that features a single-breasted cut with an open collar. The jacket is buttoned with four gray-green buttons in the front. The two breast pockets are pleated and include scalloped button flaps. Additionally, the jacket includes two angled slash skirt pockets in the front. These pockets, like the breast pockets, include scalloped pocket flaps and are buttoned with the same buttons as the front. It also has French cuffs, so cuffs that are twice the length of regular cuffs and folded back on themselves. The cut of the jacket is fitted, if not tight at the waist. The back includes a half belt secured with two additional gray-green buttons. The jacket is meant to be worn with a wide belt and includes two belt hooks that allow the belt to rest at the narrowest part of the waist, giving the wearer the impression of a slim, proportional body. The jacket flares out a bit under the belt line and has a short skirt effect. The upper right arm bears an oval-shaped badge of a green background color. Yellow letters reading "Landesverband Sachsen" frame the upper part of the badge. The lower part shows a crown atop of the coat of arms of Saxony. Though this particular jacket lacks any insignia of rank, above the left breast pocket is a ribbon bar with service ribbons from World War I.[21]

Aside from the basic design features, the most potent symbol used was the imperial steel helmet, which coincided with the paramilitary's name (Stahlhelm). The cap and the belt buckle of a typical Stahlhelm man described above from the archives of the German Historical Museum also include stylized German steel helmets. Introduced in 1916, this then-futuristic-looking helmet represented the industrial, modern era. Designed by Dr. Friedrich Schwerd, who worked at the Technical Institute of Hanover, the design harked back to medieval helmet models. Yet it was more compact. This mass-produced helmet had a modern and even futuristic look in the trenches. These helmets provided excellent protection for the head. The coal-bucket design made the helmet easily recognizable to everyone, ally or enemy. It featured a cylindrical dome that was flat on the top and provided protection to the head. The helmet had a visor that was about six inches in width that extended a little more than one inch. The visor provided protection from the sun and the elements. The helmet had a neck guard that flared out about two inches below the dome. This guard protected neck and ears. Once a soldier had been issued a steel helmet, this helmet became his personal property.[22]

Due to its form and function, the model 1916 steel helmet became the most identifiable symbol of the German frontline soldier.[23] Although slight alterations to the liner and the chinstrap were introduced in 1917 and 1918, the shape did not differ from the original model. A stylized steel helmet of this variety became the symbol of the organization, which proudly displayed it on patches, belt buckles, and caps. The Stahlhelm belt buckle in the German Historical Museum's archive collection is made of brass and includes a silver-inlay disc with a steel helmet and a wreath of oak leaves. The open wreath is crowned with the script "Stahlhelm."[24] During marches and rallies, and during induction or the founding of new Stahlhelm chapters, the men carried the black, white, and red flag of the Hohenzollern dynasty and imperial war flags. The Stahlhelm, like many other antirepublican organizations, chose these colors to show their opposition to the republic.[25]

Ultimately, the men of the Stahlhelm exuded a conservative as well as active and militaristic appearance. The Windbreakers worn by some had roots in leisure and sports clothing and gave those men a particularly outdoorsy look.[26] Both the Windbreakers and the official Stahlhelm uniform jackets were cut tight at the waist and made the wearer look thin and athletic.[27] Still, the look remained militaristic, since similar Windbreakers had been used in trench warfare. The official, and more formal, Stahlhelm uniform jacket's coloration, wool fabric, and cut closely resembled the uniforms of the Imperial Army.[28] Additionally, the breeches, the footwear, and the use of Sam Browne belts made the men of the Stahlhelm look especially bellicose.

REICHSBANNER SCHWARZ-ROT-GOLD

The Black-Red-Gold Banner of the Reich (Reichsbanner Schwarz-Rot-Gold, short form Reichsbanner) was the largest prodemocratic organization during the Weimar era. It drew its membership largely from the Social Democratic Party and other parties of the political center. By founding the Reichsbanner in February 1924, the leaders of the Social Democratic Party, the Catholic Center Party, the Democrats, and labor unions established a republican counterbalance to the Stahlhelm. Both paramilitaries were first conceived in the central German city of Magdeburg. Otto Hörsing, a Prussian civil servant, became the Reichsbanner leader. This organization also experienced an initial surge of new members, and although they probably never had more than one million active supporters, it was undoubtedly the largest single prodemocratic paramilitary group.[29]

The official Reichsbanner cap in the archives of the German Historical Museum looks similar to the Stahlhelm cap. It is also a peaked cap in military style. Its crown, contrasting the darker color of the

Stahlhelm cap, is made from khaki cotton material, although the original color before years of fading could have been a somewhat darker gray-green. The band of the cap is constructed from a deeper brown material that is heavily embroidered at the front of the band, including stylized flowers, or sun shapes. The short visor consists of polished dark-brown leather in the same color as the band of the cap. The space between the visor and the band of the cap features a chinstrap of the same material as the visor. The strap is attached to the sides of the hatband by two brown buttons. There are no badges on the band of this cap. The cockade is made of a gold-hued metal with a red field in the center. A black eagle is located within this red field. The Reichsbanner cap has a saddle shape, similar to the cap of the Stahlhelm, as well as the regular German military.[30] Nevertheless, variations of the colors and shape did exist. Some men, for example, wore blue caps of a similar design as the one just described.[31] Surviving photographs also show Reichsbanner men at times wearing blue ski caps rather than the peaked variety.[32]

FIGURE 1. Stahlhelm leaders in Berlin, ca. 1928. Note the variety of jackets. The first four officers in the foreground wear the double-breasted *Windjacke*. The speaker, Stahlhelm founder Franz Seldte, wears a tailored uniform jacket modeled closely after the Imperial Army jacket. All five officers wear the Imperial Army medals they earned during the war. Also, note jackboots, wool wrap puttees, and ankle boots with gaiters worn by the first three officers from left to right, respectively. Bundesarchiv, Bild 102–00203 / Pahl, Georg. The German Federal Archives, Koblenz, Germany.

The men of the Reichsbanner also wore breeches and an outdoor-style Windbreaker. Yet unlike the Stahlhelm, they did not seem to have had an official uniform jacket. Photographic evidence from the German Federal Archives in Koblenz indicates that Reichsbanner men wore Windbreakers with their official caps.[33] The gray color of the Windbreakers, associated with both the military and the bureaucracy, symbolized the affiliation with the state, national traditions, and Weimar democracy.[34] There were, nevertheless, more variations of the colors men wore in the Reichsbanner than in the Stahlhelm. In addition to the appearance of blue caps, some men wore green shirts.[35] A surviving Reichsbanner Windbreaker at the holdings of the German Historical Museum in Berlin is gray rather than green. The collection of the German Historical Museum does not include an official Reichsbanner jacket, further indicating that the Reichsbanner men did not have an official uniform jacket, or shirt, for that matter. This suggests that the Reichsbanner, overall, did not value uniformity or strict adherence of their members to certain visual standards.

The symbols on the Reichsbanner's belt buckle reflect the democratic attitude of its members, once against in contrast to other contemporary paramilitary groups. The eagle on the brass belt buckle, as confirmed by a remaining example in the archives of the German Historical Museum, is located in a round field surrounded by the script "Reichsbanner Schwarz Rot Gold."[36] The eagle on the buckle is similar to the eagle displayed on the official flag of the Weimar Republic, again linking this organization to German democratic ideals of the time.

The members of the Reichsbanner, as loyal supporters of the democratic Weimar Republic, saw themselves as following in the liberal democratic tradition of the 1848 revolutions and thus chose the black, red, and yellow-colored flag of liberal revolutionaries. Choosing symbols that harked back to the unsuccessful attempt at republicanism in 1848 as well as those of the Weimar Republic showed the general public that the Reichsbanner was a republican organization.

Despite this symbolism, the Reichsbanner men looked more or less like the men of the Stahlhelm. Most of them wore military-style caps, Windbreakers, breeches, militaristic footwear, and Sam Browne belts.[37] This militaristic style caused heated debates. According to James Diehl, "Military formations, and commands, uniforms, flags, and marching bands were used by the *Reichsbanner* in the same manner and profusion as they were by the rightist Combat Leagues."[38]

The attraction of military trappings among their younger followers forced the leadership to consider its useful elements. The leaders considered the uniforms as a fitting tool for recruitment because the young workers readily adopted military-like discipline and uniforms as essential parts of their organization. Like the radical young men on the Right, the men in the center of the political spectrum also looked, and at times acted, militarized.[39]

Yet there were also nonmilitaristic traditions at play. Labor festivals in imperial Germany, for instance, had included secular processions with flags and bound the participants together in emotional ceremonies. During the Weimar era, Reichsbanner leaders reminded their members that their flag was the flag of the state and consequently attached high symbolic value to the colors they carried. Yet the Reichsbanner did embrace militaristic marches as legitimate political activities. According to historian James Diehl, "The enthusiasm of socialist youth for paramilitary activity surprised many in the SPD (*Sozialdemokratische Partei Deutschlands*), especially older leaders."[40]

FIGURE 2. Reichsbanner podium with speaker and flag bearers during the festivities celebrating the Weimar constitution, November 8, 1929. The men all wear Windbreakers. The podium is draped in black, red, and yellow. Note the eagle and the saddle shape of the caps. Bundesarchiv, Bild 102–08218 / Pahl, Georg. The German Federal Archives, Koblenz, Germany.

ROTER FRONTKÄMPFERBUND

The Red Front-Fighters League (Roter Frontkämpferbund, or RFB) was the Communist Party's paramilitary. It stood at the radical Left of the political spectrum, although it was officially above party politics. Just like in the Stahlhelm and the Reichsbanner, membership in the RFB was technically open to all males willing to fight for the proletariat, even noncommunists. Ultimately, despite their official claim to non-partisanship, the Communist Party controlled this paramilitary group. In fact, the RFB constituted the largest radical left-wing opponent of Weimar democracy. It was at its core a Stalinist-communist revolutionary organization that was considerably more violent than their center-Left equivalents in the Reichsbanner. After the failed attempt to trigger a Soviet-style revolution in Hamburg in 1923, the Communist Party restructured its military arm. In July 1924, the communists founded the RFB in Halle in central Germany. By 1925 the RFB claimed to have 558 local groups with 40,000 members. The RFB's predilection to use violence against all other Weimar paramilitaries ultimately resulted in its prohibition a short time after, in 1929. By then their membership had risen to nearly 130,000.[41] Although their uniformed marches where by then illegal, the RFB continued to function underground.

In 1925, mirroring a Stalinization and centralization of the German communists, the RFB leadership decided to make a Russian-style shirt and cap, allegedly Lenin's dress, the official uniform for the entire RFB.[42] The cap's style has a proletarian background. According to the historian Daniel Siemens, the RFB "wore a kind of proletarian uniform that combined the traditional workman's cap with military insignia."[43] The RFB cap in the Weimar paramilitaries collection in the archives of the German Historical Museum indeed looks like the cap made famous by Lenin. It is a peaked cap, yet the cap does not have the militaristic saddle shape of the Reichsbanner or the Stahlhelm. Rather, the cap is soft with a crown that rolls over the band. The entire cap, which includes the crown, band, and the peak, is made of the same thin, light-brown cotton material. The peak is constructed with a stiff core and covered in this cotton cloth. Between the visor and the band, the RFB cap also features a chinstrap. The chinstrap is made from brown polished leather. The strap is attached to the sides of the hatband by two brown buttons. There is no cockade on the RFB cap band. The cap does feature a circular badge attached to the front of the crown above the visor. It has a yellow field surrounded by a red band. The band includes the inscription "Roter Frontkämpferbund" in black script. In the center of the yellow field is a red clenched fist, outlined in black.[44]

Like the cap, the official uniform shirt had Bolshevik forerunners. Although some units initially wore a light-brown version of the Windbreaker, after 1925 all units wore a light-brown shirt with a uniquely Bolshevik design distinct from the other German paramilitaries. The direct association with Soviet Russia was deliberate. The RFB shirt housed in the archive of the German Historical Museum looks more similar to Russian army shirts than the other designs described above. The shirt is made from the same thin cotton material in a brown-green color that has faded to an almost khaki coloration. This style of shirt has a closed front, so that one must pull it over their head to put it on, rather than the more common button-up style of other organizations. The collar is open and fairly wide, as it must accommodate the head and arms when dressing and undressing. The opening at the collar buttons up with two gray buttons, and the opening stops at the two breast pockets. They are pleated and include scalloped button flaps. Each could be buttoned with the same gray buttons as the collar. The sleeves of this style end in regular shirt cuffs that can be buttoned with two smaller gray buttons. The RFB shirt is comparatively thin, and its sleeves look like ordinary shirtsleeves with adjustable cuffs that button close along the wrist. Another feature that sets this shirt apart from the others is its straight, rather than fitted, cut at the waist. When worn with a belt, this extra fabric bunched up around the waist, producing an effect that the closely cut Windbreakers and the official Stahlhelm jackets did not have due to their more tailored cut. The RFB shirt was not worn tucked in and therefore had a short skirt effect just like the jackets worn by the Stahlhelm and Reichsbanner.[45]

The Sam Browne belts of the RFB featured a buckle embellished with a Marxist symbol. The symbol of the clenched fist, as found on the cap, represents the clenched fist of a worker. The buckle in the museum's archive is made from brass. It features a ring in the center that surrounds a clenched fist with a pebbled effect in the background.[46]

When the RFB marched, they carried red flags and wore red armbands. Occasionally, these red flags included yellow stars or writing reminiscent of the red Soviet flag that included a yellow star and yellow hammer and sickle. The colors red and yellow are also the colors of the RFB badge on the RFB cap, described above. Red flags themselves stood for socialism and the threat of revolution. Soviet flags carried by a German paramilitary definitely showed radical ideological leanings. The armband in the permanent exhibit of the German Historical Museum is made of red cotton and features a black circle with a clenched fist at its center. Underneath the fist the initials "R.F.B." are displayed in black letters.[47]

As the clear association with Soviet Russia demonstrates, the official RFB dress reflected its left-wing radicalism. Despite the slow Stalinization of the German Communist Party, however, the party and the RFB can by no means be considered monolithic.[48] Nonetheless, the RFB dressed like Soviet militants and thereby signaled their political leanings to those who observed them. The men of the communist paramilitary wore breeches like all other paramilitaries, in spite of their avowed disdain for militarism, which demonstrates the ways that the presence of public displays by paramilitaries influenced men's fashion trends during the Weimar years. The youthful RFB members, like those of the more conservative groups, also fancied wearing uniforms (of a sort) and voluntarily displayed military-like discipline during their own marches.[49] The success of these uniformed formations in drawing attention and bringing new recruits to the communist cause convinced the older leaders to abandon their initial skepticism toward militarism, uniforms, and marches. The young men of the radical Left, as will be demonstrated in subsequent chapters, also acted militantly—sometimes belligerently. They, like all the other paramilitaries, adopted military virtues and carried them into civilian political life, just like the young men on the Right.[50]

Yet to astute observers—for instance, the police—the Stahlhelm and the Reichsbanner looked different from the men of the RFB. Their shirt was not cut close to the waist and looked more like a smock, less respectable than a tailored uniform. The Chemnitz police derogatively called the new uniform *Russenkittel* (Russian smock). In Leipzig the police noted that the brown Russian uniforms were less impressive than other paramilitaries and gave a Bolshevik impression.[51] The brown uniforms with their exotic cut, the red armbands and flags, and the RFB fists stood out from the others. The communists put their left-wing radicalism and their contempt for both the monarchy and the republic on prominent display through their adopted style.

CONCLUSION

Ultimately, all German paramilitaries followed generally established norms and militarized Weimar political culture by readily adopting uniforms, military-style footwear, and Sam Browne belts. They all marched and participated in clash violence, to varying degrees. This

FIGURE 3. RFB leader Ernst Thälmann, saluting with his fist and wearing the RFB uniform during a propaganda march in June 1927. The shirt has an open collar and a closed front. The shirt is not tucked in. The overall appearance is distinctively Russian and revolutionary. Bundesarchiv, Bild 183-Z0127–305 / o.Ang. The German Federal Archives, Koblenz, Germany.

trend toward militarization transcended political boundaries. Still, the Reichsbanner adopted uniforms closely resembling those of the Stahlhelm. The cut of the uniforms and the color gray carried connotations within the German nation that both organizations exploited in order to win adherents. Both the Reichsbanner and the Stahlhelm displayed ideological differences almost exclusively through their symbols and their flags. The communists, however, stood out in their clear resemblance to the Bolsheviks. The uniform adopted by the Nazis, then, must be seen and appropriately contextualized within this highly militarized background of Weimar political culture. It is also important to note that the color gray was already in use by both the Stahlhelm and the Reichsbanner. The brown color of the Nazi uniform, as it developed over these years, stood out. Like the communists, the Nazis did not wear gray. Like the communists as well, the Nazis represented a more radical political ideology within the many competing parties of Weimar Germany. Unlike the communists, however, the Nazis developed their own shirt rather than taking their style from another nation. The communists wore a shirt that relied on its association with Russian designs. Still, rather than taking the black shirts of Benito Mussolini's Italian fascists, the Nazis developed their trademarked Brown Shirt.

Chapter Two

FROM A TROPICAL TUNIC TO THE BROWN SHIRT

After 1926 the uniform of the SA was unique in its color and its cut. It differed from the uniforms described in the previous chapter. Its cut was unlike traditional military uniforms or generic trench coats. Hitler's brand of fascism won the hearts and minds of many Germans with the help of the SA. Hitler's SA embodied German fascism as they gave fascist myths concrete and physical forms. In doing so, they presented a strong alternative to democracy. As the 1920s came to an end, the SA grew. The sights of brown-clad columns of men provoked reactions in the streets.

Even children realized that their parents' world was in turmoil. Author Jürgen Herbst included the description of a marching SA column in his memoirs about his childhood in the last years of the Weimar Republic. The sights and sounds of a marching SA column during a shopping spree with his uncle in the city of Braunschweig in 1931 made a strong impression on him. Herbst recalled that he walked with his uncle "past store windows . . . [when they] . . . heard music, fifes and drums, and singing. There were men marching in brown uniforms. . . . People on the sidewalk . . . stopped. Some waved and applauded, others whistled and booed. 'These men in their smart uniforms,' Herbst's uncle . . . said, 'are our hope. They will do away with the filth, decay, and incompetence. . . . They are soldiers for a new Germany. They'll bring us better days.'"[1]

Clearly, the SA evoked emotional reactions from spectators. By the early 1930s, the brown-clad columns of the SA acquired potent cultural meaning. The marchers in their brown uniforms evoked such strong reactions because they stood for a radically conservative and volkish version of a new German empire. Some Germans, like Herbst's uncle, believed the brown-clad Stormtroopers would bring a better future for the German people. Their brown color became synonymous with the entire Nazi movement.

The SA visually stood apart from the other main paramilitaries such as the Reichsbanner and the Stahlhelm. The SA uniform was also not cut like a more exotic foreign military precursor, like the shirt of the RFB. As will be seen, the color and the cut did indeed have forerunners in the German military. Yet the Nazis made important changes. These changes resulted in a uniform that modified the appearance of SA men's bodies in positive ways. It also served a signal function, easing identification at a glance, since no other paramilitary dressed like the Nazi SA. This uniform, nevertheless, was not designed and introduced from the top down. Rather, it changed over time. The changes came piecemeal from the bottom up, meaning that Hitler officially sanctioned what others had introduced and tested. Still, the modifications were part of Hitler's change of tactics in his quest for power. Visually, the early SA did not diverge much from the other Weimar paramilitaries. A brief introduction to the Nazi Party and the SA will explain why.

The early Nazi Party was not unlike many other right-wing political groupings. Like the other paramilitaries, the Nazi Party was a product of the postwar period. It was first established as the German Worker's Party in January 1919. Adolf Hitler joined the party in September of that year. By 1920 Hitler had rewritten the party program and changed its name to the National Socialist German Worker's Party, in order to broaden its appeal to the general public.[2] As most other political parties of the time, the Nazis also maintained a uniformed paramilitary, the SA. The acronym SA stood originally for "Saalschutz Abteilung" (meeting-hall security detachment). The Saalschutz was a predecessor to the SA and reflects its earliest beginnings as a militant group of activists that was willing and able to protect conservative and volkish orators during public speeches in beer halls through the use of violence.[3]

The early SA was part of the international postwar paramilitary scene; it developed in Bavaria, Würtemberg, and Austria. The SA functioned primarily in these areas until the middle of the 1920s.[4] Like the party proper, the SA did not necessarily have one founding date. Rather, the SA, as a branch of the Nazi Party, developed and changed simultaneously from its beginnings in 1920 to the expansion of proper paramilitary formations in 1921–22.[5] August 11, 1921, is considered one of the starting points, since on that day the party newspaper published an announcement that called on young men to join a special unit to function as a vanguard in the fight against political opponents.[6]

The number of SA leaders in its earliest stages reflects the rather extemporized nature of its foundation. Hitler received aid and goodwill from other paramilitaries. He secured the services of former navy lieutenant and Free Corps member Hans Ulrich Klintzsch from Captain Hermann Ehrhardt. Ehrhardt, a prominent figure in the right-wing paramilitary movement and leader of the Free Corps Ehrhard Brigade, considered the Nazis a welcome auxiliary and thus provided Klintzsch, one of his trusted subordinates, to train and organize the newly established SA as its official leader in 1921.[7] Klintzsch, however, faced an accusation of murder after Mathias Erzberger, the Center Party member and signatory of the armistice, was assassinated in August 1921. Consequently, Dietrich von Jagow functioned as interim leader from September 14 to early December 1921. Klintzsch then returned and served as leader until Hitler appointed Hermann Göring as the new SA leader in March 1923.[8]

THE UNIFORM OF THE EARLY SA

The early SA under Göring was violent in both intent and purpose. The SA was willing to fight the socialists during their May Day 1923 celebrations. They also trained for violence against the state in the form of a coup as part of a longer-term plan of action. Called up by Göring on the same May Day to disrupt the socialists' festivities, the SA stood down when they realized that police and army units defended the socialists and were willing to open fire on them, the aggressors. This incident left documentary evidence and gives insights into the early SA's purpose, as well as their uniforms. Göring ordered his one thousand well-armed SA troopers to stand down and not to fight government forces that day.[9]

Still, between 1921 and 1923, the men and officers of the SA considered themselves part of a larger antirepublican movement within the Weimar Republic. Hitler was an exceptionally gifted speaker who drew people to the antirepublican cause. He considered himself the drummer of the movement, meaning that he was a propagandist who saw himself, the men of his party, and his SA as part of a greater movement ready to destroy the republic with violence against the state.[10] Ultimately, the SA participated in the attempted right-wing coup d'état on November 9, 1923, as part of an antirepublican paramilitary coalition.[11] This failed attempt marked the end of the first iteration of the SA organization. The authorities jailed Hitler for his role in the failed coup and outlawed both his party and his paramilitary. The officers and men of the SA did not give up and go home. Most went underground or left Germany.

During this time period, the clothing worn by the men of the SA reflected the organization's initial purpose. It was intended to make the men look uniform and thus part of a coherent group. Yet the SA was part of a larger movement. The uniform they wore was therefore generic and militaristic. Only the symbols worn on armbands and flags marked the men as National Socialists. Like the Reichsbanner men, they dressed in the same generic uniform as some men of the Stahlhelm. The earliest SA uniform thus consisted of a gray ski cap, Windbreaker, breeches, wool-wrap putties with the matching footwear, and a Sam Browne belt.[12] These ski caps were not knitted woolen caps, but rather Austrian-style ski caps with a bill. They also symbolically dressed in gray, the color of the old Imperial Army's uniforms. In their gray uniforms, the SA blended in with other Weimar paramilitaries at this early stage. Even a contemporary ski cap, which the Nazis claimed as their own, was popular with other Weimar paramilitaries. As noted in the previous chapter, photographic evidence from the German Federal Archives in Koblenz, for instance, shows that some Reichsbanner units wore blue ski caps.[13]

Documentary evidence, nevertheless, also demonstrates that the SA leadership picked gray ski caps and claimed them as standard headwear for their men. The fashion caught on, and even the code word for SA men among the Nazi leadership became *caps*. In 1923, when the SA leadership ordered their men to disturb the left-wing workers' May Day celebrations in Munich, for instance, they used this code and ordered the action in a telegram, "Sämtliche Mützen sofort losschicken!" (Send off all caps immediately!).[14]

After this May Day, Göring recommended that all his SA troopers buy ski caps. He gave additional incentive by establishing collective orders that would save funds through wholesale purchases.[15] Yet the early SA leaders never directly purchased items for the men. Agency lay entirely with the men who followed Göring's advice to buy ski caps independently, in sporting-goods stores. In July 1923, Göring noted that the gray ski cap in use was popularly called SA Mütze, or "SA cap," by many. Because of the cap's growing recognition factor, he compromised and promised to pay one-third of the price of every cap so that the individual, or the local SA group, paid only two-thirds of the purchasing price as an added incentive to drive the organization toward greater uniformity.[16] In addition to saving money through ordering in bulk, the individual trooper received this unexpected discount from the leadership. Surely, this incentive made the SA cap even more popular.

If at first the adoption of a sportive ski cap for a German/Austrian right-wing paramilitary seems illogical, the cap itself had military roots. Austrian troops wore similar caps during World War I. German Alpine troops also wore similar caps.[17] The cap was constructed like a peaked cap. It was made of thick woolen fabric and included a short visor constructed from the same fabric that included an internal stiffener. What made the cap stand out, nevertheless, was the addition of a back and side panel that could be folded down. It was designed to give extra protection to the neck and cheeks. The side panel featured a downward scalloped front edge that ended in two forward sides that could be buttoned closed, either on top of the bill when folded up or in front of the wearer's chin when worn folded down. The panel could be buttoned with either one or two small buttons. Although the cap's turnups seemingly increased its practicality, it appears as if the design was more fashionable than practical. When the U.S. Army, for instance, evaluated the uniforms of the Wehrmacht in 1945, they also evaluated the ski caps that were by then in use with large parts of the German military. According to the army manual, "The turn-up may be used to protect the ears and back of the neck, with the buttoned flaps secured across the chin. The turn-up feature is unhandy and ineffective."[18] Although the flaps may have been more stylish than practical, the SA picked a style of cap that was affiliated with the Austrian military and German Alpine troopers of World War I, and the association itself may have been more important for the SA than practical considerations at that time. The leadership and especially Göring considered this style of cap fitting for the men of the SA.

Yet Göring wanted more homogeneity and envisioned some form of uniform beyond the cap. He wanted his respective troopers to look *Einheitlich* (uniform). The men were supposed to match, if only superficially. In a report to the Nazi Party about SA troopers abandoning the May Day 1923 fight, the SA chief of staff, Herman Göring, commented on the issue of uniformity among SA men in an attached memo.[19] Göring noted that the recommended uniform at that time, in addition to the ski caps, included a gray Windbreaker and gray wool-wrap putties. In essence, the early SA wore the same generic uniform as some Stahlhelm and all Reichsbanner men. Only the caps differed. Still, as noted earlier, some Reichsbanner men also wore blue ski caps, so that only the color distinguished the two groups.[20] This could lead to confusion in the case of an SA-provoked street fight, yet in these choices pragmatism played an important role. This generic uniform was widely available and could be worn on any occasion. Göring, in turn, argued in his report, "Since Windbreakers as well as fabric gaiters are garments that everyone can also wear in daily life, we can only advise all SA members to use every opportunity to purchase these items."[21]

While the early SA may have had an undistinguished uniform, the Nazi Party and the SA also had a highly recognizable symbol. A black swastika on a white disk in a red field was displayed on flags and armbands and constituted the most distinguishing symbol of the Nazis. Hitler himself claimed in *Mein Kampf* that the development of the swastika flag was of the utmost importance to him and discussed the options for the colors in the book. Within its pages, he claimed to have rejected the flag of the old empire, "for we do not desire to awaken from death the old Reich that perished through its own errors." Therefore, he continued, ". . . the new flag had to be equally a symbol of our own struggle, since . . . it was expected also to be highly effective as a poster. Anyone who has to concern himself much with the masses will recognize these apparent trifles to be very important matters. An effective insignia can in hundreds of thousands of cases give the first impetus toward interest in a movement." Hitler even claimed to have personally designed the final version of the swastika flag. Having found the right colors, symbol, and proportions, Hitler subsequently introduced flags, party badges, and armbands. According to Hitler, he introduced the armbands in the summer of 1920. He also acknowledged that his Saalschutz, the forerunner of the SA, enjoyed priority treatment by affirming that "arm-bands were immediately ordered for the monitor detachments."[22] The Nazis also coined a special name for the armband. They referred to it by the especially menacing term *Kampfbinde,* loosely translated as "battle band." Individual SA men were distinguishable by their armbands. SA troops marching together also carried a flag.

Before the 1923 coup attempt, the SA understood itself as part of an antirepublican movement. They dressed in a militaristic way like other Weimar paramilitaries. Unlike most other paramilitaries, the SA did not have peaked caps but ski caps. These caps were modeled after caps worn in the Austro-Hungarian military and German Alpine troops during World War I. Yet the cap was a ski cap and therefore also used nonpolitically for skiing. Windbreakers, breeches, and gaiters looked militaristic, yet also conformed to athletic fashion worn for hiking, for instance. The SA leadership considered breeches to be sports clothing.[23] The early SA therefore looked militaristic, yet with a youthful and athletic spin. When the SA took part in the Beer Hall Putsch in 1923, they blended in with other antirepublican paramilitaries like the Stahlhelm. They understood themselves as part of a larger group that Hitler helped to solidify. Only their red swastika armbands, their red swastika flags, and to an extent their gray ski caps, as seen in figure 4, signaled to observers that the men of the early SA were National Socialists.

THE BROWN SHIRT

Nevertheless, after the failed November 9 coup, Hitler was no longer in control of his men. He was tried and convicted of treason and spent time in jail. Göring went into hiding in Innsbruck, Austria. In Innsbruck he appointed Ernst Röhm as SA deputy leader of the chastened but not abandoned movement. Röhm could and did freely travel back and forth between Germany and Austria and maintained connections with the underground. Gerhard Rossbach, another Nazi supporter and Free Corps leader, also sought security in Austrian exile in Salzburg. Rossbach became Göring's chief of staff in the spring of 1924. A first conspiratorial meeting in Salzburg with Nazis from

FIGURE 4. Early SA in Munich on January 28, 1923. They wear gray ski caps, gray Windbreakers, and the popular gray riding pants with gray gaiters. Also note the swastika flags and the barely visible armbands. Bundesarchiv, Bild 146-1972-087-09 / o.Ang. The German Federal Archives, Koblenz, Germany.

Germany and Austria on May 17 and 18, 1924, represented the first step in the revival of the SA. Both Röhm and Rossbach were present.[24] Göring also attended, although Röhm, who was formally in charge, chaired the meeting. In this conference the delegates decided on guidelines for a reestablishment of the SA.[25] They also took the first steps toward introducing a new uniform that would change the SA's style dramatically.

Contemporaries of Hitler's and Rossbach's, such as, for instance, Winifred Wagner, claimed that Rossbach introduced the Brown Shirt to the Nazis.[26] Even modern scholarship adopted this myth.[27] Yet this is not quite the whole story. To be more precise, this popular myth is an oversimplification. Gerhardt Rossbach himself states that the brown uniform jackets he introduced were not the iconic Brown Shirts, but *Lettow Hemden* (Lettow Shirts). The difference lies in the color and the cut. Lettow Shirts are named after Paul von Lettow-Vorbeck. They were formerly used as the Imperial Army's tropical uniform tunics. Lettow-Vorbeck became a celebrated war hero in Germany because he led a successful guerrilla campaign against superior British forces in Africa. The tropical uniform tunic he and his men wore became known as the Lettow Shirt in recognition of his valor and status. The cut is the same as the Imperial Army tunics.[28] The brown color in the Lettow version is much lighter in hue than the later Brown Shirts.

FIGURE 5. Paul von Lettow-Vorbeck, mounted in the foreground, in a parade in 1919. He wears the khaki colonial uniform. Bundesarchiv, B145 Bild—P008268 / o.Ang. The German Federal Archives, Koblenz, Germany.

Rossbach himself stated in his autobiography, "I would like to note about the Brown Shirt that the Lettow Shirt I introduced was neither in color nor in cut similar to the later Hitler-Shirt." According to Rossbach, the men of the bicycle detachment of his Arbeitsgemeinschaft Rossbach (Working Group Rossbach), a cover name for his Free Corps unit, planned a bicycle trip to East Prussia in 1921. In order to be equipped uniformly, Rossbach himself purchased surplus tropical tunics, as they were worn by colonial officers, and handed them out to his bicyclists. Yet he states that "the shirts were beige-brown, and thus much lighter than the later Hitler-Shirts and adorned with mother of pearl buttons," a feature that the SA Brown Shirts at no time presented.[29]

Rossbach also specifically states that someone else invented the Brown Shirt. In his autobiography, Rossbach maintains that he introduced the Lettow Shirt as a common style of dress for his entire Free Corps and the youth organization Schill-Jugend in 1924. Rossbach furthermore explains that Edmund Heines, one of his former bicycle-detachment officers, introduced and sold the authentic Brown Shirt to the SA himself. Yet the color of this Heines-inspired shirt became darker. Therefore, Rossbach was not, as he himself emphasizes, "the inventor of the 'original' Brown Shirt, as was later on often claimed."[30] Although he did introduce a brown garment, the color of the Lettow Shirt was much lighter, and the cut was drastically different.

There is also one additional, yet obvious, difference between a Lettow Shirt and a Brown Shirt. The "shirt" in Lettow Shirt is a misnomer. These "shirts" were actually jackets. Brown Shirts are cut so that they indeed look like shirts. The Brown Shirt of the SA was always worn with a brown tie. Lettow Shirts are not really shirts but tropical army tunics. They are much longer than Brown Shirts and meant to be worn with a belt. One would not wear a tie with a Lettow Shirt, as one would not wear a tie over their suit jacket today.

Therefore, the Brown Shirt, as later worn by Hitler's SA, had a unique and very distinctive cut. The findings of an official, yet secret, investigation by the senior SA leader Otto Marxer in the SA main archives in 1935 support Rossbach's later claims that Edmund Heines was the inventor of the authentic Brown Shirt. Marxer reported that the patent for the shirt and its introduction to the SA left documentary evidence.[31] According to his report, "The brown shirt in its current form (cut, with belt hooks etc.) can without doubt be traced back to . . . Obergruppenführer [senior group leader] Heines, who . . . was said to have secured for himself some kind of copyright for this shirt."[32]

It was Edmund Heines, then, who invented the Brown Shirt. He officially patented the final cut and thus the distinctive shape of the shirt for himself, thereby claiming ownership. Ultimately, his Brown Shirt became the primary symbol of the SA and the broader Nazi movement, which was fitting because early on Heines became an overly zealous follower of Hitler. As a youth, Heines had volunteered to serve as a soldier in World War I. He served with distinction for bravery, and the army decorated him for his deeds. He left the service in 1919 as a lieutenant and, like many other officers who had no future in the postwar army, joined the Free Corps under Rossbach's command. There, Heines served as an officer in a bicycle detachment. In 1922 Heines joined the Nazi Party and the SA. Rossbach joined the Nazi Party the following year, in 1923, bringing in his new organization, Arbeitsgemeinschaft Rossbach.[33] In 1929 Heines demonstrated his overzealous streak, facing murder charges for killing a communist. He was sentenced to fifteen years in prison but granted amnesty by conservative judges in the same year. Such deeds earned him the trust of Hitler and the SA leadership. In 1933 Hitler awarded Heines the position of chief of police in the eastern German city of Breslau.[34] Interestingly, Edmund Heines seemed to have earned money with his patent on the Brown Shirt as well. A steady stream of extra income must have added to his salary as chief of police. By 1933 the two incomes combined made Heines a moderately well-off man. According to Gerhard Rossbach, for instance, Heines spent money on opulent meals in the exclusive five-star hotel Monopol in Breslau for himself and his entourage.[35]

The positive relationship between Heines and Hitler quickly soured. In 1934, after Hitler had firmly consolidated his power in Germany, he purged the SA leadership. He had both Ernst Röhm and Edmund Heines executed as homosexuals, despite their early contributions to the SA and the Nazi movement. Gerhard Rossbach, however, had disassociated himself from the Nazis in February 1926. Apparently, this decision proved to be a fortuitous one. In 1934, in the wake of the purge, he was incarcerated due to alleged connections to Röhm until January 1935. Yet he escaped with his life.[36] Later on in the same year, Otto Marxer's findings about the true origins of the Brown Shirt were filed in the main archives of the Nazi Party and not taken any further. Hitler decided to rewrite the history of the Brown Shirt over time, to avoid potentially "tainting" the shirt's meaning within the movement and its larger racial and social ideologies.

In 1936 Karl W. H. Koch published an official history of the SA, with approval by the Nazi Party. Inside, Koch mentioned Rossbach in connection with the introduction of the Brown Shirts rather than Lettow Shirts. This publication misdated the introduction of the shirt to the entire SA to April 30, 1925.[37] In 1941 another official party publication about the history of the SA also slightly misdated the introduction of the Brown Shirt to 1925, yet made no mention of Rossbach or Heines as the man who introduced the Lettow Shirt and the original Brown Shirt, respectively, to the SA.[38] Documentary evidence proves that the Brown Shirt became the official uniform shirt of the SA as late as November 1926.[39] The confusion is understandable. Some units, who joined the SA collectively with Rossbach and with Heines, had worn Lettow Shirts as early as 1923. Heines patented his shirt after becoming a Nazi Stormtrooper. Like the ski caps, the fashion caught on among the men. The shirt was popular because it favorably altered the physique of its wearers.

The Brown Shirt preserved in the German Historical Museum archive indeed has a unique cut.[40] It is much shorter than Imperial Army tunics and the then popular trench coats. The Brown Shirt ends at the belt line and has neither the flared skirt effect nor the two additional front pockets that sit below the belt line. The Brown Shirt is constructed from brown cotton material. It is cut single-breasted and has a closed collar that includes collar tabs indicating unit on the right side and rank on the left. The right shoulder has a shoulder board attached. The left shoulder does not. The shirt is buttoned with five buttons, with the first button closing the collar and the final one at the hem of the shirt being small, round, flat, and brown. When worn by an SA man, these two brown buttons would be covered by the prescribed tie and the belt buckle. The three visible buttons that close the shirt in the front are different. They are shaped like brass buttons. Yet they are made from a silver-colored metal material. The two breast pockets are slightly angled and pleated, and they have scalloped button flaps closed by two more shiny metal buttons. Because the shirt is cut extremely short, about one-third of the length of the sleeves runs longer than the shirt. The sleeves end in French cuffs buttoned by two additional metal buttons. The shirt is cut tight at the hem and includes internal tightening belts made from white cotton material that are fastened on the inside with small, round, flat, white buttons. The shirt features the belt-hook system that Imperial Army tunics had. When worn with the prescribed belt, the belt is held in place at the narrowest part of the hip by six belt hooks, which help hold the short shirt in place so as to not ride up the torso. The belt runs through a two-inch-wide loop made from the same brown material of the shirt.[41]

The brown to khaki coloration of the new shirt was eye-catching. The shirt also had an advantageous cut that enhanced the male body. The brown SA uniform visually made the wearer more appealing to the public, who had learned to value beauty and masculinity. The specific feature of an ideal male body in Western society is a muscular physique. In addition, height was a factor contributing to perceived attractiveness.[42] The clever cut of the Brown Shirt made men look both tall and fit due to its high-waisted cut that made the men's legs appear longer.

Unlike regular shirts that were worn tucked into the trousers, the hem of the Brown Shirt sat on top of the waistline. The shirt was not really a shirt, but rather an extremely short jacket that was never tucked into the breeches. The sleeves of the shirt appeared long because the shirt was cut so short. When worn according to regulation with breeches, this short-cut shirt created the illusion of a taller physique. The torso of the wearer appeared shorter because the belt was worn higher than seen on other garments. With arms and legs that looked long in relation to a torso that seemed shorter, even stout men appeared to be taller and leaner than they were. Heavy individuals with wide hips looked thinner. Meek and thin individuals appeared as if their frame was bigger and more squared above the knees. In essence, the Nazis fashioned the shirt to make all of their men appear hypermasculine at a time in which they considered their nation degenerate and especially weak. According to the Nazis, the Treaty of Versailles emasculated the German people. The Nazis thus visually reflected their ideological goals with their outward appearance.

The SA man, however, looked not only masculine and attractive but also neat. The shirt had six holes on the lower hem, which held metal hooks. Intended to hold a heavy leather equipment belt, this belt-hook design came from the German Imperial Army. The weight of the equipment worn by soldiers on their belts was evenly distributed onto the entire garment and did not pull the belt down. Because of this adoption from military tailoring, the heavy leather belt always positioned itself correctly. The belt would never be weighed down unevenly and could not slip to the hips. Another effect this cut imparted was the appearance that the SA man had recently tucked in his shirt. The belt would always weigh down the shirt. So, even if an individual ran, brawled in the street, or even periodically lifted his right arm to give the Nazi salute, the Brown Shirt would never come untucked or hang sloppily over the trousers.

FIGURE 6.
The inventor of the Brown Shirt, Edmund Heines. He poses in his shirt as SA-Sturmführer, ca. 1924–25. The belt-hook system is clearly visible. Note that he is not wearing a swastika armband. Bundesarchiv, Bild 119–1231 / o.Ang. The German Federal Archives, Koblenz, Germany.

The SA men also looked neat because, according to regulation, the shirt was always worn with a necktie. The tie lent the ensemble a rather bourgeois quality. One should remember that in the 1920s and 1930s, a male of higher social ranking would never be seen without a tie or, even worse, with an open collar. The SA uniform thus also incorporated a certain class component. SA men looked like bourgeois youths in shirtsleeves. The Brown Shirt looked like a shirt because of its extremely short cut. This gave the outfit an even more youthful and dynamic spin. The SA did not wear tunics or, for that matter, the Windbreakers so popular with the other conservative paramilitaries. They dressed more youthful than, for example, the veterans of the Stahlhelm. Yet they did not abandon a conservative and bourgeois appeal at the same time. The introduction of the Brown Shirt occurred, however, after the important leadership meeting in Salzburg where Röhm, Rossbach, and Göring met in 1924 while the SA remained underground.

Following the Beer Hall Putsch of 1923 and Hitler's incarceration in 1924, the official refounding of the SA occurred in 1926. Hitler opted to change tactics and pursue legal paths to power via parliamentary elections. Accordingly, Hitler aimed at changing his popular image from drummer of a broad antirepublican movement to leader, or *Führer,* of his movement.[43] This movement was supposed to captivate the public eye.[44] In this quest, the SA also evolved into a propaganda army. The organization's new duties and dress code functioned in tandem. As the party's public face, SA dress needed to be instantly recognizable by all. The organization's character thus shifted from one of secrecy to one of perceived transparency.

According to Hitler's first order to the newly established SA, the Stormtroopers had political purposes only. Yet the wording of the order also shows that violence clearly remained a component of SA life. For these new purposes, the SA needed both a recognizable uniform and sizable units in order to be effective. Large groups of uniformed SA were supposed to "conquer the streets" and sweep it clear of Marxist enemies. Hitler intended to give the SA a new (and triumphant) public image. Yet this image did not solely rest on violence. Ultimately, the value of the SA, according to Hitler, lay in its capability to visually impress the public.[45] This first order therefore manifested the duality of the second SA as an organization.

Hitler emphasized this point in a third official SA order. This order, from November 3, 1926, titled "SA and Public (Propaganda)," reads, "The SA faces the public in closed formations only. This is . . . one of the most powerful forms of propaganda . . . which leaves the deepest impression on every German and speaks to his heart in a more convincing and rousing language than script, and speech, and logic can ever do."[46] This was not simply one of Hitler's theories. Sociologists today confirm the persuasiveness of such public displays. Propaganda of the deed is much more convincing than verbal propaganda.[47] To accomplish this kind of propaganda, the new SA needed a uniform that differentiated them from all other German political paramilitary organizations. Along with the legal path to power came the adoption of the Brown Shirt across the entire organization.

These changes came with yet another new leader. Hitler appointed the former officer and Free Corps member Franz Pfeffer von Salomon as the new SA leader in 1926. Pfeffer von Salomon introduced reforms that structured the SA along military lines. Military uniforms are usually designed in a top-down manner. Typically, they are controlled by an organization's leadership and then implemented and required for all members.[48] As mentioned above, the story of the SA uniform was different. It developed piece by piece and started with the Brown Shirt. Initially, Hitler had nothing to do with this process. The Brown Shirt became popular at the grassroots level in 1924, after the Salzburg meeting.

The introduction of Heines's patented Brown Shirt therefore occurred in stages. Documentary evidence shows that SA units adopted the shirt at varying times, with some units sporting the shirt earlier than others. Viktor Lutze, the district and SA leader of the northern Rhineland, and later national leader of the SA, sent a letter to the leadership of the party in Munich in August 1925 requesting clear guidance regarding the correct dress for the SA.[49] Lutze expressed worry about the lack of visual uniformity among his SA and had sent earlier notes without any official reply. This fact contradicts the mistaken April 30, 1925, date for the introduction of the shirt to the SA as claimed by Karl W. H. Koch. Lutze received a reply from the party leadership after only a few days, stating, "The members of the SA wear the Hitler-cap, Brown Shirt with brown necktie (to order through Müller, Solln . . . [in the vicinity of] Munich, Number 26 Lindenallee), and a gray pair of sports pants with wool wrap puttees." The ski cap, the breeches, and the wool-wrap puttees remained the same, gray, civilian sports clothing. Therefore, 1925 started a transitional period from the old gray to brown. The shirt-and-tie combination initiated this change. The caps and breeches became brown later to give the uniform a more coherent look. Still, the Brown Shirt and tie were supposed to be ordered exclusively from one retailer in a small town close to Munich, which made the switch to the Brown Shirt difficult on a large scale.[50]

THE BROWN SERVICE DRESS

The change of regulating the color of the cap from gray to brown was included in the tenth official order to all troopers. This order regulated public behavior and dress and was announced on November 14, 1926. SA Order Ten described the *Dienst-Anzug*, literally "service-dress." Notably, the word *uniform* does not appear in the order. This wording was a result of the party's new legal path to power. The SA had officially abandoned its roots as a clandestine army. Semantically, the SA could not wear a uniform due to the military connotation. Instead of developing a garment based on a civilian model, however, the SA simply changed the name of the attire from the militaristic SA "uniform" to "service dress." SA Order Ten introducing the service dress included minor changes to the policy given to Lutze in 1925. The cap was now supposed to be brown rather than gray. According to this document, the service dress of the SA consisted of "the brown shirt (necktie and cap) with insignia." The insignia included "color patches, numbers, stars, strings, trimmings, shiny metal buttons on cap and breast pockets, armband, etc." The Brown Shirt without the insignia could be worn by all members of the party. The order indicated that the color of the pants should now be brown as well. "Ridiculous fashion styles of pants," like the then fashionable knickerbockers, were forbidden. Breeches in gray and black hues, however, were not strictly banned. The breeches and the footwear, in fact, could not be mandated. They could only be kept similar. Still, the outfit was completed by a wide belt, "if possible, with shoulder strap."[51] This order made Heines's shirt the official uniform shirt for the SA and the entire Nazi Party. Party officials were required to wear the shirt during official functions. Additionally, regular party members were allowed to buy the shirt for themselves, even if they were not in the SA or full-time Nazi Party administrators.

With this standardization of the uniform, the production and further development of the Brown Shirt became centralized. The party also monopolized the sale of the new "service dress." Only the party, or officially licensed businesses, could sell the new uniforms. From 1926 on, the SA Wirtschaftsstelle (Economic Office) in Munich distributed official Brown Shirts, caps, and ties made from the iconic brown fabric. With centralized distribution, the party no longer contracted production to the retailer Müller mentioned above. However, the party had not created a single office just for the procurement of uniforms and paraphernalia (belts, insignia, marching equipment, and so forth) quite yet. The SA Wirtschaftsstelle was not the only entity that could produce or outsource the production of the shirts.

Party policy directed, "Where large SA sections exist women's groups can be formed to produce shirts and ties."[52] Women could sew the uniforms with the help of a preexisting pattern. The fabric for these shirts and ties, however, was also supposed to be ordered from the center in Munich. Centralization and monopolization were products of the SA's new image and its existence as a legitimate propaganda troop. These processes ensured that all SA uniforms looked more or less alike and that the party would always earn part of the revenues. However, the full uniform was expensive. It took time for ordinary SA men to purchase each element of the entire outfit. Many SA men came from the lower-middle class and the working class, and many were unemployed.[53] Because of that, despite the strict guidelines, it took years to fully transition all SA men from gray to brown.

The 1926 party rally was the first mass demonstration of the SA in which some units wore the new Brown Shirt. It took place in a city without mass support. The 1926 rally signaled the rebirth of the Nazi movement, which aggressively entered the heart of the Weimar Republic, the city of Weimar itself. The rally took place during the transitional period. Hitler chose to wear the old Windbreaker like those of his men who did not have the means to buy a Brown Shirt right away. However, the 1926 party rally marked the transition to the new SA image.[54] During this, and the following party rallies, Hitler and his SA leader, Franz Pfeffer von Salomon, ensured that the SA leadership could control any further changes and improvements on the brown uniforms through official questionnaires. The Nazis were open to change.

Hitler was, for instance, willing to experiment with traditional clothing and with a jacket to be worn over the Brown Shirt as the 1927 party rally proved. Breeches were optional for all Bavarians. SA Order Ten, introducing the new service dress, made special provisions for Bavarian SA men. The order specified that Bavarians could wear the traditional Bavarian lederhosen, short leather pants made of elk hide.[55] SA leader Pfeffer von Salomon and Hitler wore this specifically Bavarian garment with the new shirt. Bavarians were the only members allowed to combine traditional dress with the service dress of the SA. This was a concession to Bavaria as the home state of the Nazi movement and as the adopted home of the émigré Austrian Hitler. Hitler had served in a Bavarian unit during the First World War. Bavaria was also home to a strong nationalist-conservative movement during the Weimar period. Thus, Hitler allowed his Bavarian SA to wear an especially conservative piece of attire. Yet Hitler, Pfeffer von Salomon, and the SA leadership wore the Brown Shirt at the party rally in 1927 rather than the outdated trench coat. Leading by example, they modeled the new outfit for the attending masses.[56]

Pfeffer von Salomon wore the Bavarian shorts and a very short jacket in addition to the mandated uniform items. The jacket, however, was not adopted by the SA. Interestingly, the Nazis feminized this very distinctive jacket, named *Kletterweste* (climbing vest). This jacket became part of the uniform for young girls in the Bund Deutscher Mädel (League of German Girls, or BDM), the female branch of the Hitler Youth.[57] The Nazis tested certain elements, rejected some, and then introduced other elements to other Nazi organizations. It is interesting to note that although the Nazis propagated fundamental gender roles, they did dress young girls in a jacket that was originally worn by the highest-ranking (male) SA leader. The girls in the BDM did not all own the jacket. Nevertheless, well-off girls had the right to purchase the jacket because it was officially part of the BDM uniform. The girls also wore a white shirt and a black skirt with the jacket. Like the boys in the Hitler Youth, the girls wore the distinctive black neckerchief with the braided leather ring. The *Kletterweste* further masculinized this feminine outfit. It gave the look a more rugged feel and gave the girls a more athletic and militaristic expression. Even German girls looked tough and wore proper uniforms with BDM insignia and signs of rank, thereby participating in the Nazis' ideal image-construction process.[58] Nevertheless, before the jacket became a girls' jacket, some SA men, like Pfeffer von Salomon, purchased the jacket.[59] The climbing vest never became part of the officially regulated SA uniform, not because it appeared too feminine but rather because it would have made the uniform more expensive.

The official uniform by 1926 consisted strictly of only the brown cap, Brown Shirt, and brown tie. This uniform standardized the upper bodies of SA men and was relatively cheap. The desired effect was therefore apparently sufficient. Pfeffer von Salomon summarized his impressions on the propagandistic effect of the new uniform in a critique of the rally. According to Pfeffer von Salomon's SA order from August 22, 1927, his SA had "given the German people a clearly visible proof of the power that fills our movement and will lead us to victory." Pfeffer von Salomon explained exactly what he meant when he commented on "the powerful uniformity of the SA."[60] The leadership of both the party and the SA was aware of the propagandistic

FIGURE 7. Hitler and his SA leader, Franz Pfeffer von Salomon, in 1927. Pfeffer von Salomon wears the Bavarian leather shorts. He also wears the climbing vest, discussed above, over his Brown Shirt. Bundesarchiv, Bild 146-2020-0004 / o.Ang. The German Federal Archives, Koblenz, Germany.

effect of the new uniform. According to the leadership, large numbers of men dressed in the new uniform were, together, a very potent sign of the movement's rebirth.

Yet the new uniform still had room for improvement. On August 25, Pfeffer von Salomon sent another order to the entire SA requesting feedback. This order highlights an interesting process regarding SA dress policy. This process includes consultation and market testing. This belies the formally hierarchical structure of the SA and shows a limited feedback loop. If requested, feedback was welcome. Even though a specific change might not have been anticipated, a new feature might just be incorporated into the dress code if it was practical, popular, and looked attractive. Pfeffer von Salomon ordered lower-level and midlevel leaders to report in written form on the experiences of the party rally. The high command specifically wanted to know if "the new insignia worked well" as well as whether "chinstraps for the caps [should] be introduced? They very much enhance the look, yet they also make the caps more expensive and are useless on our caps."[61] The feedback request shows that some SA units coming to the rally sported caps with chinstraps. When the strap was worn under the chin, the cap appeared more aggressive. The visor shaded the eyes of the wearer. The chin also looked harder. A cap held down by a strap suggests dynamic movement, a positive feature for their desired image.

Heinrich Hoffman, Hitler's personal photographer, took a few pictures of Hitler with the new SA cap including the chinstrap at the 1927 party rally. Hitler, however, wore the new cap only a few times on this occasion. He usually addressed audiences without a head covering. During his dictatorship, as supreme commander of the German armed forces, Hitler wore the saddle-shaped military-style cap as worn in the German Army. Yet as leader of the Nazi movement during the Weimar Republic, the charismatic leader refused to be shown wearing the cap of a simple SA man. Totalitarian leaders like Hitler needed to stand out from their uniformed followers in order to visually symbolize their leadership role. After Hitler decided on a uniform for himself, he always appeared in the same outfit and changed it only when his perceived role in society changed. Wearing the SA cap did not have the same symbolic value as wearing the cap of a German Army officer. However, the cap was adopted as a mandatory piece of the regular SA "service dress."[62]

Through questionnaires after rallies, the Nazis established feedback channels to improve their uniforms via input from the party base. This signifies that the base had a voice in the construction of the SA image. The SA, at least in this sense, was more democratic than one may expect. For instance, an SA unit from Munich had embellished their caps with a colored strip of fabric between the brown upstanding earflaps and the brown top of the cap. The fabric had the same color as the unit's collar patches, which indicated what geographical region an SA unit came from. With the colored fabric on the cap, the region could be identified even if one stood behind a trooper. The party communications show how the higher leadership asked lower-level and midlevel leaders for input. Both of the noted improvements to the cap—the chinstrap and colored fabric—eventually became part of the standardized SA cap. The SA developed their look in a centralized

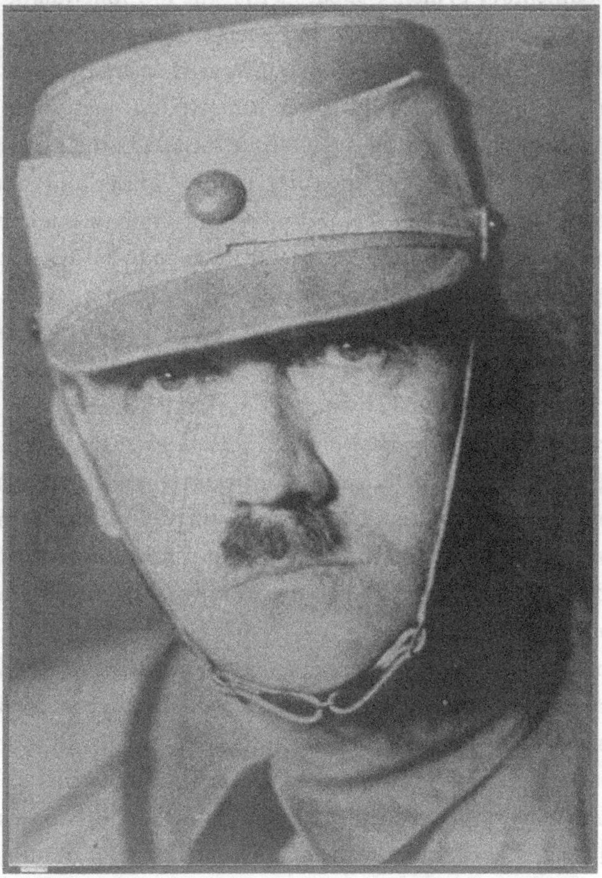

FIGURE 8. Hitler wearing the SA cap. The chinstrap could be worn above the visor or under the chin. With the strap under the chin, the chin appears harder. The overall impression becomes more martial. Bundesarchiv, Bild 146-2020-0005 / Hoffmann, Heinrich. The German Federal Archives, Koblenz, Germany.

manner. Mirroring military command structure, input was wanted, yet only if requested from the SA or NSDAP leadership.

In this manner, the ski cap changed even more. The shape of the cap altered slightly. The cap became stiffer rather than the traditional soft ski-cap style. In later versions, the cap became rigid and could no longer be folded, meaning that the earflaps on the later versions became purely stylized and no longer functioned as their predecessors had. An additional layer of fabric still appeared as an earflap that one could unbutton, yet the layer was sewn permanently to the side of the cap and served no practical purpose. The entire impression looked stiffer with a higher crown. These later brown SA caps had a distinctive coffee-can shape.

Documentary evidence suggests that the introduction of a stiffer cap with higher crown might have served a sinister and practical purpose related to style and image. A stiff cap with high crown, fastened with a strap, could soften a blow. This was an important change, given the rising tide of violence the SA, in their conspicuous uniform, provoked during the early 1930s.[63] Hitler and Pfeffer von Salomon wanted to grant their SA more protection through the introduction of a rubber foam–lined metal skullcap to be worn under the SA cap. In an SA-wide order titled "Head Protection," from August 1930, the SA leadership argued that 80 percent of all injuries suffered by the SA in fights with Marxists were injuries to the head. Since a protective helmet was legally not allowed, the leadership introduced this "substitute head protection" in order to give their men a "more secure feeling." The SA effectively introduced an illegal form of an improvised and intentionally concealed steel helmet.[64] The introduction of the chinstrap and the new style of cap make sense when one considers these measures. The SA was now well equipped for clash violence in the streets.

The centralized surveys and questionnaires established by Pfeffer von Salomon in 1926 allowed for the coordinated improvement of the existing uniform through the rest of the decade. They allowed for the organic introduction of fashionable, practical, and protective elements. As the incorporation of the Brown Shirt showed, the Nazi leadership initially acted opportunistically and adopted popular trends after the troopers helped establish them. This creative adoption with intellectual incoherence allowed the Nazis to appeal to different audiences. Although this method was practical, opportunistic, and comparatively cheap, it was also messy and complicated in the application. This can be seen in the fact that up until 1935, Hitler himself did not exactly know where the Brown Shirt came from.[65] Nevertheless, once a specific feature of the uniform had reached a certain level of popularity, Hitler decided on its general adaptation. He did not have to come up with an original idea; he just determined official changes after his own taste.

The signs of rank and insignia, for instance, underwent changes in a similar method over a number of years. The procedure was disorganized. Yet in this particular process, Hitler showed an incredible amount of agency and reserved the ultimate decisions for himself. In 1929 Hitler and Pfeffer von Salomon published an SA order regarding the improved signs of rank. Again, the new insignia for officers became more colorful. The military-like signs of rank with a complicated structure, designed to accommodate for the growth of the SA, were supposed to help officers stand out from their men.[66] Hitler fussed over little details when it came to the uniform and insignia, which resulted in further confusion and complicated rule changes. In March 1931, Hitler allowed his SA men to wear the eagle clasping the swastika, a right that originally only officers enjoyed.[67] In the same month, Ernst Röhm, who had returned as SA chief of staff, gave an order to his men specifying that the eagle was to be worn on the tie and the party badge on the cap.[68] Hitler, however, did not approve. Only two months later, in May, Röhm sent out yet another order about the insignia. According to Röhm, Hitler had settled the issue during a leadership conference and decided that the eagle was worn on the cap and the party badge on the tie.[69] This decision-making process regarding the uniforms of the SA is comparable to the way Hitler generally approached decisions regarding the Nazi image. If something was popular with a certain section of the German population and could be integrated, such as, for instance, the popular socialist May Day festivities, then Hitler officially sanctioned and thus incorporated it.[70] In this way, Hitler established an SA uniform that perfectly suited his needs. It was supposed to get attention, impress supporters, and intimidate opponents. It also provided security. Some SA men engaged in clash violence wearing the hidden foam-lined metal helmets under their caps.

CONCLUSION

Hitler himself knew that the visual impact of the SA cannot be neglected. Nazi voting patterns in Weimar Germany have been studied extensively. No single social group consistently voted for the Nazis.

Rather, the Nazis were able to draw votes from multiple different sections of society. The Nazis attracted the upper classes as well as the upper-middle class. On the legal path to power, they transformed themselves into a people's party that offered something for everyone. When liberals and conservatives lost voters after 1930, the Nazis became a party that then integrated the middle-class voting bloc. The Nazis became a catchall party attracting voters from many layers of German society.[71] For a party that appealed to many distinct groups, the uniform, and thus the visual impression, was important. The fascist message broadcasted differed slightly from audience to audience. Nevertheless, the way this message was delivered remained constant. The uniform, in this context, is the major visible feature of cohesion.

Regulating and standardizing the new SA uniform also served an important function. The fact that the SA wore a party uniform according to strict regulations and with insignia of rank led to the SA's association with protective organizations like the army. This had its advantages. Susan B. Kaiser argues that "a well-regimented appearance is expected in protective organizations, because such an image is viewed as a sign of efficiency and competency."[72] The SA standardized their uniforms to appear both efficient and competent.

The brown Nazi uniform carried cultural symbolism originating in the military that endowed a cultural conception of respectability on the Nazis.[73] Hitler and the SA leadership fashioned the SA image by combining the nineteenth-century affinity for the military with new cultural elements, in the form of sports garments coupled with a bourgeois tie. Additionally, the cut of the Brown Shirt was unique. It visually altered the physique of its wearers and made them look tall and fit. Unlike a military uniform or the dress of the other paramilitaries, the Nazi uniform transformed all men into attractive and neat-looking people. The Brown Shirt was ironically more democratic in this sense. Nevertheless, this uniform was the result of a lengthy process.

The evolution of the SA and its uniform occurred simultaneously. The Brown Shirt first developed in a decentralized manner and with private initiative. With the official incorporation of the new brown uniform into the SA, this process changed. The further development of the uniform occurred in a centralized manner. Yet surveys tracked popular trends, which only the leadership could then legitimize. The result was a new uniform well suited for Hitler's purposes.

By the early 1930s, the shirt was the image-bearing hallmark of the Nazi movement at a national level. The diary entry of Hamburg resident Luise Solmitz from March 6, 1932, shows the impact the uniform had on contemporary observers. Hamburg was far from the original southern German birthplace of the party's movement and its shirt. According to Solmitz, "It is peculiar, what role brown plays in the life of this Brown Shirt leader [Hitler]; born in Braunau, headquarters in Braunschweig." Interestingly, Despina Stratigakos hints at the opportunistic attitude the Nazis displayed when it came to the construction of their image. According to her, Hitler did not like the color brown.[74] Yet by 1926 the color brown had come to embody the Nazi movement.

Compared to the other paramilitaries in the streets of the Weimar Republic, the SA stood out. This was intentional. The Brown Shirt made the SA men in the street look attractive, tall, and muscular, yet also aggressive and intimidating. The distinctive color and cut of the Heines shirt had a signal effect that triggered clash violence. Large numbers of SA men provided more safety for one another when such violence occurred. Still, the numbers also provided difficulties. The uniforms needed to be mass-produced, distributed to local outlets, and then sold to the individual SA troopers.

Chapter Three

THE BROWN GARMENT OF HONOR, MATERIAL CULTURE, AND SOCIAL CONTROL

Although they frequently caused clash violence, the SA represented themselves as conservative defenders of order. The Nazis actively used violence to shape a specific image. The goal was to look attractive to supporters and intimidating to everyone else. The contradiction between discipline and violent indiscipline was thus intentional.[1] The creation of this dual image was not an easy task. The German fascists, however, succeeded in this task by establishing a certain degree of discipline among the troopers. This discipline can be divided into two specific types: first, discipline in violence; second, discipline during public performances. The SA established and maintained both kinds of discipline within their organization.

Although violence may initially seem chaotic, SA men were ordered to act bravely, and thus disciplined in the face of bodily harm. SA men were not allowed to avoid violence by flight. Heroic defenders were not allowed to flee the Marxists. To flee was considered cowardly behavior. On the one hand, defeat of the SA by the Marxists could be rewritten as a heroic battle against all odds. Fleeing SA, on the other hand, appeared weak and would undermine efforts to create the desired image. Even worse, the leftist press could exploit these situations for their own propaganda. SA officers, therefore, disciplined their men to act in desired ways during clash violence. Stormtrooper officers used uniforms to successfully transform their unsavory SA men into well-disciplined teams.[2]

Additionally, the SA was supposed to leave a positive impression during public propaganda marches and rallies that did not include the likelihood of clash violence. The SA needed to act with military-like precision and discipline to make the correct impression and cultivate their dual image. This was problematic since the SA was a voluntary organization during the Weimar era. The SA leadership did not have the right to punish their troopers for bad behavior. Ultimately, the SA succeeded in visually impressing Nazi sympathizers with military-like order and Brown Shirted uniformity during marches.[3]

The SA uniform was a fitting tool for social control at a time when officers relied on voluntary behavior to construct a well-disciplined image for use in public propaganda. The Nazis accomplished this by applying a two-pronged approach to ensure bravery and discipline among the men of the SA. First, the Nazis used modern capitalism and marketing techniques to their advantage. Second, the Nazis appealed to the honor of the men by using the uniform as a technique to reward men for adhering to the behavioral standards propagated by the Nazi leadership.

CONSUMPTION AND CONSUMERISM

On the surface, it appears as if there was an interconnected relationship between consumption and consumerism and the development of Western democracy specifically. Hitler, nevertheless, also used the modern concepts of consumption and consumerism masterfully for his own causes. The uniform of the SA was key to this approach. The men of the SA were voluntarily acting as consumers within the Nazi ideological machine. Indeed, the development of modern consumer culture and the demise of liberal democracy in Germany therefore occurred simultaneously, reinforcing one another.[4] As the example of the SA shows, German fascists applied the energies and financial resources of consumers in their quest to first destabilize and then dismantle democracy.

Officially, however, the Nazis opposed modern consumerism.[5] Yet the SA provided well-off SA men with the opportunity to indulge their desires in consumerist fashion in special stores that provided uniforms and equipment of various qualities and price ranges. The financially secure SA trooper had a choice and could buy officially sanctioned, fashionable embellishments to complete his outfit.[6] The social stratification of consumers is fostered by a difference in quality, as seen in the manner of production and the precise form of consumption.[7] The Nazis thus maintained an ambiguous relationship with consumerism.

Therefore, the Nazis also provided the men with the option of simple consumption in the name of the movement mostly because many SA men lacked the financial resources to purchase more than the necessary parts of the uniform. These men engaged in consumption rather than consumerism. The consumption of services and experiences, such as health care and travel, was indeed important. SA troopers additionally engaged in the acts of purchasing a shirt, tie, and cap.[8] The consumption practices of individual SA men fostered the development of a collective identity. In this way, the uniform provided avenues of agency to the men and simultaneously allowed Hitler to harness their physical energies and their financial resources into the service of the Nazi cause.

The act of buying the uniform was a disciplinary measure in and of itself. SA recruits had to set up a savings plan, either by themselves or with the help of credits extended to them by the party. It took discipline to obtain a complete basic uniform, consisting of a shirt, cap, and tie. For an unemployed SA man in a time of severe economic hardship, food and housing costs were more important than a fancy uniform. An unemployed SA man would have found it difficult to save enough money for a complete uniform because the officially licensed uniforms were expensive, as may be seen in a surviving catalog. This catalog is complete with telephone and bank-account numbers. The Nazis copied a specific American consumer model by establishing mail-order catalogs and call-in order services.[9]

Troopers could call in an order, transfer the money, and receive their uniform in the mail. In this undated catalog, an SA service tunic is also included. According to John Angolia, the SA leadership introduced the first of these tunics to officers in 1932, so the catalog can be roughly dated to the post-1932 period.[10] This catalog shows a wide variety of uniform items, leather accessories, flags, and additional gear. The most affordable uniform cost roughly 6 Reichsmark (RM) for the basic Brown Shirt in the cheapest (that is, lowest-quality) fabric. The least expensive tie cost about 0.85 RM. The cap in the cheap, soft version cost 2.40 RM. The belt and shoulder strap then cost an additional 5.30 RM.[11] Thus, the most inexpensive regulation uniform cost 14–15 RM, making it fairly expensive for the time. The weekly allowance for an unemployed SA man in Hamburg in 1930, for instance, was only 10 RM.[12]

SA leaders demanded that their men purchase the full uniform. However, many SA members found it difficult to come up with the financial means. Sturmführer Weber, a leader of one of Hamburg's reserve SA troops, proclaimed in a report to his superiors dated April 23, 1931, in the midst of the global economic recession, that his men did not have complete uniforms because they were so expensive. Weber exaggerated the prices to excuse his inadequately uniformed men. He argued, "Unfortunately, clothing is still not satisfactory." He excused the situation by stating, "Of course, these are only obstacles of a financial kind. . . . [T]he procurement of the most necessary clothes . . . [consisting of] leather putties, cap, belt, and shoulder strap, call together for at least 3000 [RM]." He admitted, "Paying is not something I can order. I am dependent on the financial situation of my men. I have reported that the reserve unit be ready for inspection by May first. . . . [T]he most urgent items will be procured by then."[13] Weber meant only the basic outfit. He implied that his men would at a later point of time complete their uniforms. Weber's tactic to add up the uniform prices for all of his 310 men resulted in the outrageous sum of 3,000 RM. He thus came up with an estimate of a little under 10 Marks for every man. Of course, Weber tried to create the impression of an excessively high price in his report so that his tardiness might be excused. Nevertheless, Weber's excuse shows that even for many older and wealthier men in an SA reserve unit, it was difficult to save enough for the complete outfit. In the crisis years of the early thirties, the uniform was expensive for most SA members. Saving for and buying each successive uniform item was no doubt an act of individual discipline. The high price made Hitler's brown garment of honor even more exclusive.

In order to keep this source of revenue, the party monopolized the sale of the new uniforms. Only the party or officially licensed businesses could sell Brown Shirts. From early 1926 on, the SA Wirtschaftsstelle (SA Economic Office) in Munich distributed official Brown Shirts, caps, and ties to special retailers. Centralization and monopolization were products of the SA's new image and its legitimate existence as a propaganda troop. These processes ensured that all SA uniforms looked alike and that the party earned a portion of all revenues. Demand quickly outgrew the capabilities of the Wirtschaftsstelle. Thus, the Nazis created a Brown brand with its own transportation and supply logistics, stores, and a central administration office. By 1928 the SA ran this Reichszeugmeisterei, a kind of party-equipment office, or quartermaster office.[14] A guideline for the formation of new SA locals from 1929 stated that new SA recruits must order their shirts, caps, and ties with the "Zeugmeisterei South in Number 50, Schellingstreet, Munich."[15] This office outsourced the production of uniforms and paraphernalia to private companies and controlled quality and prices. These companies were allowed to stamp, or otherwise mark, their product with an official Reichszeugmeisterei (RZM) seal that also included a product number. Between 1929 and 1933, the number of local RZM offices grew. An SA regulations leaflet from February 1, 1933, gives addresses for eleven RZM offices in Düsseldorf, Dresden, Hannover, Munich, Berlin, Hamburg, Breslau, Magdeburg, Frankfurt-Main, Vienna, and Königsberg.[16] By 1933 the RZM had offices in all German regions, as well as in Austria, that functioned as logistical distribution hubs.

Simultaneously, the party established many Braune Läden, or "Brown Stores," which received merchandise from these RZM hubs. The RZM procured the merchandise, and the Brown Stores were licensed to sell the official products. In these stores one could get everything a dedicated Nazi needed to complete his service dress or equipment. In contrast to a cash-strapped SA loyalist, a well-off SA man could indulge in a virtual shopping frenzy at the local Brown Store. The rich not only bought the basic uniform items in much better quality, although for a higher price tag, but could also buy matching pants, sports outfits, camping gear, and more. Men with money could buy portraits of Adolf Hitler, Franz Pfeffer von Salomon, and other leading Nazis. It seems as if the Nazis possessed a keen sense for business, contrary to anticapitalist Nazi claims. If there was money to be made, the Nazis found a way to get it. The Nazis used the capitalist system and liberal bourgeois business practices to their financial advantage. Nazi leaders clearly understood how to sell Brown paraphernalia and earn money even in times of financial crisis. Both consumption and consumerism thus played into the hands of the National Socialists.

In 1932 Ernst Röhm ordered in an SA regulation leaflet (*SA Verordnungsblatt*) that all SA members must buy only RZM-licensed products. He made the order more appealing by offering a 5 percent discount and issuing warnings against buying knockoff Brown Shirts from cheaper, nonlicensed retailers.[17] Again the leadership found it necessary to make concessions to the men. Breaches of discipline and the purchase of bargain shirts appear to have been common. The leadership wanted to use the men as a captive market, yet they realized this was impossible with the current standard and given the national economic situation. Accordingly, the leaders adopted compromises that acted more as the proverbial carrot than the stick. The Nazis tried to monopolize the RZM by directing negative propaganda against companies that tried to sell cheap, imitation Brown Shirts.

Evidence in the form of contemporary advertisements suggests, however, that the men continued to find alternative ways to acquire the desired garments from unofficial sources, including homemade or inexpensive knockoffs. In an effort to counter these tendencies among the men, the RZM produced professional advertisements. The boundaries between political propaganda and advertisement during the Weimar era were fluid. Advertisements for the Brown Shirt reflected Nazi attitudes toward masculinity and beauty. The advertisements depicted the ideal SA man as healthy and fit. This ideal overlapped with general cultural preferences based on Greek models of beauty that commonly found expressions in Weimar-era attitudes toward the human body. Nazi advertisements also followed the American model and were accompanied by a short text, or slogan, to emphasize quality and to make a connection to a specific lifestyle or subcultural market.[18]

In order to persuade new recruits to buy the RZM-brand Brown Shirt, the officially licensed producers came up with the slogan *Nur beim Zeugmeister* (Only from the RZM). The slogan was usually accompanied with visual graphics, or cartoons, as depicted in figures 10 and 11.

FIGURE 9. A Brown Store in 1931. Note the rich window display that includes uniforms, flags, and paraphernalia attached to an SA tavern in Berlin. Bundesarchiv, Bild 102–04636A / Pahl, Georg. The German Federal Archives, Koblenz, Germany.

FIGURE 10. Advertisement from a 1929 party-rally brochure. Federal Archive, Document Archive, Berlin, NS 26 304. Reprinted with permission.

Figure 10 is an advertisement from a 1929 Nazi Party rally brochure. The rally had the character of a festival and included competitive sports, a brass band, and Nazi speakers. On such occasions, the Nazis generally combined political propaganda with entertainment. Brochures like this included a multitude of advertisements for Nazi products and services. This brochure, for instance, includes advertisements for SA field kitchens, SA sports clothing, flagpole tips, a photography studio, and an insurance company. The featured cartoon is captioned by the slogan *Nur beim Zeugmeister.* This advertisement includes the negative stereotype of a dubious businessman, who is depicted as short, fat, and with a stereotypical bourgeois bowler hat. This rather suspect entrepreneur offers a knockoff Brown Shirt to an SA man. The tall and unyielding SA man, decked out in all the paraphernalia of a Brown Store, including hiking backpack, rejects the imitation brown shirt offered to him. The party tried to associate cheap, off-brand shirts with shady business practices and, ironically, with capitalist attitudes guided by profits. The depiction of the SA trooper clearly shows how the RZM advertisement reflects masculine ideals of SA subculture.

Figure 11 shows a page from a 1932 rally brochure. The full-page advertisement for the RZM Nordmark, the party procurement office for northern Germany, features a trim, young SA man tightening up his uniform belt. Again, the SA trooper is in full uniform, looks appealing and energetic, and is framed by the slogan *Vorschriftsmässige SA*

FIGURE 11. Advertisement from a 1932 Nazi rally brochure. Federal Archive, Document Archive, Berlin, NS 23 405. Reprinted with permission.

Ausrüstung nur beim Zeugmeister (Regulation SA equipment only from the party procurement office). The silhouette of the trooper highlights the trim fit of the shirt. This advertisement features a positive stereotype, playing to the cultural preferences of radical young men. These types of advertisements address the vanities of the ad's intended audience and simultaneously suggest that only legitimate brand stores offered quality shirts. The fact that the party advertised in brochures aimed at their most loyal and vigilant members shows that it had serious difficulties keeping their men in line. The evidence suggests that knockoff shirts and homemade shirts remained a popular option.

No matter where the men obtained the shirts, documentary evidence suggests that the men enjoyed being seen wearing their Brown Shirts in public. The leader of Hamburg's SA Troop 6, Sturmführer Bisschopinck, made remarks about the popularity of the uniform and disciplinary problems in an August 4, 1928, order to his men. Due to an alarming tendency among his troopers to be absent from SA duty without an excuse, when public marches in uniform were not on the agenda for the day Bisschopinck felt compelled to warn his troopers that they must attend. He complained that "Troop 6, with strength of 73 men, was recently never stronger than 25 to 30." Therefore, he felt compelled to "order that . . . whoever misses service two times will be fired." He warned his troopers, "We are not a parade troop that only shows up for service when we are to be seen parading through town. . . . Only those men who are willing to serve the high goals of the SA have room in our ranks."[19] Bisschopinck's troubles indicate that the troopers fancied wearing their uniforms in public, but did not want to engage in other SA activities they perceived as boring. The consumer behavior and cultural preferences of the men played into the hands of the officers. Although Bisschopinck saw sufficient reason to criticize his men, the popularity of the Brown Shirt facilitated the original purpose of the SA as envisioned by Hitler in 1926.

Yet not only the rank and file were fond of their Brown Shirts. Officers also liked to be seen in public wearing their uniforms. To regulate the use of the shirt, Hitler and Pfeffer von Salomon ordered in SA Order Ten, "The service dress can only be worn with the permission, or on order, of the troop leader. If one, for instance, wants to wear the service dress when hiking, the hike has to be designated a hiking patrol on duty, or propaganda trip by the leader." Order Ten specifically stated, "The leaders from Sturmführer upwards may give this permission [to wear the uniform] to themselves."[20] It was a special privilege of SA officers that they could wear their Brown Shirt anytime they chose.

Uniformity and discipline were the goals, yet the Brown Shirt itself was not perfect. The uniform did not offer any protection from wet and cold weather. The SA leadership overcame this obstacle with simple advice. With SA Order Ten, issued in the fall of 1926, Hitler and Pfeffer von Salomon addressed this issue early on. Hitler ordered, "Windbreakers are allowed without insignia." Yet he followed this line with a qualifier: "Against the cold, it is better to wear long woolen underwear. . . . However, the dress within one troop always has to be uniform."[21] The uniform enhanced bodies and was therefore to be displayed. Wearing long underwear was a better option than covering the garment with a coat. Again, the leadership was forced to make concessions. They could not provide appropriate clothing and had to make do with compromises.

The shirt was also too warm in the summer months. During the summer, dirty collars became a problem. The summer heat caused the men to sweat, which in turn quickly soiled the shirt's collar. Yet again, the SA leadership came up with a simple solution that even allowed for extra revenues. Hitler and Pfeffer von Salomon issued an SA-wide order on June 5, 1930. The leadership noted, "To avoid repeated sweating through of the collar of the service shirt and to avoid the wear and tear caused by repeated washing, many men wear badly fitting white [button-in] collar liners and neckerchiefs, gray neckerchiefs, etc." Although the men did this in an attempt to protect their shirts from dirt, "this disturbs the uniformity of the honor garment drastically. The highest SA leadership thus orders effective immediately the introduction of easily washable brown [button-in] collar liners." The leaders gave reasons beyond uniformity as well by arguing, "This collar liner is made in such a way that a perfect fit is guaranteed." Of course, the leadership again subtly tried to order their men to spend their money at a Brown Store. "With the introduction of this brown collar liner the wearing of white collar liners, neckerchiefs, etc. is prohibited. These brown regulation collar liners are only to be procured through the RZM and official party offices." The men needed to provide collar sizes when ordering. "Price per item, including shipping and wrapping, is 0.75 RM."[22] White civilian collar liners on a Brown Shirt disturbed the ideal picture and therefore could not be tolerated. This demonstrates the substantial shift in regard to the uniforms from the early SA to this later SA as party propaganda troop. Through these shifts, the party managed both to keep its monopoly on the uniform and to make extra money in the process.

The Nazis clearly recognized the monetary value of their merchandise. They even voiced the belief that part of the reason for the Brown Shirt prohibition in some German states in June 1930 was this extra source of revenue.[23] The states of Bavaria, Baden, and Prussia prohibited the uniform due to rising levels of violence triggered by the SA.[24] Yet the state did not have the power to take the private belongings of SA men. In an order received by the police headquarters in Dortmund, the Prussian minister of the interior, Heinrich Waentig, informed the police, "In order to maintain peace, security and order, the public wearing of the so-called party uniform of the National Socialist German Worker's Party, and its subauxiliary and side organizations is forbidden within the Free State of Prussia." The minister "urge[d] all police to enforce this prohibition, also if necessary, through the threat and use of incarceration and fines."[25]

Incarceration and fines, however, could be easily avoided, as the further elaborations of the interior minister show. If the police caught a man in the illegal garment, "The delinquents are to be led to the closest police station. Personal data should be registered, and the delinquents should be advised to get civilian clothes." After putting on civilian clothes, the uniform had to be handed back to the "delinquent." The minister then ordered his police to send him "home with the advice that, a second offense would result in the confiscation of . . . the uniform pieces by the police." The minister finally admitted to his police forces that "since only the public wearing of the uniform is prohibited, police intervention is out of the question, if the party members wear the uniform in a closed meeting (in a hall or gymnasium) . . . the way to and from these localities can only be gone to in civilian clothes."[26] The prohibition was meant to reestablish peace in the streets of Prussia, yet the order shows that the police did not even have enough power to confiscate the offenders' uniforms. Weimar democracy did not allow more thorough action or control against the Nazis, which played to their advantage. The Brown Shirt could not be taken from a trooper legally. Hence, the fascists retained an important tool.

An order given out by northern SA leader Viktor Lutze in 1930, during the ban of the SA uniform in Prussia, indicated how the SA circumvented the law in other ways. Lutze told his men, "Because of the prohibition of the SA service dress, it is likely that within individual troops the necessary pressure, for newly arriving SA men to purchase the service dress and for the rest to complete their service dress, is lacking." Therefore, he ordered, "At least once a month, every troop leader has to hold a rally in a closed room in order to check if the already purchased equipment is being handled correctly. He has to take care that the service dress is being completed." More important, he ordered, "Newly inducted SA-men can become full members only after they go through a probation period. During this time, the new SA-man must purchase the uniform and is supposed to do only office duties. Only when he is in possession of a full service dress can a transfer to full membership status occur." Lutze also made statements about the intent of the law. He told his men, "With the prohibition of the service dress the new German government intends not only to lower the propaganda value of the SA, but also to hurt the SA economically as badly as possible." Lutze tried to order his men to buy the uniform by stating that "it is the duty of every SA man, even during the time of prohibition, to purchase the necessary pieces of equipment at his

RZM, and in doing so spoil the plans of the Marxist government."[27] Lutze thus ordered his men to simply ignore the law. Yet breaking the law was not necessary, since bending the law was quite an easy task.

During the prohibition of the Brown Shirt, the SA simply met in uniform in closed rooms or on private land. During this period, SA men going to a meeting and on the way back home were ordered to cover up the Brown Shirt with an overcoat or carry their uniform in packing paper under their arm.[28] Government regulations and economic hardship did not matter. The SA still required each of their members to own a complete uniform.

Pfeffer von Salomon had an even better idea when faced with the hardship of prohibition. Once the Brown Shirt was prohibited, he suggested that every SA man buy a white substitute shirt—from the RZM, of course. Pfeffer von Salomon could not force the rank and file to buy another shirt. However, he could use marketing techniques to persuade the men to do so. The order he distributed on July 10, 1930, one month into the prohibition period, consequently reads like a page from a mail-order catalog. The order began by assuring the men that this shirt would last. "The shirt is produced in the most durable quality. . . . [It] is not thin and threadbare, and thus after two washings an unusable rag." Rather, even with an "unheard-of cheap price, [it] is an indestructible garment, which withstands use over years." Despite the deep economic crisis, the Nazis thus marketed a second uniform shirt to their SA troopers. They had no actual authority, however, to force the men to buy this garment, as with the rest of the uniform components. The Nazis used capitalist marketing tactics and emotional appeal to overcome this obstacle. The white shirts cost 5.60 to 6 RM per piece and had to be ordered from the RZM.[29] Of course, the authorities easily spotted columns of white-shirted SA. The Prussian state legislature tried to also ban the white shirts but was unsuccessful.[30] White shirts were simply too common. This demonstrates the success of the SA as a disciplined propaganda troop. Even in white shirts, the SA intimidated the police and local bureaucrats.

Regardless, Nazi lawyers quickly won a legal battle resulting in the repeal of the ban. After the Nazis went to court over the shirt issue, all states repealed bans on the Brown Shirt, recognizing it as a lost cause.[31] For the Nazis, their Brown Shirt had become too important to give up without a fight. Hitler and Pfeffer von Salomon opportunistically used the prohibition period to showcase the perceived weakness of the democratic state. In the end, the democratic constitutions of the states of the Weimar Republic did not allow a total prohibition of the Brown Shirt. According to the Prussian minister of the interior, Carl Severing, Nazi lawyers identified at least four laws that overruled a prohibition of the Brown Shirt. Therefore, the authorities lifted the ban in 1931, after a period of about nine months.[32] Without a doubt, the prohibition of the shirt heightened the shirt's symbolic value for the men.

THE HONOR GARMENT

The Nazis did not only channel voluntary energies connected to capitalism. Like in the military, Hitler also used the uniform as a tool for social control since it allowed for "the reliance upon external controls through observability." Only those SA men who behaved according to a set of strict regulations could wear the uniform. Social control, in the words of Nathan Joseph, "starts with the decision by the heads of the uniformed organization to extend and refuse the privilege of the uniform to some or all of its personnel. The first mode of control through uniforms is, therefore, that of permitting or forbidding members to exhibit their organizational affiliation through clothing." When Hitler and Pfeffer von Salomon introduced the uniform, it became a symbol of the Nazi movement. The actual brown garment thus became a cultural artifact with its own identity. Joseph contends that "the uniform seems to have an existence independent of the group or its wearers. . . . The uniform is not only an emblem but also a reminder of the behavior appropriate toward this emblem; it becomes a third factor in the interaction between wearer and other." Joseph acknowledges that the Nazis took this technique to the extreme. The Brown Shirt became an "impersonal objectification of the group. The identification of the uniform with the group reaches its epitome with the *Ehrenkleid* of Germany—the uniform as an 'honor garment' that transfers to its wearer the accrued glory of an organization or nation."[33] The Nazis' skilled use of the Brown Shirt to associate it with core cultural values fostered appropriate behavior.

The use of a uniform as a tool for social control came naturally to Hitler, who learned this technique in the Imperial Army. In the Imperial Army, the uniform had a mythical status linked to national honor. The garment represented the physical manifestation of the men's sense of honor. Both the Brown Shirt and the *Grauer Rock* (gray coat) of the Imperial Army functioned in similar ways. According to an undated set of SA uniform regulations, the "service dress is a garment of honor. Its wearer is a representative of the movement in public."[34]

Even though the men were easily observable, the options for punishment were limited. Thus, breaches of discipline occurred frequently. Therefore, Pfeffer von Salomon outlined possible forms of punishment for SA men in an SA order from November 7, 1926, titled "Discipline." According to Pfeffer von Salomon, "Discipline has to rule the SA. Without discipline the entire organization would be senseless, without purpose and utterly useless." In this order, Pfeffer von Salomon addressed the limits to punishments. "The superiors do not have the ability to, in a real sense, punish or use force to reach discipline, since service in the SA is done voluntarily." Addressing his officers, he continued, "Yet, the superior also serves as volunteer. He is not forced to deal with elements unfit for service. He can chase anybody back home, whose training and use would call for more violence than the superior is allowed to use." He then called on the men's sense of honor by stating, "Therefore, every SA leader has to keep his men as disciplined as other organizations do with the help of violence. The SA can use only those men who consider service as [a] duty of high honor and consider it the highest achievement that one today could reach for people and freedom, and who know that discipline belongs to this service."[35] Pfeffer von Salomon acknowledged that his men should be self-disciplined, yet theory rarely reflected reality.

If an SA man did break the rules, the "Discipline" order also contained a small catalog of acceptable punishments. The tone of the order is almost paternal, although Pfeffer von Salomon ultimately included a veiled threat of violence. Nevertheless, the list of officially approved disciplinary measures included, first, a "simple reprimand (informal rebuke)" and, second, a "strict reprimand (formal rebuke in front of the entire SA group)," in an attempt to use humiliation and peer pressure as a means to bring the behavior of all in line. The third-highest degree of punishment is worthy of note because the officers, in a patriarchal fashion, could order a "temporary prohibition to wear the SA uniform." The uniform was important enough to the troopers themselves that by taking away the privilege of wearing the Brown Shirt, the men felt chastised to a degree beyond being publicly berated. This was followed, fourth, by "temporary demotion." Temporary and ultimate exclusion from the SA served as middle-ranking disciplinary measures. The ultimate form of punishment for an SA man was the exclusion from the Nazi Party proper, followed by the "withdrawal of the right to wear any earned badges of merit."[36] The SA leaders seemed to know that ultimately, a paternalistic attitude alone would not be sufficient, and these standards illustrate the foundation that could be built on to implement real punishment for misbehaving SA men.

Therefore, Pfeffer von Salomon stated specifically as a last disciplinary measure, "If SA men take personal revenge on a delinquent beyond these punishments, then that has nothing to do with official declarations. This cannot be asked for, nor suggested officially. Every kind of involvement by officers should be avoided."[37] It seems that to Pfeffer von Salomon, tacit condoning of informal punishments such as beatings, or other forms of violence, seemed necessary. However, this punishment was applicable only after a complete forced dissociation from the SA and the Nazi Party. The SA leaders never had the legal power to truly punish the men. Rather, it was the men's individual agency bolstered by group identity and a shared sense of honor that played into the hands of the officers.

One could dishonor the garment and thereby the SA with cowardly or otherwise undisciplined behavior. In his SA Order Ten, Hitler ordered ruthless violence and actual bravery in, oftentimes bloody, street brawls. If a uniformed SA man acted cowardly in the street, he dishonored the uniform and thus the entire Nazi movement. Consequently, Hitler banned offenders from wearing the uniform again. Hitler and Pfeffer von Salomon demanded bravery by commanding, "Every SA-man who in service dress flees, or is seen being beaten up, is detrimental to our image." Again, the order made clear that it was the duty of officers to ensure that cases of cowardly behavior in public were first recorded and then punished. "If one is beaten up, or cursed at, in service dress, or is forced to flee (an orderly retreat also counts towards this) he [the officer in charge] has to report this incident within three days to his superior for investigation. Not reporting, or a late report, will be punished with exclusion."[38] If someone did not act according to this specific order, the individual offender and his troop leader would be chastised. The image was too important to be tarnished by men who shied away from violence. Hitler ordered his SA troopers to act aggressively when their officers deemed it appropriate.

Hitler and Pfeffer von Salomon made their brown honor garment even more exclusive by allowing only young and healthy men to wear the Brown Shirt. According to Peter Longerich, "The youthful element dominated the SA."[39] This tactic affiliated the shirt, and by proxy the movement, with the dynamics of youth and power. The physically disabled were also not allowed to cover themselves in the garment of honor because they could not give the necessary impression of strength.

Although the SA was an organization open to all veterans of the war, handicapped men could not represent the movement in the uniformed SA. An order from Pfeffer von Salomon's headquarters in Munich from August 25, 1927, therefore noted, "The physical demands of the SA will rise. Because of that, in addition to the steps taken against the entirely unfit and the crippled, an age limit is also necessary." Pfeffer von Salomon instituted an age limit of thirty-five years for regular SA men. Older men could organize in reserve SA units.[40] The regular SA man was thus healthy and under thirty-five. Image was a large element behind this decision. Hitler wanted to create a youthful image based on an ideal masculine perception.

Older and disabled SA men could not uphold such a youthful and healthy image. Again, the SA strove for uniformity, even when it came to age and health. However, this ideal presented problems. In 1933 SA officer Arthur Böckenhauer reviewed Hamburg's entire SA in a general assembly. When his troopers marched by, Böckenhauer was shocked because his troopers did not follow the rules. The party leadership therefore appears to have had a difficult time achieving its aim. Böckenhauer saw men who were too young for the SA and men who were too old, and, even worse, he had witnessed a "a whole string of men . . . whose condition does not only not allow SA duties, but who have for the SA entirely unacceptable physical handicaps, which are detrimental to the image and the value of our organization."[41] His troop leaders had disregarded the health order and taken in physically handicapped war veterans. These men, he feared, would destroy the desired healthful, strong, and energetic image. Ultimately, Böckenhauer himself could be held responsible and reprimanded by his superiors.

Immediately after the review, he commanded all of his troop leaders in written form, and in very harsh words, to weed out individuals who were too young or too old or who had physical handicaps. He warned his subleaders, "If such men, who are not fit according to service regulation, are left within the SA or are in an SA unit, the subtroop [Hamburg's SA] will in the future make individual leaders responsible." Böckenhauer, however, was careful not to offend the SA men whom he considered unfit for service. The young and the old could serve the movement in the Hitler Youth or Reserve SA units, respectively. The handicapped SA men of Hamburg, even if they were of the right age, could not be kept. Their only option was to join the party. The SA image was much too important. According to him,

"The subtroop does not wish to offend these men, but rather pities the men for their bodily ailments." Yet, he continued, "Nevertheless, this does not change the fact that these men, as painful as it is, have to be removed from the troop."[42] Because of these age and health restrictions, the SA looked uniformly healthy and youthful—as well as exclusive. The SA thus reflected the fascist ideal as a dynamic movement.

The rules for behavior and discipline were explicitly connected to the uniform. The officers had to enforce strict rules when the men wore their Brown Shirts. The men were not allowed to smoke and drink, if the officers deemed it detrimental to the SA image. Order Ten stated, "Smoking and drinking in service dress is only allowed with permission by the troop leader."[43] The total prohibition of tobacco and alcohol was unfeasible. The brown uniform conformed to the cultural values of the men. Drinking and smoking also belonged to their social world and could not easily be forbidden by officers, not if officers wanted compliance in other matters.

Some troop leaders did not trust their men. In August 1931 Böckenhauer, for instance, ordered his troop leaders to post sentries in the toilet facilities and the barroom of a rented meeting hall. These sentries enforced the ban on tobacco and alcohol for the SA during the rally.[44] It should come as no surprise that young men liked to imbibe. Alcohol remained both a problem for the leadership and a natural part of everyday life for the troopers. However, drinking usually happened after public appearances, in bars frequented by SA men and sympathizers, or otherwise at night. Keeping their men as sober as possible when under public scrutiny was part of the duties of SA officers.[45]

Intemperance was not the only reason for breaches of discipline. Rowdiness in public and lack of discipline toward superiors provoked complaints and punishment. Böckenhauer, for instance, had witnessed an SA man misbehave. During a nightly propaganda march in Hamburg, when the men were to throw their burning torches on a bonfire, one man had not thrown the torch according to regulations. Böckenhauer, as highest-ranking officer present, took offense and approached the man, who gave his name as SA man Fels. Böckenhauer gave Fels an immediate verbal warning and then wrote down Fels's name and the number of his unit as displayed on his collar. Böckenhauer wrote to Fels's immediate superior that "there can be no doubt that this behavior and mannerism was undisciplined."[46] This kind of petty rule breaking resulted in a paper trail and definitely in punishment for Fels. There were other breaches of discipline, which seemed to have been punished with similar, almost parental, forms of punishment. On the trip to see their leader by train in the spring of 1931, some SA men were "hanging out of the windows" of the railroad cars. As punishment, these offenders "were not allowed to see Hitler."[47]

In order to create a unified and disciplined image, Hitler and Pfeffer von Salomon did not allow digressions from dress regulations and thus used a control function of uniforms, which is the organization's insistence on nondeviation from the regulations. According to Nathan Joseph, this "is made possible by the existence of precise uniform regulations."[48] When Hitler and Pfeffer von Salomon allowed the SA to wear the uniform as sign of affiliation, they accompanied this order with a strict set of regulations in three orders.[49] The lower-level leadership then checked on the status of their men. Uniformity enhanced the propaganda value of the SA.

Thus, SA men were not allowed to add items to their uniform that showed affiliations with other political groups. SA Order Ten stated specifically that all nonregulation insignia, such as, for instance, "cockades, deaths heads, swords, crowns, arrows," and the like, were prohibited.[50] The order implied that the men liked to embellish their outfits with such militaristic and royalist symbols.

The Nazi image, however, was clean and exclusive. Only Nazi symbols were allowed on the Nazi uniform. The members of the SA could not show their affinity or affiliation with other right-wing groups. The SA was exclusive in demanding that the troopers demonstrate loyalty only to the SA. Hitler and Pfeffer von Salomon prohibited the personalization of uniform items and even provided a list of nonregulation insignia. The SA could not show symbolic signs of divided devotions. The Nazis recruited young men with deeply held preexisting values and practices. The SA leadership attempted to teach the men to abandon previously cherished values in favor of total devotion to the Nazi cause. The Nazis therefore walked a fine line. They tried their best not to alienate royalist conservatives in their movement while simultaneously asking these conservative elements to trade their imperial symbols for the swastika.

CONCLUSION

Especially in the last years under Pfeffer von Salomon, when the SA grew in numbers, inner strife became the norm. Tensions between the party, the SS (Schutzstaffel, or protection squadron), the SA, and even an SA uprising in Berlin in August 1930 ultimately forced Pfeffer von Salomon to resign. After a short interim period, Hitler appointed Ernst Röhm in November 1930 as chief of staff once again. The fact that Röhm was gay was well known and caused resistance among some SA leaders. Still, Röhm was a professional staff officer and talented organizer who was up to the task of disciplining the growing organization. Therefore, Hitler held on to Röhm despite his unpopular sexual orientation. Hitler, in his defense of appointing Röhm, argued that the SA was a rough-and-tumble organization of fighters and thus embraced violence and seemingly even sexual deviance.[51] Again, this highlighted the dual character of the SA. The Nazis needed inner discipline within their propaganda troop. Yet violence toward others was embraced, if not encouraged.

In this way, the SA created a dual image and presented a strong alternative to the allegedly chaotic republic.[52] Hitler constructed a large uniformed and disciplined SA that personified fascist ideals in the streets. Hitler accomplished this with the aid of the modern forms of consumption and consumerism and by attaching cultural values to the uniform of the troopers. Additionally, uniformity suggested to observers that the Nazis were a monolithic bloc. The uniform disguised discontent among the men of the SA. In this way, the uniform aided the Nazis in suggesting internal cohesion and in projecting a coherent and disciplined external image, even if that was not always the case. Image clearly mattered more than reality in this case.

Uniformed marches were deeply rooted in Weimar political culture. Young men of all political orientations enjoyed uniforms, marches, and voluntary disciplined group behavior. Therefore, Hitler needed only to tap into this potential energy in order to construct his SA. Since absolute obedience to superiors could not be enforced, the SA leadership was rather lenient toward its men. The highest form of punishment an SA leader could use against undisciplined, or even rebellious, troopers was exclusion from the SA and from the party, coupled with the threat of a beating. Nevertheless, that would have been counterproductive. The SA needed to present strength in numbers and function as a large consumer base, so this form of punishment was impractical. It was therefore the preferences of the troopers that played into the hands of the officers and gave them uniformed masses.

The popularity of the garment also allowed for less obvious and very modern forms of social control. Only young and healthy men could wear the uniform publicly to represent the Nazi movement. Thus, collectively, the actors in political theater always appeared young and energetic. By amplifying the advantageous cut of the shirt through the clever use of young, healthy models, so to speak, in addition to the use of fairly new forms of mass advertising and sales techniques, the Nazis were able to establish an especially youthful, energetic, and fit image.

The sale of the garment also allowed the Nazis to earn considerable amounts of revenue from every SA man, especially after the successful monopolization and centralization of the sales business through the RZM and the Brown Stores.[53] The coupling of the traditional principle of the honor garment with modern forms of marketing and product branding furthermore pushed the sales of the shirt and other uniform items and flushed revenues into Nazi coffers. Capitalist sales techniques and the popularity of their uniforms were useful to Nazi leaders. It helped to enhance the dual image they aimed to project, and they earned valuable monetary resources.

Chapter four

ASSEMBLING THE TROOPERS—THE LOGISTICS OF MILITARIZATION

Adolf Hitler stated in his SA Order Number One that the SA's "work should . . . be done . . . in enormous mass parades" on November 1, 1926.[1] However, the individual SA group (*Gruppe*), as the smallest structural unit of the mass organization, did not include many men. With the restructuring of the SA in January 1926, Franz Pfeffer von Salomon instructed the SA that each group should be made up of between six and twelve male friends and neighbors. Approximately five to eight of these groups made up a troop (*Truppe*). The next higher unit was the storm (*Sturm*), each containing between two and four troops from the local area. Nevertheless, no single Sturm could muster thousands of men at the same time. This level was achieved within the next higher unit, the SA standard (*Standarte*), which combined between two and five SA storms (*Stürme*) from a region. Between two to five Standarten made up an SA brigade (*Brigade*).[2] The assembling of thousands during party rallies and propaganda marches therefore called for the concentration into Standarten and Brigaden, effectively necessitating the movement of men from farther away.

The Nazis used their SA most effectively when they assembled in large brown columns. Only travel allowed the Nazis to reach the desired effect when local SA units converged and created the impression of a large, monolithic body of uniformed SA troopers. They used automobiles, trucks, motorcycles, and even bicycles to move the troopers to strategically important locations.[3] They also used field kitchens to stay self-sufficient and independent of local infrastructures. This was necessary since the spaces the fascists invaded were typically socialist or communist territories. The point was to intimidate and to trigger clash violence. The fascists' advanced use of technology and military-like logistics made this possible. Ultimately, this shows how the SA moved their men cost-effectively, quickly, and relatively safely to reach the desired effect in distant locations. This also demonstrates the growing role of the SA as a military organization as well as the further militarization of politics by the Nazis.

Support could also be strengthened by sending SA troopers into locations with strong Nazi backing. Travel enabled the SA to participate in local festivities. The Nazis incorporated local traditions successfully. Local populations carried and maintained the Nazi vision when they allowed Nazi participation in ritualistic movements through defined spaces. In this way, Nazi symbols and uniforms saturated regional processions. Ultimately, local festive processions gained new political implications and became the basic form of Nazi ritual and its most important tool in mobilizing public support.[4] Usually, these local processions incorporated SA troopers who traveled.

SA MOBILITY

The SA's ability to travel did not exclusively rest on the use of advanced motorized means of transportation. The SA used the admittedly more mundane bicycle to cover shorter distances. The use of bicycles by urban proletarian groups for propaganda tours into the countryside has a long history. Socialists had a highly sophisticated club life that included many recreational athletic organizations, such as bicycle clubs.[5] Similarly, there were recreational bicycle tours that simultaneously functioned as forays into contested territory in the early years of the SA. For example, the SA of Bad Tölz assembled their SA bicycle troop on Sunday afternoon, August 15, 1922, for an outing. The tour also included the consumption of alcohol and was followed by ritualistic occupation of public space and the shouting of Nazi slogans.[6] Still, this form of travel-based SA activity was combined with leisure in good weather. Later, however, the SA militarized the political bicycle ride. These rides were not outings of a recreational nature but rather orchestrated missions incorporating specific, identifiable objectives and a means to reach as many of these set targets as possible. SA riders appeared in disciplined formations wearing their uniforms. As the case of Hamburg's SA shows, these tours also occurred during the cold winter months. In the harsher weather, they did not include alcohol and placed more emphasis on covering ground instead of leisure activities.

In the winter of 1928, Hamburg SA leader Arthur Böckenhauer, for instance, ordered his men to form a "strong bicyclist detachment." On the Sunday of January 22, his men covered the villages surrounding his city with Nazi propaganda to prepare for the Hamburg City Council elections on February 2. The detachment transported propaganda parcels into the villages of Farmsen-Berne, Volksdorf, and Wohldorf-Ohlstedt. Böckenhauer ordered his men to hand deliver one thousand parcels to the approximately thirty-six hundred voters in these villages. They contained a recent copy of the Nazi newspaper *Völkischer Beobachter*, a copy of an illustrated Nazi journal called the *Illustrierter Beobachter*, and two flyers. Nevertheless, the order also contained the specific note that leftover packages must be returned since the availability of propaganda material was limited and those materials would be utilized elsewhere.[7]

According to the order, the village of Farmsen-Berne included a large low-income home. The SA leader estimated that this home alone contained at least nine hundred individuals eligible to vote. The men of the bicycle detachment hand delivered their propaganda parcels to each one. They were not, for example, allowed to simply hand a pack of parcels to the janitor with instructions for delivery. Each of the people living in this welfare home received the personal attention of an SA man. Since not everyone anticipated such a visit, Böckenhauer assured his men that this kind of personalized election canvassing was legal. The staff was also not allowed to prohibit the Nazis from disseminating their propaganda in the home.[8]

Böckenhauer, however, ordered his men to do something else in addition to canvassing. After each household received a knock on the door and got free Nazi propaganda from a dapper young man, the entire troop also rode through the village in formation. The order specifically read, "After the distribution of the parcels is finished, the entire bicycle detachment engages in a propaganda tour of the village and then continues on its way to the next village." The impact of this tactic should not be underestimated. Sometimes this display was the first time a person in the countryside saw a genuine SA man. Just a short while later, all villagers had the opportunity to witness an entire group of SA riding their bicycles in a tight formation led by an officer. The cyclists left not only written propaganda material but also the impression of a large mobile group of young uniformed men. The impact of the men riding in such a way contributed to the construction of a dynamic and masculine Nazi image. To learn from the experience and in order to account for every parcel, Böckenhauer also ordered his officers to give an official report three days after the ride.[9] This highly organized SA propaganda ride was thus comparable to a military operation. The Nazis systematically militarized the political bicycle ride to methodically cover the countryside.

The Nazis, however, used technology not only to cover ground and combine units into large masses. Technology also helped to shape the Nazi image in important ways. The motorcycle, for instance, gave the SA image an ultramodern dynamic. During the Weimar era, the motorcycle represented the most cost-effective way to mechanize transportation. The lost war and the Depression years caused Germans to favor the motorcycle rather than the car, as cars represented a more expensive option. In popular entertainment as well as newsreels on the silver screen, motorization equaled modernity. SA men using two-wheeled mechanized means of transportation additionally engaged in heavily gendered image construction. The motorcycle industry and advertisers gendered the motorcycle and its riders as particularly masculine.[10] Motorcycles, therefore, allowed the SA to represent themselves as especially modern and hypermasculine men, despite the economic crisis.

The use of popular modes of transportation, like the motorcycle, furthermore, allowed for a shifting of allegiances to the Nazi cause by motor-sports enthusiasts. The affinity for motor sports and especially motorcycle racing cut across social boundaries and represented a mass phenomenon. The Nazis cleverly incorporated popular spectacle and leisure to win the support of wide swaths of German society in this manner.[11]

Bicycles and motorcycles represented only the tip of the iceberg when it came to SA mobility. Again, the fascists learned from the Left how to be effective. The Nazis copied the use of motorized transport on trucks in political propaganda from the socialists as well. They did this because motorized transport was more impressive than transport by bicycle. One could, for instance, decorate the trucks with flags and slogans to make them propagandistically more effective. Motorized speakers could appear in more than one location in a short amount of time. The Nazis also used this fast and impressive way to travel. Since renting trucks was expensive, the Nazis tapped into the financial resources of their middle-class constituency. The fascists in Hamburg, for instance, received aid from sympathetic truck owners and owners of trucking businesses who donated the use of their vehicles.[12]

The transportation of troopers into areas without strong Nazi support oftentimes triggered clash violence.[13] The fascists thus militarized not only the bicycle tour but also the propaganda ride by truck. This form of militarization, however, was marked by additional security considerations rather than a focus on discipline alone. The Nazis sought to secure their men during truck rides since political opponents or the police could easily locate decorated trucks and employ counter-measures before arrival at their destination. In May 1927, for instance, the regional SA leadership for the northern German city of Hanover mandated that special security measures during transport by truck be taken. According to the northern SA leadership, "SA transports on trucks have, if possible, to be accompanied by two motorcyclists in civilian dress." One of these undercover motorcyclists had to ride "far enough in advance that special occurrences (police, enemy raid, etc.) can be reported in time to the group leader, so that he in turn can order the necessary counter-measures." The second motorcyclist, however, "rides in the rear, to be able to personally, or by telephone, report incidences and to always keep up the lines of communication."[14] Ensuring the safe passage of transports was important to the Nazis. Evidently, protecting trucks was important enough to spend financial resources on the extra gasoline for the two additional motorcycles. The transport of SA on trucks was secured in a military-like manner to ensure smooth and safe travel.

As the SA grew in the early 1930s, it perfected the use of motor vehicles, which further demonstrates its growing role as military organization. Private motor vehicles could be made available to a wider circle of users. A private motorcycle owner, for instance, could make himself and his motorcycle available for Nazi services. To do this, the fascists again used the financial resources of their middle-class supporters. To allow the SA to have a small fleet of privately owned vehicles, such as motorcycles and cars, Pfeffer von Salomon ordered the establishment of motorized SA units in April 1930. According to Pfeffer von Salomon's order, the motor SA was supposed to consist mainly of motorcycles. According to his order, every SA Sturm had to establish a "motor storm." Every SA man in possession of a motorcycle or small car who was willing to put their private property to the use of the SA was to join this special SA troop. According to Pfeffer von Salomon, there was no cap on the motor storm's size. Each was permitted to have an unlimited number of motorcycles, restricted only by the availability of the bikes themselves. Yet the number of cars, according to the same SABE order, was not to exceed more than two per unit. Additionally, Pfeffer von Salomon specified that only one SA man could be responsible for their assigned SA vehicle. The cars and motorcycles belonged to the party if the owners were on duty. The leader of each motorized unit was supposed to have not only a motor vehicle himself but also technical expertise.[15] The motor SA therefore mostly used the highly gendered motorcycle and ensured that the masculine effect was even further enhanced through the ability of the motor SA officers to do maintenance and repairs themselves.[16]

By emphasizing motor SA subculture, the motor SA became even more masculine and showed a further militarization of the SA. The men of the Silesian motor SA, for example, sang:

> What ratters and roars and thunders so,
> As if the devil came riding
> Criss-cross through Silesia's land?
> A brown, wild, swashbuckling army!
> And you ask what are those troops?
> Then it rings out in jubilance,
> Tari, tara, It is, it is Hitler's Silesian
> Motor-SA.[17]

The men of the Silesian SA considered themselves a hypermasculine army with noisy intimidation tactics. SA leader Pfeffer von Salomon's order specifying who could be transported with the motor SA also points to a militarization of the SA. According to his order, the transportation of "civilians" was strictly prohibited. The militarization of private vehicles in the service of the SA becomes even more obvious when one considers the following explanation of the use of the motorized SA. According to Pfeffer von Salomon, these units were intended to be used for general SA service purposes as well as "driving exercises, propaganda marches, [and] signal corps exercises."[18] Thus, the SA motorized its units and then militarized their use.

In March 1932, Ernst Röhm furthermore widened the circle of potential Nazi motorists when he specified the use of vehicles for the Nazi movement during election campaigns. His order, titled "Deployment of the Motor Units in Election Campaigning," documents the growth of the Nazi vehicle fleet and shows that the Nazis meticulously coordinated the use of vehicles to ensure that resources were used as efficiently as possible. According to this order, the Nazis made use of motorized SA and SS and additionally established an independent organization for all men with motor vehicles who did not belong to the SA or SS.

The Nationalsozialistisches Kraftfahrkorps (NSKK) was open to all Nazi Party members.[19] The National Socialist Motor Vehicle Drivers' Corps was thus a third motor-vehicle organization within the Nazi

Party. One should not forget the age restrictions enforced by Pfeffer von Salomon. Financially secure older men with cars could also be useful and thus made up a separate organization. The NSKK provided an opportunity for older and well-off men to actively participate in the Nazi movement despite age and class distinctions.[20]

According to Röhm, the motor SA's main purpose was for "short notice meeting security, propaganda in the countryside, [and] poster and flyer hand out." The NSKK, on the other hand, was supposed to "provide Nazi politicians with vehicles."[21] The Nazis were generally highly motorized, yet through their organizational structure did not have to pay for the vehicles they utilized. Ultimately, the motor SA expanded from 100 Sturm units in October 1931 to 680 in August 1932, with 26,105 individuals enlisted. The number of NSKK members grew from 300 in 1930 to 10,000 in 1931.[22] The Nazi vehicle fleet in Saxony grew in similar numbers. In February 1931, the Halle SA listed 15 vehicles, Eisleben 12, and Bitterfeld 8. The Erfurt automobile unit had 10 members. By April 1932, the Erfurt SA had 396 motorcycles, 180 cars, and 53 trucks, as well as 700 men.[23] As these numbers suggest, members of the middle class readily sacrificed their free time and made their vehicles available to the party and the SA. The SA used fleet vehicles based on private initiative. They lent the SA a modern masculine image and functioned as logistical tools to militarize the SA.

Ultimately, even this enlargement of the SA motor vehicle fleet was not enough for Nazi purposes. As an August 8, 1932, an NSDAP ordinance leaflet shows, the SA even purchased vehicles for their fleet for the use of SA officers. The SA could purchase vehicles for their specific use with their own funds. Officers could pick their own company cars, so to speak. Yet the leadership had to approve of the choice and could deny an officer's selection in favor of a cheaper option. These valuable assets, however, were not just given to the officers without stipulations. The leadership checked periodically to ensure that the cars of SA officers purchased by the SA were used appropriately. According to the leaflet, all vehicles used by officers could be inspected for technical issues at any time. These inspections could be ordered from above and were performed by a specialist. However, not only the vehicles were taken care of. Accidents could be costly. Hospital and lawyer fees could be a drain on Nazi funds. Thus, the SA leadership decided that all men driving cars and riding motorcycles for the movement should pay dues into an accident insurance fund for all SA, SS, and NSKK drivers. Uninsured men could not operate motor vehicles for the movement.[24]

The Nazis had learned the value of bicycle propaganda rides from the socialists. However, only the Nazis had a large middle-class constituency that allowed them to use their private property. Ultimately, the middle class enabled the militarization and mobilization of Nazi propaganda efforts performed by the SA. This represented a significant advantage over the socialist parties with a proletarian mass base, since the fascists could easily concentrate larger groups of SA in contested rural areas.[25] Bourgeois resources allowed the Nazis to make their image even more progressive and modern by enabling the use of modern aviation technology.

The Nazis had learned from the socialists to use technology to transport speakers and larger groups via motor vehicles. Still, the Nazis not only perfected the effective use of ground transportation but also went one step further. They pioneered the use of airplanes to transport speakers. Flying allowed the fascists to make their image even more progressive and ultramodern. The Nazis chartered airplanes during election campaigns to reach wider audiences. Yet as with other motor vehicles, the Nazis developed their own flying SA units for propaganda purposes. The SA image was therefore marked by cutting-edge modes of transportation. Röhm's office in Munich ordered the establishment of flying SA units called *Fliegerstürme* (flying storms) in April 1932.[26] The financial resources of the middle class, however, were evidently not enough in this case. Groups consisting of trained pilots and mechanics sprang up, although they lacked the accompanying airplanes and equipment. While the SA could train their own pilots, the procurement of airplanes, hangars, and tools proved cost prohibitive.

Faced with the challenge of finding adequate aviation resources, Röhm sent out a second order to his flying enthusiasts that July. Three months after the original order, the leadership clarified that only units fit for use in propaganda and messenger duties could claim the title of SA *Fliegersturm*. These units included pilots and ground personnel who were SA members. Most important, they had to be in possession of hangars, operational airplanes, and tools.[27] Although the SA used private pilots within their ranks for party purposes, the documentary evidence suggests that the enthusiasm for flying was greater than the actual ability to provide private airplanes. Nonetheless, the SA did establish flying SA units. Their specific reasoning was strategic.

Airplanes could be used for reconnaissance purposes. The establishment of flying units thus furthermore highlighted the SA's military value.

With the use of bicycles, motorcycles, cars, trucks, and even airplanes, the Nazis possessed the ability to move large groups of SA with style. Often, the destinations for these groups were rural and regional

festivities. In this way, the Nazis joined, as well as militarized, regional processions.[28] Yet the fascists also militarized the urban political festival. The Nazis did not invent this form of political celebrations. Once again, they copied from other political parties and movements from both the Left and the Right. The Nazis, however, concentrated their men on a scale much larger than other parties at that time. The concentration of large numbers of men caused logistical problems. The militarization of political festivals by incorporating strict rules for all, however, allowed the Nazis to stage mass rallies.

SA PRESENCE AND MASS SPECTACLE

The working class organized in the Social Democratic Party had long-standing traditions of secular festivals. The leftist tradition of celebrating May Day with concurrent political festivities stemmed from the imperial era.[29] Such festivals were secular in nature yet drew on religious predecessors and were thus rich in symbolism. These became common occurrences in almost all locations that had organized labor movements. These festivals included music, speeches, and visual symbolism. The environment at the festivals was festive, yet also emotional and reflective. They were advertised in published programs and could last for several days. These festivities incorporated a working-class character since participants sang, ate, and consumed alcohol together.[30]

The ideological right in the Weimar era copied this idea and created their own political festivals. They, however, gave their festivals a militaristic spin. During German Day, first established in 1921, right-wing paramilitaries marched together.[31] During the Weimar era, these right-wing festivals also became mass meetings. The Stahlhelm, for instance, congregated in the tens of thousands during their 1925 Front Line Veterans' Day rally in Magdeburg.[32]

The Nazis copied these mass spectacles, yet they perfected the practice by enlarging the scale repeatedly. Hitler's ability to concentrate SA storms, standards, and even brigades in one geographic location for mass parades during political festivals became his most important propaganda tool in this era. The massing of hundreds and even thousands of local SA units enhanced the propaganda effect tremendously. Contemporaries, historians, and sociologists have long noted the importance of frequent spectacular rallies, parades, and mass gatherings for the Nazis' political success. Mass displays had two important psychological functions.

The first of these functions involved the viewing audience. The Nazis mastered this practice through a display of standardized symbols and masses of uniformed men. This massing demonstrated the power of numbers as well as the disciplined dedication to the Nazi cause. Witnesses to such mass spectacles are much less likely to oppose a uniformed group than a single uniformed trooper. Massed display of power replaced the legitimacy of a single SA man as representative of the movement. The individual witness became helpless.[33] The uniform thus became a metaphor for the movement. The individual wearers were submerged. The SA functioned as a seemingly monolithic body of uniformed men.

The second function of mass displays involved the participants. The joint process of presentation and witnessing facilitates a power transfer in two directions. The spectator transferred the power of the masses to the party. The uniformed participant also drew pleasure, strength, and thus a dynamic attitude from the communal experience. The individual participants are themselves witnesses to their unified dominance. They draw strength from the suggestion of their own massed power.[34] The marchers derived a feeling of empowerment from the experience. The Nazis knew about these psychological and sociological properties of mass assemblies and ultimately used their uniform to enhance these effects. Of course, intimidation had its uses in clash violence. Thus, the Nazis vigorously worked on mastering the assembly of large groups.

The most important, and naturally the largest, annual public display of the party occurred during the summer at the *Reichsparteitage,* the nationwide party conventions. The annual party rallies from 1926 until the outbreak of World War II served as mass propaganda events. Important logistical problems were solved through trial and error. Party members and SA from Germany and Austria congregated together in one city for a few days on each occasion. Thousands of SA members marched together, listened to speeches by Hitler, and generally celebrated themselves. The Nazis moved, fed, and housed masses of people in order to achieve this effect. These Nazi activists then engaged in a collective consumption of services, such as cheap or free food, with lodging provided by the party. Additionally, the experience of new sights and experiences through travel represented an invaluable form of community building.[35] Yet lodging and food presented both logistical and security challenges. Through detailed military-like orders, the SA leadership anticipated every possible scenario and enabled the Nazis to overcome these difficulties.

Before traveling to the 1927 party rally in Nuremberg, the first party rally in which Hitler himself and a significant number of his SA men wore the Brown Shirt, Pfeffer von Salomon gave out specific orders regarding every detail of the trip. Regarding the train ride to Nuremberg, the order mandated that every traveling group place one man in charge. All others had to obey him. The train riders were not allowed to hang flags out of the train cars because of the danger of confusing the swastika banners with railroad signals. Upon arrival in the Nuremberg station, every detachment or transport was to report to the "quarter office" to receive additional instructions.[36] Traveling by train was thus made as smooth as possible. Discipline during train rides was essential. Officers ensured that no SA member was unsupervised during any part of the trip.

To ensure the SA displayed a disciplined public image, strict supervision continued on arrival. According to Pfeffer von Salomon, no uniformed trooper could wander off. All SA units were ordered to stay together. Additionally, officers were not allowed to leave their men unsupervised. Pfeffer von Salomon gave out a strict itinerary to these groups. After arrival, all units marched together to their quarters, reported to the officer in charge, and regrouped. After this had been achieved, they all received food, communally, and then participated in a torch-lit march through the city. If officers and men wanted to go sightseeing or visit a local bar, they could do so together at a prearranged time on the following day. Before their limited leisure time, however, the men had to march through town again. For the SA musicians, reveille was early because they had to be marching ready by six in the morning. All SA bands marched with music to give the town itself a wake-up call. All other men could sleep until six, when the musicians began and roused the rest of the group. All the men then attended a flag consecration at eight, followed by yet another march through the city at nine thirty. The official program concluded by three in the afternoon. After that, everyone was provided with food. Only then did the SA leaders give their men time to enjoy themselves. Yet they warned the men to stay together in their respective groups under the supervision of an officer.[37]

The food supply for such large numbers presented logistical difficulties. In some instances, the men relied on simple sandwiches. Premade sandwiches made by female Nazi sympathizers attained mythical status. Women, though not able to join the SA, functioned in an auxiliary role when it came to food preparation. Nazi women participated by working in SA soup kitchens, collecting donations, and preparing their renowned sandwiches. In fact, the *SA-Stulle* (SA sandwich) became a hallmark of Nazi rallies. Women generally supported the social welfare efforts of the SA and fed unemployed SA members.[38] Fascist women adhered to the gendered roles of the Nazi movement by performing domestic tasks. However, the feeding of men at assemblies soon surpassed the traditional SA sandwich.

Similar to transport, the SA accomplished supplying its men in a highly sophisticated and militarized manner. Previous experiences in the army served Pfeffer von Salomon well. In preparation for the 1929 party rally, Pfeffer von Salomon distributed orders for the entire SA regarding the supply issue. To be more flexible, Pfeffer von Salomon ordered the establishment of mobile SA kitchens on June 20, 1929. He decreed, "The goal is the self-supply of SA units out of their own cooking utensils and with their own supplies of food." He explained to the troopers why this was necessary. According to Pfeffer von Salomon, there was a supply problem during rallies, both large and small. The Nazis depended on the existence of facilities that allowed large-scale food preparation. He also clarified that through the introduction of these kitchens, "We are in the position to concentrate our SA in those locations we deem effective, rather than in the places that have built-in mass kitchens and in which 'one' is willing to supply us. The larger the concentration, the larger our problems would become."[39] Mobile kitchens allowed the Nazis to operate independently of the political affiliations of the owners of restaurants and hotels. Yet despite logistical problems, the law presented additional difficulties.

Although the Nazis actively militarized travel, they could not utilize proper military field kitchens that had the capability to be hauled into rough terrain. Rather, the SA kitchens were "to be light weight and easily transportable and as cheap as possible. . . . [The kitchen] should be transportable via truck or in the baggage car of a train and SA-men should be able to cover smaller distances by hauling the kitchen on its own wheels."[40] Off-road capabilities were unnecessary and, more important, prohibited under the military restrictions of the Treaty of Versailles. Still, the SA actively pushed militarization to the limit.

Without women to prepare the food in all locations, Pfeffer von Salomon found it necessary to elucidate on the procedures. He told his men, "The food preparation has to be fairly easy. Peeling potatoes,

the butchering of livestock, and difficult cooking instructions must be avoided. The ingredients should be storable for months and even years.

They must be able to overcome primitive transport conditions. . . . The food should be uniform and its preparation should be familiar in the entire SA so that the borrowing of raw material from other units is possible." The men were not supposed to expect luxuries. According to their leader, "Variety is less important because we never supply ourselves for longer periods of time. The dish can be the same every time the SA kitchen is responsible for food supply." Nevertheless, the men did not have to worry about anything other than having "flatware and eating utensils with carrying equipment (backpack, or bread bag)."[41] Bread bags and backpacks for eating utensils and mobile kitchens stocked with nonperishable and basic cuisine definitely represented the increased mobilization and militarization of SA activities. Pfeffer von Salomon expanded the potential reach of his Brown Shirts through these changes. Regardless of the facilities available in a specific city, the SA could feed the men he ordered there, no matter their number. Their use of mobile SA kitchens allowed them to leave their strongholds and saturate strategically important areas right before elections.

The new SA mobile kitchens were tested during the 1929 party rally in Nuremberg. On June 25, 1929, several days before the rally, Pfeffer von Salomon sent an order to the entire SA regarding the issue of self-supply. In this order, Pfeffer von Salomon acknowledged that the food supply in the previous year had been lacking and that these problems would now be avoided. Pfeffer von Salomon then attempted to solve the problem of monotonous food over a period of several days. "The different meals in Nuremberg, cooked with the same raw material, will look and taste different through the adding of different ingredients." The trick, of course, lay in the ability of the individual cooks to use the standardized raw materials in different ways and thus create the illusion of variety. Again, nothing was left to chance. Pfeffer von Salomon ordered SA cooks to arrive two to three days early in order to receive instructions in cooking and to cook test meals under supervision. The cooks did not have to experiment with unfamiliar facilities and raw materials because an experienced cook would run them through every planned meal and cook it with them at least once before the troops arrived.[42]

The second-to-last point of the order highlights the importance of the introduction of field kitchens. Pfeffer von Salomon demanded that every SA man attending the rally eat only from the mobile kitchens and not from any local restaurants or pubs. This was intended to be a supervised trial run, and, in order to make this experiment work, each individual man had to eat what everybody else was given. "The mass supply of food belongs to the program of the party rally and is thus part of the SA service [one is on duty while receiving meals]. The mass supply of food is even one of the most important points and one of the most important mass exercises of the party rally. . . . Every SA man must take part. . . . No SA man is allowed to leave the mass quarter during the designated meal times."[43] The 1929 Nuremberg rally was ultimately a field-kitchen experiment. Pfeffer von Salomon ordered the establishment of field kitchens with the most basic instructions. It was to be mobile and cheap. The centrally planned kitchens were then tested in a trial run. The experiment worked, and the field kitchens became part of the regular inventory of local SA groups.

The SA also made the housing of SA units that traveled to far-off destinations a priority. During the most impressive displays of the SA, the annual party rallies, housing had a twofold function: barrack-style housing kept the men in larger groups for both safety and supervision. The SA dressed like an army, and they traveled like an army. When they arrived by the thousands to take over a city for a few days, they lived in spartan conditions. According to one SA leader, Alfred Conn, the trip to the 1929 party rally in Nuremberg was such an experience. On arriving in Nuremberg by a chartered train, Conn marched his men to their quarters at a large school, where they received a free field-kitchen meal. Indeed, this atmosphere gave Conn and his men the feeling that they were actively engaged in the struggle for the soul of Germany.[44] Some men slept in large tent cities, others in gymnasiums or barns. All such makeshift locations belonged to Nazi sympathizers and were provided free of charge. Pfeffer von Salomon preferred these mass quarters not only because they were cheap but also because they were safe.

As anticipated, the SA's aggressive behavior sometimes resulted in clash violence at these events. In the 1929 rally in Nuremberg, the "Marxists" struck back. Clash violence erupted between toughs on both sides. Like an army, the SA leadership evaluated the lessons from this event in order to make sure it was not repeated. Pfeffer von Salomon then circulated an SA-wide order summarizing the "battle." These orders were usually brief. However, the 1929 rally evaluation took up four full pages.[45] This rally was an important exercise in assembling masses of people and testing their temerity under pressure.

Left-wing activists infiltrated Nazi rallies in SA uniforms, sometimes gathering information and sometimes creating confusion and chaos. These fake SA men walked into mass quarters, spread fake news of Marxist brawls, and severely disturbed the discipline, which in turn increased the likelihood of a real brawl. To avoid these shortcomings, Pfeffer von Salomon gave orders regarding housing and the avoidance of spies in SA uniform. He ordered, "During large concentrations of SA, or during rallies in larger cities, the SA-men must be available to their leaders constantly. No city furlough and off time! . . . Never bring new men to larger meetings. . . . Under no circumstances are non-SA party members allowed to stay with SA-units." He also stated specifically that "nonregulation service dress is forbidden!"[46] An opponent of the Nazis wearing an SA uniform might not even know he wore outdated signs of rank on his collar. Nevertheless, every SA trooper was literate in reading these signs and thus easily noticed small inaccuracies.

To ensure security, Pfeffer von Salomon declared that as "a fundamental rule, never let anybody enter the SA-mass-quarters. No visitors, family members, civilian party comrades, merchants, [or] SA-men from other units are allowed. Establish effective guards that will patrol streets and bars and catch SA-men who left their groups. Visibly marked SS security patrols are the most effective. I order hereby every SA-man found without his group is to be immediately let go without mercy."[47] Staying together, a strict adherence to uniform regulations, and the use of SS patrols curtailed opposition infiltration into the SA as had happened in Nuremberg. If officers enforced all regulations, the assembly of large masses of SA in one city for the weekend was not only possible but safe as well. Officers watched with scrutinizing eyes during mass events. Infiltration, or even open brawls, with this political army became dangerous for any Nazi opponent.

Mass assemblies were highly effective and inexpensive because of the Nazis' skill in applying practical solutions to logistical problems. The nature of these communal events for the individual SA man can be compared to a field trip. There was travel, the excitement of new sights and experiences, and the communal homosocial experience during the different events. To an individual, these annual trips could be life-changing experiences. According to Conn, the 1929 Nuremberg rally was a "great and unforgettable experience," which was hard to describe. He wrote that one simply had to experience it for himself.[48] For local anti-Nazis, these events can be compared to an invasion. From that perspective, an opposing political army brought violence into the strongholds of socialists and communists. This aggressiveness was a hallmark of Nazi propaganda.[49] For the Nazi sympathizers in such locations, the entire event was an exceptional spectacle of enormous proportions.

The massing of SA from all geographic regions of the Weimar Republic was such a successful spectacle that the inhabitants of cities that experienced a rally voted in higher proportions for the Nazis. Their success is therefore measurable. The 1928 electoral results for all German cities demonstrate this. The Nazis fared badly in most industrial centers, with results far under the 10 percent mark in city council elections—except for the cities of Koblenz, Munich, Nuremberg, and Weimar, where they had remarkably high levels of support. The explanation in the first three cities is relatively clear. In their stronghold in Bavaria, they earned 10.7 percent of the vote in Munich and 10.6 percent in Nuremberg. The strong allegiances to the army in Koblenz explain why a decent percentage of voters were attracted to the militaristic message of the Nazis. In Koblenz the Nazis won 10.4 percent.[50]

The Weimar result, 10.6 percent, stood out because the relative popularity of the Nazis in Weimar defied simple explanations, unless the fact that Weimar was the only non-Bavarian city in which the Nazis chose to hold their annual rallies is considered. Therefore, evidence strongly suggests that the 1926 party rally impacted the election results for that city.[51] This spike in voting loyalty is a testament to the success of SA tactics. They could impress, yet also successfully engage in clash violence with numbers on their side. This left a positive impression on the residents of Weimar. On the national level, 1928 was a bad election year for the Nazis, yet Weimar showed how success could be achieved on the local level. The fascists learned that the massing of their uniformed SA had the effect that the SA leadership aimed for.

CONCLUSION

The Nazis' mass spectacles were pure political theater. The SA actors in these political dramas wore their brown costumes with pride and gave the entire movement a strong, dynamic image. When Alfred Conn marched by Hitler and Pfeffer von Salomon during the 1929 Nuremberg rally, he recalled that the SA men had glowing eyes and were showered with flowers.[52] No other mass organization in the Weimar era repeatedly accomplished such dynamic displays of power. The ability to concentrate the sheer numbers of uniformed men allowed the Nazis to accomplish such feats by promoting the movement to the masses.

When it came to actually assembling large groups, the organization made use of experiences from these rallies and used bicycles, trucks, and railroads to transport men. One such large rally occurred on April 12, 1931, in Weimar. Röhm ordered the SA from the provinces Thuringia and Upper Franconia, the district Halle-Merseburg, and the cities Chemnitz, Plauen, and Leipzig all to appear in Weimar. Hitler spoke at this meeting. Röhm routinely ordered thousands of SA men to come and listen to their leader.[53] He had the logistical capacity that had been introduced, tested, and optimized years earlier.

The plan that Hanover's SA leader prepared when Hitler was to speak in Oldenburg on May 5, 1931, demonstrates the attention to detail. Free food for the men was factored in again. After the arrival of SA groups, each had one hour and fifteen minutes to eat free food from the mobile SA kitchen. After lunch, thousands of men marched past Hitler and Göring in a parade lasting approximately two hours.[54] After the onset of the economic crisis in 1929, food functioned as propaganda when large sections of the rank and file of the SA were unemployed.[55]

The opportunistic Nazis learned about mass parades from both the Left and the Right. Nevertheless, logistical experiences made by bourgeois officers in the Imperial Army and the financial capabilities of bourgeois Nazi supporters allowed the Nazis to perfect the techniques they copied from their political opponents on both sides. Perfecting these techniques allowed the Nazis to be aggressive since they could move and support thousands of men for days at a time. The Nazis symbolically invaded territory where they did not have a strong backing. They were able to do so because they were independent of local organizations and independent of the party affiliations of the locals with their mobile kitchens and travel infrastructure. Their mass approach to parades and rallies ensured that the local populace was impressed by the sheer masses of Brown Shirted men. In this way, the Brown Shirt symbolically represented the movement and conquered the streets, as Hitler had ordered in his initial order to the SA.

The Nazis could move thousands of men from multiple locations all over Germany into one specific town or city before important elections. The Nazis could move their propaganda army with astonishing speed and drilled routine into politically contested locations, where they might encounter local resistance. These brown shock troopers flooded the streets in organized columns with marching bands playing popular army marches and Nazi songs. The Brown Shirts projected the image of youthful dynamism. Mass assemblies enhanced the propagandistic effects of the uniform even more. Military experience permitted the SA to move thousands in a cost-effective and consistent manner and even to master logistical and security problems.

The middle- and upper-class constituency of the SA brought in private motor transport. The financial burdens of logistics, transport, food supply, and shelter were in large part shouldered by business owners who supported the Nazi cause with donations. The Nazis used bicycles, chartered trucks and buses, and public transportation by rail, and they even established independently mobile motor and flying SA units. The SA also mastered the housing and food issues by finding cheap quarters in private houses, hostels, and barns of party members. For these party members, it was an honor to house members of the Brown Army. With the use of mobile field kitchens for large stew dishes and donated precooked or durable food, like sandwiches, smoked meats, cakes, and fruit preserves, the Nazis could feed hundreds, sometimes even thousands, of men for a few days at a time. Such logistical proficiency was essential for the Nazis to mobilize the forces necessary to saturate electoral hot spots and proletarian neighborhoods in the cities. Such practical efficiency freed the Nazis to contend for power in crucial areas and gave their image a dynamic and aggressive spin.

The SA drew power and organizational skills from widespread military experience among its members. The SA was not an army, yet it acted like one at times. The growing role of the SA as a military organization became more and more clear. It functioned as a spare-time propaganda troop that engaged in street-level clash violence and protected Nazi speakers. The military-like posturing and the imitation of military insignia, ranks, and discipline among SA men helped to shape the aggressive SA image in important ways. They used this image during the late Weimar elections masterfully. As the SA grew in numbers, a further, even more overt, militarization was demonstrated via visible changes to the service dress. Shortly before the Nazis came to power in 1933, they made important changes that influenced the SA image yet again.

Chapter five

THE PROFESSIONALIZATION OF A CIVIL WAR ARMY

Gerhard Rossbach notes in his biography that the early SA was a volunteer organization with specific ideals connected to real political goals. The SA sought to represent antirepublican sentiment and to fight a civil war in the streets. These goals united these volunteer political soldiers. Thus, the early SA retained a degree of freedom. The later SA, however, was marked by militarism. Rossbach argues that militarism abuses the political soldier because it takes the freedom away from him. The later SA had no freedom and was thus militarized. To Rossbach, it appeared as if the SA militarized. Hitler, however, meant to make his SA more professional. Hitler decided to change his relationship to conservative bastions in the democratic state rather than fight a civil war against the state. He therefore changed his relationship to the army.[1] This change did not come quickly. Yet it became necessary to make the SA appear more like a professional military to bridge the ambiguity between SA violence and discipline in a time of extreme growth.

The 1928 national elections were a turning point in Nazi strategy. Because the Nazis were unable to win voters for their cause in proletarian urban and industrial centers, Hitler decided to concentrate his efforts on rural areas and the middle class. He also started to openly court the Stahlhelm and the military. After his electoral breakthrough in 1930, this became more difficult. From 1931 onward, the SA counted more members than the actual German military.[2] Hitler sought to improve SA discipline and order, on the one hand, and increasingly saw the SA as a paramilitary force that could conquer the streets, on the other. As the SA grew in numbers up until 1930, violence dramatically increased. After 1930 the level of violence spiked again and exploded in 1933–34.[3] Yet especially during this time period, Hitler's goal was to win the middle class and the favor of the military.

PROFESSIONAL SOLDIERS AND PROFESSIONAL UNIFORMS

Because it became increasingly difficult for Hitler and his SA leader Franz Pfeffer von Salomon to keep the growing SA under control,

Pfeffer von Salomon resigned in August 1930 and Hitler reappointed Ernst Röhm as SA chief of staff in January 1931.[4] The SA then underwent a thorough professionalization along military lines under Röhm until 1934. This militarization was intended to bring the SA image closer to that of a respectable militia capable of taking over responsibilities within the state. This was important because Hitler knew that he could come to power only if the military at least tolerated his SA. Yet the militarization of the SA under Röhm cannot only be seen in changes made to the command structure and the specialization of the administration.[5] These changes were also made on a more mundane level. Changes to the uniform of the SA aimed at bringing the SA image closer to that of the military and making it look more respectable.

Shortly before they came to power in 1933, the Nazis introduced a brown business-suit jacket and a long woolen coat to the SA. The Nazis also standardized the hue of the entire outfit. Pants, jackets, and coats all matched for the first time in both cut and color. These changes made the SA service dress look more like a traditional military uniform. The SA appeared more professional. Additionally, Hitler and his SA chief of staff Röhm streamlined the SA's administrative structure and introduced clearer guidelines regarding the command structure and signs of rank. These new elements represented a permanent change to the uniform. The brown outfit with cap, tie, Brown Shirt, and the mismatching elements (riding pants and high boots) became the "traditional uniform" of the *Kampfzeit,* the Nazi term for the Weimar era. In the late Weimar period, the Brown Shirt represented only part of an SA man's collection. Ultimately, the men of the SA had outfits for different occasions, just like men in the military. With this wardrobe, the Nazis wanted to make a positive impact on conservative elements. Yet this apparent further militarization also alarmed Hitler's opponents.

The newspapers of the social democrats and police reports, for instance, clearly show that the Nazis still invaded contested territory and acted aggressively. The paramilitary structures of the SA did not go unnoticed by political opponents. The social democrats, who wholeheartedly defended Weimar democracy, noted the militarization of politics by the Nazis during the early 1930s. On August 28, 1930, the editors of the most prominent social democratic newspaper, *Vorwärts,* published an article describing the purpose and structure of the SA. The article also included a list of 215 dead and wounded victims of Nazi attacks between April and July alone. The growing aggressiveness of the Nazis caused concern among those who held democratic values. The headline of the article, "The Organization of the Killers," made it clear to all readers that, according to the social democrats at least, the SA was a paramilitary gang of murderers.[6]

The article also clearly described the military-like structure of the SA. The editors argued, "With the SA and the SS, Hitler and his followers created formations that were organized like the military. Their purpose is terror and violence, their means are brass knuckles and revolvers." After giving a brief review of its leaders, the editors scornfully called the organizational structure "Military Antics." The men of the SA saw themselves as political soldiers for their movement. According to the editors, "Only those who are willing to unquestioningly and under all circumstances follow the orders of the highest SA leader, and the leaders appointed by him, can become members. Every SA member must simultaneously be a member of the Nazi Party."[7]

The social democrats further described the perceived relationship between the SA and the military. According to them, the geographical command centers of the SA ominously overlapped with the local command centers of the Reichswehr, the German army established after the First World War. The editors of *Vorwärts* commented on the fact that all higher SA officers were former officers of the Imperial Army. They correspondingly noticed, "The internal organization is comparable to that of the Reichswehr. As in the military there are special service branches: Intelligence Service, Signal Corps, Musicians, Medical Orderlies, etc."[8] The article ends on a bellicose and defiant note: "It is the task of the worker's organizations and the social democrats to energetically oppose Nazi attacks." However, although this *Vorwärts* article called for a united front against the Nazis, the national elections of September 14, 1930, signaled the beginning of landslide electoral successes for the Nazis in subsequent national elections.[9]

Not surprisingly, the social democratic press outlined both alleged and real connections between the SA and the military. This suspicion can be explained by the customary distrust between organized labor and the military during the imperial era. Nevertheless, the police, as politically neutral guardians of Weimar democracy, also noted the outward similarities between the service dress of the SA and the uniforms of the Imperial Army and the Reichswehr. The German military used different colors on their collar patches to distinguish different service brands. The Berlin police noticed a militarization of the SA service dress when they followed suit. They noted in a report that, according to a decree given out by the SA high command on April 22, 1931, "the visual distinction of the tactical and strategic SA leaders purposefully follows the principles applied by today's Reichswehr and by the former army. Just as . . . military leaders are distinguished by a deep red color as [a] distinguishing symbol on their uniforms . . . so is . . . a deep red color also introduced as [a] distinguishing symbol for tactical SA leaders." The police also noted the similarities in the dark red of SA and military generals, black for technical troops, and blue for medical personnel. In addition, "The metal coloration of insignia, trims, etc. are . . . borrowed from the former service branches of the military."[10] Not only the decorations and insignia on the service dress of the SA reminded the police of the actual military.

The colorful tops of the SA caps that Pfeffer von Salomon considered introducing in 1927 also awoke the suspicion of the Berlin police.[11] They noted that on festive occasions of the SA, just as during parades of the Reichswehr, "special efforts are put on colors as for instance the colored tops and sides of caps."[12] These "special efforts" to incorporate military-like trimmings as well as the increased militancy of the SA evoked more reactions within the social democratic press. In October 1931, the editors of the *Greater Hagen City News* mockingly called this emphasis on color "war paint."[13] Still, the content of the article reveals that the social democrats and the police did not see eye to eye when it came to the aggressive posturing of the SA.

The editors of the *Greater Hagen City News* gave their article the headline "Do We Live in the Third Reich Already?" According to this article, the police did not intervene when the Greater Hagen SA broke the law by wearing their Brown Shirts when traveling to a rally in Braunschweig. In Braunschweig the SA service dress was tolerated during that October, whereas in the Prussian town of Greater Hagen the Brown Shirt was prohibited. The passive inactivity of the railroad police outraged the editors. The "1000 men of the National Socialist civil war troop left the train during the short stop clamoring and rampaging." They did this under the eyes of the hopelessly understaffed police force. The editors called for strong resistance to this literal invasion and reminded their readers that they should follow the law. If the Reichsbanner was illegal, they would not wear "their green uniforms." The law-abiding socialists accused the Greater Hagen police of turning a blind eye. Yet reactions were not uniform. The police in Königsberg used their rubber truncheons when the SA overstepped their boundaries. The end of the article highlights the increasing political violence in the face of invading Nazi armies. When the SA returned from Braunschweig late at night, a social democratic raiding party awaited the SA outside of the train station.[14]

While police forces either looked on or stepped in, and while the social democrats tried to put up resistance in kind, the SA acted brutally and self-assuredly. Only a little more than a month after the *Greater Hagen City News* published their article about the SA, the SA command gave out an order signed by Hitler himself. In Decree Number Five from November 28, Hitler and Röhm streamlined the command structure and adapted it to the problems caused by the rise in membership. Evidently, the actual term for SA members was not previously agreed on. They decreed that the entire SA consisted of SA men. These SA men then were divided into leaders and men.[15]

Since not all SA locals could be led by the same level of officers, the order contained guidelines regarding rank and position. Hitler and his SA chief of staff established military-style rules that established which rank could hold each position in the organization. Just as in the military, some positions could be held only by persons who had attained a certain rank. For instance, *Obergruppenführer, Gruppenführer, Oberführer,* and *Standartenführer* belonged to the higher leadership, the equivalent to the rank of general in the military. The midlevel leaders, officers in the military, had to be *Sturmbannführer* or *Sturmführer.* Low-level leaders, likened to noncommissioned officers in the military, had to have attained the rank of *Truppführer* or *Scharführer.* All others were simply SA men.[16]

The military professionalization of the SA during this time becomes palpable in the next point of the decree. Hitler specifically ordered that individuals who formerly held high-level leadership positions and were readmitted, men who had high ranking positions in other right-wing paramilitaries, or men who held rank in the Reichswehr could join the SA with an elevated rank because of their former positions and experience in other similar organizations. Experts achieved higher ranks immediately after signing up. They did not have to work their way up in the hierarchy.[17] Ultimately, many SA men who joined before this order were disgruntled. Yet the need for military specialists in the SA was more important, and thus Hitler upheld the enticement for specialists to join with a higher initial rank.[18]

Just as in the regular military, all other SA men rose in the ranks according to merit rather than according to the time they held a specific rank. Ineffective and lazy officers were not promoted simply based on the time they invested. Only efficient work and dedication to the movement allowed the men to attain promotion to a higher rank. Naturally, Hitler also decreed who had the power to promote whom. He copied a military-like structure for his SA with flexible and separate power structures. The commission directory attached to the order listed the commissions for the separate power structures, the position held by the leader of each commission, and the ranks that SA men had to hold for the respective commission. These structures included a built-in flexibility because the ranks necessary for a position could be multiple. For instance, to be eligible to be a midlevel administrative leader such as a *Zeugmeister*, responsible for a regional *Zeugmeisterei*, the ranks of *Untergruppengeldverwalter* (subgroup financial administrator) or the next lower rank of *Zeugmeister* were eligible. A position could also be held by a temporarily appointed leader who did not officially hold the necessary rank. As in the military, this structure allowed for smoothly functioning administrative machinery that fluidly allowed upward movement within the ranks. As this example shows, the administrative offices included officers responsible for finances and brown merchandise. Hitler and Röhm also streamlined the responsibilities for leaders of the motor SA, the musical corps, and the medical corps.[19]

The second attachment to this order made up the rank directory. This directory included the ranks and the manner in which these ranks should be addressed by others, and, most important, it detailed descriptions of the appropriate rank insignia. The official names for SA ranks usually did not resemble military ranks. Nevertheless, the way the ranks were displayed through insignia was very similar. For instance, insignia for officers included stars and oak leaves, displayed on colored collar tabs. The insignia and the colors representing generals, officers, and specialists, such as motor-SA officers and doctors, clearly show that they were copied from military models. Both the commission and rank directories sketched out an intricate command structure that clearly illustrates militant tendencies. The uniforms and structures of the SA resembled that of a political army. The editors of the *Greater Hagen City News* shared this notion when they called the SA a "National Socialist civil war troop."[20]

As noted by the Left, the military specialization of the SA also included attempts to reshape the uniform along military models. Since additional items made the uniforms more expensive, Röhm ordered on July 7, 1932, that although it would have been convenient to introduce changes for all SA men and leaders, the SA would introduce a new service tunic, a new cap, and a new overcoat to officers and those men who could afford the items. He did this for experimental purposes only. Röhm, just like Pfeffer von Salomon, used the men of the SA to try out new items and get feedback before deciding whether to make them part of the regular service dress. The SA, as described in previous chapters, had mastered market research. Thus, "Until further notice, . . . the Brown Shirt remains the service dress of the SA."[21] The Nazis still wanted to change their image and make it more professional, as the rest of the order clearly indicated.

The order reflects the understanding that the SA was on the verge of becoming a state organization and showed this by introducing suitable garments that resembled items worn in formal military dress. In this order, Röhm argued, "The National Socialist movement is in the final battle for political power." He also admitted that the Brown Shirt "takes the climatic conditions in Germany too little into account" and that the men had to "put up with that." To remedy this situation, Röhm "ordered the implementation of test runs to prepare now for later improvements on the service dress of the SA." The SA leader included a list of uniform items to be introduced or modified. These new items included a new service tunic and an overcoat. The SA leadership anticipated changes to the service cap, pants, footwear, and the belt. Also included on the list of anticipated changes were modifications to the signs of SA rank and insignia. The first of two additional enclosures provided a detailed list of the color codes for collar tabs, the color of the numbers displayed on these tabs, as well as the colors and significance of braids and buttons. The second enclosure included a detailed description of the cutting pattern for the new service tunic and riding pants.[22] If an SA man wanted the new tunic, he could have one made by a talented female supporter or a professional tailor by using the same standard pattern.

As opposed to the Brown Shirt, the new service tunic resembled an open-collared suit jacket, like those on business suits, or the style of tunic traditionally worn in the military. The single-breasted tunic is closed in the front with four metal buttons. Like on a military tunic, the two breast pockets and the hip pockets are slightly angled, pleated, and scalloped. All four pockets are closed by the same metal buttons. The tunic is tailored close fitting at the hip and flares out toward the bottom.[23] The service tunic changed the way an SA man looked from sportive to more conservative.

Since the jacket was more expensive to produce than a Brown Shirt, Röhm stated in his July 1932 order, "I especially want to draw attention to the fact that no leader must put financial burdens on their men. Additionally, the preparations for the manufacture of a fabric in fitting hue and quality are not finished yet, so that an early acquisition might result in later modifications." Even new SA recruits were required first and foremost to purchase a Brown Shirt. Nevertheless, the SA leader also appealed to a sense of modesty and camaraderie among his men. Röhm specified that "I advise all SA-leaders and men that are able to purchase the new tunic, to consider their poorer comrades, who oftentimes do not have the necessities of life."[24] Although the new tunic made the SA look more professional and less radical, the cost of the tailor-made tunic was prohibitive for many men.

The considerations for a new SA cap were, however, of a practical nature. The original ski cap was soft and gray. By 1932 the cap was rigid and brown. Although this specific shape and brown color were iconic, the order admitted, "The present service cap is not ideal." According to Röhm, the fact that the cap could not be folded and easily stowed in a bag or a backpack presented problems. Supposedly, a foldable cap would serve the SA better since all men shared an affinity for sports and hiking.[25] Nevertheless, the ability to easily stow the cap in a backpack indicated the increasing military character of the SA since it facilitated physical exercise.

The SA chief of staff had three different models for a new cap in mind. He ordered three SA units to receive and test the caps in the field. Röhm decreed that the designated parts of the groups Schlesien and Berlin-Brandenburg were to test out two model caps, both without a bill. The officers were to "report soon on popularity and the test results." The groups Hochland and Austria were to test a model along the lines of the traditional soft ski cap. The groups West and the NSKK, the Nazi drivers' organization, were to test a cap modeled after the service cap of the military.[26] The cap tests were still in their initial stages, yet a prototype cap based on a military model was part of the envisaged SA image.

To be able to serve the purposes of the Nazi movement, even in the toughest winter weather conditions, the SA also envisioned a brown long overcoat. The color of the coat, the new tunic, and the riding pants matched in hue from this point forward. This order illustrates that further standardization of color was planned rather than accidental. The order shows as well that some of the new image changes remained in the realm of wishful thinking. The footwear to be worn with the new matching items could still not be mandated and did not match. The order stated, "High brown or black boots, or brown or black lace-up boots with matching leather, or fabric putties can be worn as footwear." Men with no financial means to purchase these could also wear "low shoes and unicolor, or sports socks in appropriate colors." Röhm advised his officers to carefully monitor the footwear situation and ensure that all men had rugged footwear. Yet he also noted that officers were supposed to assist their men in paying for footwear in case of need.[27] The Nazis seemed to actively try to copy military uniforms, yet real boots for all remained unattainable.

Although footwear remained a problem for the Nazis, since it disrupted their plans to present a uniform image, the SA image nonetheless moved closer to military models. This went beyond military-like clothing cuts and shaped caps, overcoats, and service tunics. Röhm's order also included a new wider belt. Additionally, he introduced a distinction between different service dresses. For example, all SA men had to know how to wear their service dress for regular duty and how to embellish their dress for parades and festivities. Just like regular drill instructors, all SA officers were supposed to wear a signal whistle with a two-toned braid.[28] As the social democratic press and the police already noted, the effort the SA put into the different colors on insignia and on the uniform itself was enormous.

Color codes in military uniforms are rather complicated. In the imperial German military, the color of trimmings not only denoted service branch but also showed what federal state a military unit was stationed in. In the Imperial Army, all German soldiers wore the same gray uniform, yet the colors of the trimmings and cockades on the caps could specify regional affiliations. For instance, the state colors of the state of Mecklenburg are blue, yellow, and red. An imperial service man from Mecklenburg wore a blue, yellow, and red cockade on his cap. Röhm's order shows that the SA actively copied this military tradition. The order contained an enclosure detailing the colors for the different SA groups. According to the enclosure, SA men from Mecklenburg wore blue collar tabs with yellow numbering. The braids on this uniform were twisted in the same colors. The buttons were golden.[29] This order thus documents the efforts of the SA to attain a color-coded uniform that could be viewed and comprehended like the uniform of a soldier.

In September 1932, the SA leader gave out a decree that showed further militarization and specialization efforts and indicated how the men viewed themselves. The leadership designated the service dress an "honor garment" that one could dishonor with inappropriate behavior. Therefore, the new service dress had to be complete, clean, and in excellent condition, or men risked doing their uniform a disservice. Röhm's decree seemed to summarize and reinforce the previously discussed order, yet it also shows that some men pushed the limits of militarization. The order noted that men were forbidden to wear a steel helmet with the SA service dress. Moreover, the decree listed the equipment of every SA man. Just like service men, SA men were required to have a backpack with straps to fasten a rolled-up overcoat or blanket, camping gear, a mess kit, and a canteen.[30] The SA applied military-like structures, uniforms, and equipment during this transition into the new decade. In the early 1930s, they also began practicing military tactics again. This development was important. The Nazi SA, increasingly perceived as an army, caused fear of civil war among their opponents.

An October 20, 1932, situation report from the Munich police department reflects the anxieties of democratic state institutions in the face of these developments. The police report also shows how the Munich police interpreted the intentions of SA men and leaders and their hopes and dreams for the future Third Reich. They initially acknowledged, "Through the taking over of meeting and speaker protection during the last elections, the SA leadership put extraordinary demands on their men." The report immediately suggested, "These people took up these financial and physical burdens in the specific hope to help their party to ultimate victory and themselves to a job." The police report continued: "People in the SA believed the future army would get its new recruits from the ranks of the SA. It may sound unbelievable, but simple people, that never even served in the army, saw themselves as battalion and regimental commanders of the new military already because of their leadership positions in the SA." Because of these tendencies and fears that Hitler could not retain the radicalism of his men, the contemptuous report warned of imminent danger of civil war.[31]

After this warning, the Munich report confirmed the earlier discussion of the social democratic press and described the military character of the SA. It stated, "According to several recent measures it is doubtful that the highest SA leadership considers toning down the military character of the SA. They are planning to build a flight school for the entire Reich." Even worse, "The training exercise activities of the SA . . . have increased lately. Often, night exercises occur, during which, with the help of hypothetical war scenarios, attack and defense tactics are practiced. During these training exercises, tactics are partially used, just as in the current military." The fact that SA members had to be healthy and undergo physicals by SA doctors before declared fit for service, the age limitation of thirty years for regular SA, and the fact that the SA had reserve units made up of older men strengthened the military character of the organization.[32] The police and the social democratic constituency watched the SA change their public image from that of a propaganda troop to that of a military organization. They increasingly dressed and behaved like a Nazi army. Some men likely anticipated becoming officers when the transformation was complete.

CONCLUSION

The SA uniform and its additions made the ever-expanding mass organization look coherent and professional. The SA did, however, have discipline problems and regional differences in the interpretation of their own ideology. The *Traditionsanzug,* the traditional dress of the SA as first introduced in 1926 and developed until 1929, differed from the new uniform introduced in 1932. After that time, all newly produced and sold uniform items matched in hue. Before that, the lower body did not match at all. SA men wore trousers and footwear according to what was sportive, militant, and affordable. Thus, all riding pants varied in both color and cut. All footwear differed as well. After 1932 all SA men wore the same uniform above and below the waist. A left-wing SA man from the North looked the same as a right-wing Stormtrooper from the South. The uniform thus suggested a monolithic movement, which the Nazis were not.

The uniform also suggested professionalism. Only the newly appointed leaders were true experts. These professionals in administration, military questions, and SA health services gave the SA an air of respectability. These experts were also allowed to join with higher ranks. With this privilege also came the privilege to purchase an SA uniform tunic and long woolen overcoat. These specific items were also worn by the military. Hitler and Röhm granted officers and financially stable SA men the right to symbolically dress like the Reichswehr with these additions.

When compared to the *Traditionsanszug,* the new tunic and overcoat made the SA look more traditional and less radical. The youthful and energetic flair given to the Stormtroopers by the Brown Shirt and tie were never truly lost because they remained in the wardrobe of every trooper. Still, if the weather was colder, or the situation called for a more professional look, the SA could also look less radical and tone down their shock value with the newly introduced items. This was important to the Nazis during their critical rise to power.

Ultimately, the service tunic and the overcoat became standard dress items for all SA men in the beginning of the official Nazi period, in 1933. The stiff brown SA cap stayed the same until late into the Third Reich. The SA leadership never adopted the test versions of the military cap discussed above. Although Röhm and some of his men had different plans, the SA never became the core of a new Nazi military but rather got absorbed into the military itself. Still, the men of the SA did make the impression that they could become legitimate soldiers, and both SA men and those watching from the side lines noticed. In 1933 the Nazis also started making myths about themselves and their actions during the Weimar period. The following chapter will evaluate such myths focusing on the Brown Shirt.

Chapter Six

CLASSLESS HEROES—THE CENTRALITY OF THE BROWN SHIRT IN MYTHIC NAZI FILM AND LITERATURE

After the Nazis dismantled German democracy in 1933, they set to work making myths about themselves and their path to power. They depicted the Weimar period as *Kampfzeit* (time of struggle), marked by their active resistance against the democratic state. According to the fascist interpretation of the Weimar period, the republic brought economic chaos, sowed division, and led to subsequent national frailty. According to this Nazi version of history, the Germans were suffering economic hardship caused by the lost war and the Depression. Social class and political affiliations further divided the German people. This discord made the Germans, and by proxy their state, weak and vulnerable. Consequently, according to this interpretation, fighting against the republic was an honorable deed for the salvation of the German people and the rightful German state.

In power, the Nazis dedicated time and financial resources to a rewriting of history along the above-described lines. A three-film series created and reinforced positive myths about how the SA and the Hitler Youth fought the republic. The films also highlight the importance the Nazis lent their Brown Shirts during the Weimar years. According to Nazi myth, for instance, twenty-two-year-old SA man Horst Wessel and fifteen-year-old Hitler Youth Herbert Norkus both died because their uniforms made them conspicuous in the communist-dominated proletarian neighborhoods of Berlin. Their real, albeit short, lives posthumously served as the bases for fictional characters that Hitler's propaganda minister, Joseph Goebbels, used as inspiration for two propaganda films. The first, *Hans Westmar,* recounts the fictionalized story of an SA man based on Wessel. The second, *Hitler Youth Quex,* relates events around fictional Heini Völker, based on Norkus's life. Another fictional character, this one not based on a real historical figure, is SA man Fritz Brand, the protagonist of the film *SA-Mann Brand,* which is the final film of the 1933 trilogy.[1] The most successful of these three films, *Hitler Youth Quex,* was produced for 320,000

Reichsmark. By January 1934, not even one full year after its release, one million Germans had seen the film.[2] Up until 1942, the Nazi authorities made the film mandatory viewing for the Hitler Youth. Ultimately, approximately twenty million Germans viewed the film. These mythical stories thus served to actively shape Nazi culture in the midst of its development.[3]

The Nazis used not only film as a medium to create and strengthen positive myths about themselves and their uniforms by combining fact with fiction but print media as well. *Die SA Erobert Berlin* (The SA conquers Berlin) is a novel published in 1933 by Wilfrid Bade about a fictional Berlin worker, Schulz, who finds his way to the Nazi SA. Like the first two films above, however, some characters in this novel are based on real historical figures.[4] Readers would have recognized the names of Berlin SA man Horst Wessel and the Berlin SA leaders Joseph Goebbels and Kurt Daluege. Another book that fitted into this genre, *Männer im Braunhemd* (Men in the Brown Shirt) is an attempt by SA officer Karl W. H. Koch to synthesize the stories of real men of the SA into a coherent fictionalized narrative.[5] Published in 1936, this account retraces the history of the SA from its earliest beginnings and includes many authentic photographs. Just like the films and the novel, this book amplifies myths and legends the Nazis created about themselves.

These myths always include hypermasculine, heroic Nazis who struggle against great odds to achieve ultimate victory. Historian Jay W. Baird analyzes the myths, contending that the Nazis cultivated an affinity for heroism that was already present in both high and low German culture. This heroism, according to Baird, centered around the themes of struggle and redemption in death. Baird retraces the lives of several Nazis who died for their cause during the Weimar years. The list of Nazis scrutinized by the author includes both SA man Horst Wessel and Hitler Youth Herbert Norkus. According to Baird, Joseph Goebbels centered the Wessel myth around "resurrection and return." Goebbels and Hitler Youth leader Baldur von Schirach used the themes of heroic death and transfiguration as the main hallmarks of the Norkus myth.[6] In mythic self-depictions, the importance of the uniform to the individual Nazi becomes evident.

The importance of the Brown Shirt becomes clear when one scrutinizes Norkus's actual Hitler Youth record. Herbert Norkus was a member of Berlin's navy branch of the Hitler Youth. Consequently, his uniform was not brown, but blue. The navy branch of the Hitler

Youth wore traditional navy shirts with the wide, striped collar. Yet the director made Heini Völker, the on-screen persona of Norkus, a member of the regular Brown Shirted Hitler Youth. Ultimately, on the silver screen, the fictionalized characters of Heini Völker and Hans Westmar both highly value their Brown Shirts and wear them with pride. In both cases, the Brown Shirt is made highly visible and serves as a tool to recruit followers. Marching groups of Nazis suggest strength and unity, which contrast the purported weakness and inherent divisions of the republic. This sense of unity aids in leading the German people into the Nazi fold. Interestingly, the myths themselves started with real, and even controversial, historical figures, which developed over time into stereotypical hero figures who fought and died for the establishment of the Third Reich. The connections between heroism, as identified by Baird, and the uses and functions of the Nazi uniform as a tool to overcome class barriers, as depicted in Third Reich–era film and literature, confirm how integral the Brown Shirt is to the construction of mainstream political culture in Nazi Germany. These connections, furthermore, highlight the importance of the Brown Shirt to the Nazis of the Weimar era.

Franz Wenzler directed the first film in the trilogy: *Hans Westmar, One of Many: A German Destiny from the Year 1929*. Wenzler cleaned up Horst Wessel's biography and filmed a propaganda piece with an overdrawn cast of characters that represent Nazi archetypes. The protagonist is the young, tall, and blond university student Hans Westmar. Throughout the film, Hans meets several love interests. In one of Berlin's SA homes, Hans meets Klara, a Nazi sympathizer. Hans also gets to know Maude, a decadent German American visiting Germany. Finally, Hans meets the young proletarian Agnes, daughter of an unemployed, alcoholic communist man. Each of these women is a potential love interest for Hans. Another woman, however, is clearly depicted as a communist antagonist: Mrs. Cohn. With her name, her short stature, and her dark hair, in opposition to Hans's blond locks, Wenzler evoked another, oppositional, stereotype in Mrs. Cohn. Cohn is a Jewish adviser to the other three (male) communist antagonists in the film. One of them, Camillo Ross, is a German communist whose mustache lends him a resemblance to Joseph Stalin. The second, Kuprikoff, is the Russian party leader of Berlin and speaks with a heavy accent. With almond-shaped eyes, a goatee, and a workingman's cap, he looks suspiciously like Lenin. Finally, Kupferstern is a communist and member of the German parliament. With a short stature, a large nose, and thick, round glasses, his character, like Mrs. Cohn, is depicted as a stereotypical Jew.[7]

Like the cast, the plot is unpretentious. On arriving in Berlin from Vienna, Hans lives the life of a privileged student. He is a member of a dueling fraternity, yet student life does not satisfy the young man. In the classroom, the lectures given by pacifist teachers make Hans angry. In the streets, the overwhelming presence of communists also antagonizes him. The nightlife and the cosmopolitan flair of the city push him to the decision to actively work against pacifism, internationalism, and communism. He therefore joins Berlin's SA and crosses class lines by temporarily abandoning his studies to work first as a taxi driver and later as a construction worker—effectively proletarianizing himself. In the SA home of Berlin's Storm 1, Hans finds friends and support among the uniformed men of the SA. Klara, a young woman, takes care of the men of the storm. When Hans is shown entering the SA home, Klara is washing the men's Brown Shirts.[8]

At this moment in the film, which reflects the reality of the time, Berlin's SA is weak in proletarian neighborhoods. The shirts make the men stand out. Therefore, Hans and another SA man from Storm 1 do not dare to wear their Brown Shirts when they accept an invitation from the communists to speak at one of their meetings. Once there, they find that the communist meeting itself is chaotic. The uniformed men of the Red Front-Fighters League, or RFB, sit on the stage with dangling legs in an extremely undisciplined manner. The parliamentary member Kupferstern gives a speech in which he names the social democrats as primary enemies. The Nazis, according to Kupferstern, are just rowdy young boys that the communists will beat to a pulp—not even worth their time. When the communist member of parliament asks which one of the invited Nazis is about to speak, he addresses them as *Braunhemdchen* (little Brown Shirts), demeaning them with the diminutive. Ultimately, Westmar gives a speech to the assembled communists, antagonizing the crowd to start a riot. Subsequently, an SA man of Berlin's Storm 15 is murdered by three communists. This shocks the German communist Ross, yet his Soviet superior, Kuprikoff, argues that the Nazis will hide from now on.[9]

Kuprikoff, however, did not consider the stubbornness of Berlin's SA in general and of Hans Westmar in particular. The next scene shows all of Berlin's SA storms assembled in full uniform and ready for a march through the city. Before the march in the proletarian neighborhoods and past the communist headquarters, the SA officer in charge shouts in a booming voice, "Comrades! We are not hiding!" The troopers then march through the city. They are led by the Nazi flag, a brass band, and Hans. Reacting quickly, the communists assemble to attack the marching Nazis. Although they succeed in brawling with several men, which leads to their arrest by the police, the rest of Berlin's SA successfully march to the communist headquarters. Right in front of the building, and within earshot of Kuprikoff, Westmar is promoted and gets command of a troop of his own in the communist neighborhood of Friedrichshain, sparking a turf war.[10]

The communists, now alarmed, decide to eliminate Westmar because the young Nazi hero immediately dedicates all his energies to his own storm. He denounces his middle-class life to his mother and proclaims that he will become a worker. He then runs off to the SA home of Storm 1, where Klara just finished sewing the two stars of a troop leader on Hans's Brown Shirt.[11] As troop leader, Westmar dedicates himself tirelessly to his work and enlarges his troop from twelve to one hundred SA men. This in turn enrages the communists, who see a formidable challenge to their dominance in the streets. Kupferstern and Kuprikoff, however, decide on a new tactic and order the young communist Agnes to keep tabs on Hans. Nevertheless, Westmar's growing troop is formally elevated to the status of storm.

Westmar's new storm, together with all the other Berlin SA storms, escapes the hostility of the city's proletarian neighborhoods during a trip to the countryside. The Berlin SA travel on open trucks in their full uniforms. They carry with them the regular swastika flags of each SA storm, as well as the Romanesque SA standard designated to the SA of the entire city. After the trip, the men sleep in the straw of a barn—still wearing their uniforms. When the call of a bugle wakes them, they rise, attach their shoulder straps, and put their hats on—remarkably unwrinkled. The troopers then assemble for roll call and listen to the words of their leader, who informs them that they will exercise in the open air to strengthen themselves. Berlin's SA is then shown leaving the courtyard in front of the barn in perfect military order. Following the flags of the Berlin SA, the brass band and the troopers march in practiced perfection around the corner and out of sight. On the trip home, the uniformed Hans Westmar holds the standard of Berlin's SA and is framed by two storm flags. The trucks are preceded by a motorcycle with two uniformed troopers, reflecting reality in this method of excursion travel.[12]

Back in Berlin, the communists increasingly realize they are unable to counter the dynamic Nazis. The presence of the Brown Shirts is impacting the elections, and ever-growing numbers of voters cast their lot for the NSDAP. In this situation, Agnes represents the communists' last chance of turning the tide. She is supposed to spy on Hans and, if possible, lure him into a trap. Yet the girl cannot escape young Hans's charms and warns him of the impeding danger to his life. With nowhere to go after she betrays the communists by telling Hans of the plot, Agnes contemplates suicide. Of course, the SA man rewards Agnes's loyalty by taking her in. From then on, the two form a close bond.[13]

With only three days to go before the elections, Hans has successfully integrated himself into his proletarian neighborhood. He works as a construction worker, has a proletarian girlfriend, and has a proletarian SA storm. As storm leader with three stars on his collar, he leads his storm through Friedrichshain. When marching through this working-class neighborhood, Hans mimics the tactics of the communists. The band accompanying his storm plays shawms, a traditional communist instrument, rather than brass instruments and drums of traditional marching bands that accompany other organizations. Thus, when the storm comes marching through the city, people expect a troop of RFB rather than SA. Additionally, Hans uses uniformed SA to chant Nazi rhymes into the backstreets of Friedrichshain. The SA storm in Friedrichshain successfully, then, co-opts both techniques, the shawms band and the chanting of slogans, to rally their supporters. Yet Hans did not steal only these techniques. A scene with Agnes and Klara sewing Brown Shirts for Berlin's SA shows he also stole Agnes from the communists.[14]

At this point in the film, all of these changes become too much for Kuprikoff and Kupferstern. The communists decide to shoot Hans Westmar—and succeed—with the help of Hans's landlady. Then, the men of his storm carry their gravely injured storm leader down the stairs of his apartment building, all displaying their uniforms in full view. Subsequent orders to communists to finish the job and murder Westmar while in the hospital put off the German communist Camillo Ross. To protect their leader, the uniformed men of Hans's storm stand guard at the hospital entrance. Ultimately, all the men of his storm pass by his hospital room, giving the Nazi salute at the door. Hence, one by one, his men march by one final time in their uniforms.

During this act, the men do not wear their boots, in order to be quiet and keep the disturbance of the other patients to a minimum.[15]

After Hans succumbs to his injuries, the film jumps to the SA leader's overly militaristic wake. Unsurprisingly, his coffin is draped in the Nazi flag. In place of a steel helmet, an SA hat rests on top of the coffin. Upper-class fraternity brothers and proletarian SA flank the coffin, in their respective uniforms. Then, the funeral procession is attacked by communist riffraff. After the police step in to calm tensions, the funeral once again exudes military ritual, including flags, uniforms, and mourners raising their arms in the Nazi salute. The final scenes show SA marching through the Brandenburg Gate on the eve of Hitler's ascension to power. Hans Westmar is shown as a ghostly figure marching in full uniform in the sky. The chinstrap of his SA cap is down, and the storm flag he is holding is waving in the wind. He is marching along to the tune of the "Horst Wessel Song." At this final march of the film's climax, the communist hecklers—miraculously—become quiet and deliberately turn their proletarian fists into the open hands of the Nazi salute. Camillo Ross does the same, and so ends the highly embellished depiction of Horst Wessel's life.[16]

Hitler Youth Quex, the second film in the trilogy, is also based on a real figure. Directed by Hans Steinhoff, the film's cast of characters is made up of easily identifiable protagonists and antagonists. The protagonists, unsurprisingly, are Nazis and Nazi sympathizers. The antagonists are once again communists, in keeping with *Hans Westmar.* However, in *Hitler Youth Quex,* our main character is a teenager named Heini Völker who lives with his mother and his unemployed, communist father, who is also a World War I veteran. The family lives in abject poverty in a proletarian neighborhood of Berlin. This quarter of the city is dominated by the leader of the Communist Youth International, Stoppel, who also leads a band of adult communist thugs. Although the teenage Heini does not have a girlfriend, the communist youth Gerda and the Nazi Ulla both vie for the attention of the handsome boy. Ulla Dörries is a member of the League of German Girls (Bund Deutscher Mädel [BDM]). Ulla's brother, Fritz, is the leader of the local Hitler Youth group. The group also includes another Hitler Youth boy, Grundler. All the city's Hitler Youth are led by *Bannführer* Kass, who, like Heini's father, is a veteran of the Great War. The antagonistic communists in this film, unlike the first movie, do not have Jewish partners at their sides. That, however, seems to be the only difference regarding the rather unsophisticated and certainly unflattering depiction of communists. The story line and the centrality of the uniforms, however, are strikingly similar between *Quex* and *Hans Westmar*.[17]

Unlike Hans Westmar, young teenager Heini Völker, is born into a proletarian family. Völker's mother and father suffer from their impoverishment. Since Heini's abusive father is an alcoholic (and a communist), Heini does not spend a lot of time at home. Due to these dynamics, Heini catches the eye of Stoppel, who tries to recruit him for his Communist Youth International. Stoppel invites Heini to a weekend camping trip with his group of junior communists. Heini, who is attending a trade school and going through an apprenticeship in a print shop, is happy to join. He is looking forward to leaving the cramped and dirty quarters of the city. He is also excited about the prospect of swimming.

On their day of departure, at the train station where Heini is supposed to meet up with the communist youth group, however, a different troop of boys and girls catches Heini's attention. The boys of Berlin's Hitler Youth and the girls of Berlin's League of German Girls march in two columns onto the platform of the station. On the one hand, the Nazi youths in their full uniforms with backpacks, camping gear, and troop pendants impress Heini.[18] The unruly, loud, and disrespectful behavior of the communist youths, in contrast, makes a stronger negative impression on the boy. The communist youths carry a red flag on the platform yet wear no uniforms. Neither does Gerda, the communist youth who is smitten with Heini Völker. That night in the campground, some of these kids steal the sandwich given to Heini by Stoppel. The boys and girls drink beer and hard liquor, smoke cigarettes, and dance together. Stoppel and some older boys also play cards. This proves too much for the clean-cut boy who neither smokes, drinks, nor seems to have much interest in girls. Heini is heartily disappointed in the Communist Youth International. He did not get to swim, and he is left hungry after becoming prey to the older boys. Despondent, he sneaks away from the camp, determined to sleep by himself in the woods.

Once distanced from the noise of dancing and frolicking youth, Heini hears a different tune and follows it. The sound of the Hitler Youth hymn guides the teenager to the Nazi camp at the shore of a lake. From cover on the periphery, Heini witnesses the uniformed boys and girls standing at attention in their gender-divided groups as they listen to a speech by their adult leader, Kass. The youths act disciplined, and the camp gives the impression of militaristic order. The tents for boys and girls stand separated. The camp also has a large flagpole with the Hitler Youth flag. The militaristic impression of the Nazi youth is heightened when Heini Völker gets caught staring in awe at the camp by a Hitler Youth picket on guard. The boys recognize Heini from the train platform as a young communist and chase him off. Some of the Hitler Youth boys, however, voice regret during a stew dinner around the campfire. They show empathy and state that Heini should have been allowed to stay. Heini, who left one camp and was chased away from another, lays down to sleep, alone and without shelter, in the woods.[19]

Heini, however, does not despair. Awoken the next day by the sounds of a bugle, he is mesmerized by the scene in front of him as he watches those in the Hitler Youth camp from a safe distance. He watches them go for a swim in their black Hitler Youth swimwear. Later, they stand at attention in full uniforms to raise the Hitler Youth flag above their camp.[20] They then line up for a hike in ordered and gender-separated columns and march off into the countryside. Heini's feet are shown marching in place as he watches the uniformed fascist youth march off to the sounds of their brass band. Following the all-male band, the boys wear the Brown Shirt and black neckerchief, long riding pants and boots, or short khaki pants with sturdy shoes. The girls, marching behind the boys, wear the white shirt and the black skirt of the fascist female organization with their matching black neckerchiefs.[21]

Without dinner, a good night sleep, or breakfast, Heini evades Stoppel, who sets out to look for him, and hitches a ride back to the city in the back of a truck. Back at home, he tells his mother about the boys with the swastika. In an enthusiastic tone he relates to her how they cooked, swam, and exercised together. The song they sang, the Hitler Youth hymn, especially impressed Heini. When his father hears this kind of talk, his abusive nature takes over. He forces his son to sing "The Internationale," the hymn of the communists. Intimidated, Heini complies. Still, unbeknownst to Heini, his next encounter with the Nazi youths is not far off.

The following day at trade school, two of the Hitler Youth boys, troop leader Fritz Dörries and a member of his group, a boy with the last name Grundler, are handing out Nazi flyers. Unlike many of his classmates, Heini takes a flyer and talks to the young Nazis. Stoppel and Gerda watch the scene unfold. Stoppel, aware of Gerda's charms, sets her on Grundler, who promptly falls for the ruse and hands the flyers over to Gerda. Of course, the communist girl destroys them after distracting the gullible Hitler Youth boy with her attention. Heini, meanwhile, finally gets to talk to the leader of the local Hitler Youth group. Fritz Dörris, son of a doctor, invites Heini to his home for dinner. Ulla, Fritz's sister, wears her BDM uniform even in the privacy of her home while serving pancakes.[22] When Fritz introduces Ulla and Heini, he explains to his sister that Heini would like to become a Hitler Youth himself. The viewer then watches Heini enjoy a meal and the hospitality of these young fascists rather than going hungry, as happened in the communist camp. The juxtaposition of the Hitler Youths treating Heini as a proper guest versus the communist youths stealing his food may not be subtle, but the message is clear: the Hitler Youth is the superior group.

Although Heini expressed his wish to join the Nazi youths, or perhaps because of it, his father and Stoppel try to convince him to join the communist youth group instead. The young boy would like to attend the grand-opening evening celebration of a Hitler Youth home in a cellar in his neighborhood that Fritz and Ulla invited him to. Instead, his father wants Heini to attend a communist meeting to be inaugurated into their youth organization, pushing the two further apart. The opening of the Hitler Youth abode angers Stoppel, who quickly organizes an attack on the boys in their cellar. Heini is torn. Ultimately, he makes up his mind and decides to attend the Nazi meeting and buck his father's authority.

The uniformed Hitler Youth in their rented cellar are aware of the dangers within the proletarian neighborhood. Fritz, the leader, sends out Grundler to stand guard. Grundler, who had initially neglected this duty, puts on his cap and lowers his chinstrap to secure it. He positions himself at the door to the cellar, looking particularly grim and alert. When Stoppel's thugs attack the cellar, all Hitler Youths are shown putting on their caps and pulling down their chinstraps.[23] The arriving police arrest the young Nazis as well as Heini, who arrived at the scene late. At the police station, Fritz sees Heini and expresses his disappointment. To him it looks as if Heini was part of the attack by the communists. Heini is unable to explain himself.

A chance to redeem himself, however, arises quickly enough. Stoppel finds Heini at work at the print shop and lets Heini in on a sinister plan. The communists want to use rifles and dynamite stashed in a secret location in the neighborhood to eliminate the Hitler Youth and their cellar for good. Heini, however, who cannot tell a lie, proceeds to tell Stoppel that he will warn the fascists. As soon as Stoppel leaves the shop, Heini uses the telephone to warn Fritz and his sister Ulla at home. Both are wearing their respective uniforms when Ulla answers the phone. In addition to her skirt, shirt, and neckerchief, she also wears the brown *Kletterweste* (the same one that was tested for the SA men but ultimately relegated to women's wear) and a black beret, completing her BDM uniform. She tells Fritz what Heini said, yet Fritz voices his suspicion while putting his shoulder strap over his Brown Shirt, complete with the Hitler Youth armband and the leader's lanyard.[24] From this point in the film until the end, Ulla and Fritz are shown only in their full uniforms.

A massive explosion ripping through the neighborhood opens the next scene. The explosion is signaling to Heini and Stoppel alike that the Nazis destroyed the secret weapons cache of the communists. From now on, Heini's life is in danger. Stoppel even intimidates Heini's mother in her own apartment. The boy's mother cannot live with the added fear of her son's assassination in addition to the poverty and the domestic violence she regularly suffers. After Heini comes home and admits that he saved the Nazis, his mother recognizes the mortal danger her son is in. She puts Heini to bed in the kitchen, a room that also serves as Heini's bedroom, and turns on the gas stove to sacrifice them both.

Remarkably, in the following scene, Heini awakes in a hospital bed and learns that his mother did not survive. He is now left alone with an abusive father in a hostile neighborhood. Heini, however, does not have to go back home. He finds support among the Hitler Youth, especially Ulla and Fritz, who take care of Heini. The most important scene of the film shows the siblings visiting Heini in the hospital with two other uniformed Hitler Youth boys. Ulla and Fritz thank Heini for the warning and hand him a package with a complete Hitler Youth uniform. Heini had earned it by putting himself in harm's way. The Nazi youths formally apologize to Heini and extend the official invitation to join the Hitler Youth with this gift. After the adult Hitler Youth leader, Kass, talks to Heini's father, Heini is shown walking with a suitcase in his new uniform next to Kass, effectively leaving his old, moribund life and entering his new one. The two Brown Shirted Nazis then go to a Hitler Youth home featuring an enormous flag.[25] Heini will share a room with Grundler, who, as viewers now learn, is an orphan.

As a member of the Hitler Youth group, Heini makes a name for himself rather quickly. When Heini is on kitchen duty and Grundler takes his time finishing a meal, Heini takes the cup that Grundler was about to take a drink from. Because of his speed, reminiscent of quicksilver, Heini receives the nickname Quex from Grundler. Quex enjoys the life in the Hitler Youth home and is not allowed to go back into his old neighborhood. Even so, his safety cannot be guaranteed. Grundler, again, meets Gerda, the communist. After Gerda's flirtatious demeanor in the earlier episode with the flyers, Grundler slips and tells her where Heini now lives. Gerda immediately relates the news to Stoppel. Heini, however, does not fear the communists and asks his leader, Kass, for permission to work for the Nazis in the dangerous quarter of the city that he knows so intimately. Kass warns the boy that his uniform is not a "parade piece," adding that someone wearing the Brown Shirt needs to obey his leaders. Heini, always obedient, listens to Kass. Nevertheless, he later accidentally runs into Stoppel. The older man tries to scare Heini, who is still not intimidated, and warns him one final time that he is not allowed to return to his neighborhood wearing the Brown Shirt.[26]

Preceding the next elections, uniformed Hitler Youth boys distribute Nazi propaganda materials in Stoppel's territory. Then, an injured Fritz runs into the Hitler Youth home and announces to the *Bannführer* that all of his boys have been badly beaten and that he needs immediate backup. Quex volunteers and convinces his leader, by reminding Kass of his own honor and bravery in the Great War, that he should be allowed to help Fritz. Kass agrees and sends Grundler with Heini into the communist quarter. Grundler, however, sends Heini on an errand and lets Gerda destroy a load of Nazi flyers. The returning Quex then beats Grundler and gets Ulla to help him print new flyers in the print shop. Ulla is impressed with Quex and kisses the teenager.[27]

Meanwhile, the communists have already spotted Heini Völker and are rallying their thugs to hunt down the Nazi youth. Although Stoppel, at the last minute, has a change of heart and tries to send the assassins in the wrong direction, they catch up to and stab Quex. The dying youth is then found by the rest of his troop. The unfortunate Heini dies in Fritz's arms muttering the Hitler Youth hymn with his last dying breath. The scene cuts away, and the film ends with marching columns of Hitler Youth—another similarity between Hans Westmar and Quex.

The third and final film in the series, *SA-Mann Brand,* is an entirely fictional account, yet the mythical importance of the uniform links this film with the first two. Another similarity is that all three feature casts of characters who appear flat at first and develop nuances only when they are turned toward fascism. *SA-Mann Brand,* directed by Franz Seitz, shares a similar plot with the previously summarized films. The list of protagonists is topped by the twenty-six-year-old proletarian Fritz Brand. He is a convinced Nazi and an active SA man. The young man still lives with his unemployed father, a social democrat, and his mother. They live in an apartment building owned by an older Catholic couple, Anton and Genoveva Huber. Another apartment in the Huber house is occupied by the war widow Margaret Lohner and her sixteen-year-old son, Erich. The Lohners are Nazis. Erich is taking part in Hitler Youth activities, although his poor mother cannot afford to buy him a Hitler Youth uniform. The list of protagonists ends with Anni Baumann, the daughter of a communist, who is a love interest of Fritz Brand. The antagonists are once again communists, this time led by the Soviet leader Alexander Turow and the German-born youth section leader Spitzer.[28]

The movie starts where the plot of the other two films thickens. Fritz Brand is an SA man. The communists want to eliminate Brand. Anni, the daughter of the communist Baumann, however, warns Fritz of the impeding danger when he returns from an SA evening in his uniform. After Fritz safely returns to his parents' apartment, his parents are shown sitting at the dinner table. Fritz joins them, but his Brown Shirt angers his father. The angry old social democrat tugs on Fritz's Brown Shirt sleeve and tells him to "take off the carnival costume" when he sits down at his table.[29]

Next door at the Lohner apartment, such quarrels do not sour family evenings. Mother and son are both devoted Nazis. Yet they are poor since their only income is from the mother's piecework sewing. Erich and his mother in this scene are sitting at the table by the light of a lamp when she tells Erich to go to bed, since he must get up early to take part in a Hitler Youth hike. Erich sighs deeply and proclaims that Hitler Youth activities would be more fun if he also owned a uniform like the other boys. Unlike Fritz Brand's father, widow Lohner would love to see her son in a brown uniform. Yet no matter how hard she works, she simply cannot afford it. Erich consoles his mother by relating that his youth leader told him that it is not the Brown Shirt that makes a man, but the spirit.[30]

The Baumann family is red. Nonetheless, Anni Baumann, the young daughter, is secretly in love with Fritz. Her father and her brothers are abusive and follow the lead of both Alexander Turow and Spitzer when they suggest using Anni to get to Fritz Brand—much like Gerda's role in *Hitler Youth Quex*. In this case, Anni declines to do anything of the sort. When the Soviet leader threatens to have Brand murdered, Anni finally agrees to collect information for the communists from Brand. Turow also makes sure that Fritz loses his job. The young SA man, however, does not despair. He visits Erich and his mother as they celebrate Erich's sixteenth birthday. She surprises him with a Brown Shirt. A studio portrait of his dead father in an imperial soldier's uniform with spiked helmet as well as a shadow box containing his father's Iron Cross and another medal appear in the background, framing his birthday presents. Mother Lohner saved her money not only for a Brown Shirt with Hitler Youth armband but also for khaki shorts, a Hitler Youth hat, a belt with shoulder strap, and a black neckerchief with the braided leather loop to surprise her doting son.[31] When Fritz Brand enters the apartment of his friends and neighbors, he also gives Erich a studio portrait of Adolf Hitler.

In the next scene, however, Fritz learns that the government made the SA, the SS, and the Hitler Youth illegal. Fritz is shocked and visits the Lohners to tell Erich and his mother that the new Brown Shirt he is wearing is illegal—a devastating blow to the young fascist. Both adults know that Erich will be disappointed. Fritz must explain to the sad teenager that the government outlawed the Nazis. Erich is more or less speechless. He can only reply that he was excited about his new uniform and that he is upset. The timing could not have been worse for Erich. The SA men in their tavern, meanwhile, raucously proclaim that the government can take their uniforms, but the government cannot take away their spirit.[32]

The men of the SA put this spirit on display immediately. Fritz Brand, in the next scene, gets shot during an altercation with the communists in a tense moment of the film. Although the ensuing hospital stay is lengthy, the men of Fritz's storm eventually visit him—in their uniforms, no less—bearing good news. They show him a newspaper that contains an article about an SA march of four hundred thousand men. The SA is no longer illegal. Fritz is thrilled and asks the other SA men to bring him his uniform as quickly as possible. Buoyed by the good news, Fritz Brand miraculously heals and then discharges himself from the hospital. Ultimately, Fritz and his young neighbor

Erich Lohner lead the SA march through a proletarian neighborhood, both in their full respective uniforms. The Nazis march behind a brass band and, illustrating the true changing sentiment in the city, are protected by a police cordon. The SA makes up a long procession, as the standard and no less than seven storm flags suggest. The SA finishes their march without incident. Tragedy awaits, however. While still riding the adrenaline rush of the day, Erich Lohner is shot and mortally wounded by a communist through a cellar window as he walks home alone.[33]

The rest of the plot unfolds from here rather quickly. Although Erich was not as lucky as Fritz, his death was not in vain, because this personal tragedy occurs in tandem with Hitler's ascension as German chancellor. Erich, then, leaves a legacy of martyrdom for his just—from the perspective of the filmmakers—cause. The SA, exercising their newfound power and armed with rifles, then arrest Turow. Other communists are loaded on a truck and driven away under SA and police guard. The uniformed men of the SA also force Fritz Brand's employer to hire him back. The SA is then shown marching in a large victory parade at night with brass bands playing the "Horst Wessel Song." The men carry torches, and all pedestrians stop and raise their hands to the Nazi salute as the SA march by, in parallel with the end of *Hans Westmar.*[34]

In all, these cinematic displays, with their unpretentious plots, served an important mythmaking purpose in the Nazi era. Yet film was not the only way in which these Weimar-era stories of struggle and eventual Nazi triumph were told. Horst Wessel, or rather a fictional representation of him, also appears in a novel first published in 1933 that depicts the story of Hitler's Stormtroopers during the Weimar era. The Nazi chronicler Wilfried Bade, who officially dedicated his book to the SA, wove a story that connects facts, myths, and fiction about the Nazi Stormtroopers in Berlin. His cast of characters includes fictional characters, as well as characters based on both Horst Wessel and Joseph Goebbels. In his *Die SA Erobert Berlin* (The SA conquers Berlin), the life of a fictional worker, Schulz, is retold from 1926 to 1933. As in the films, Schulz finds his way into the ranks of the Berlin SA, rises in the ranks, and witnesses the final victory of the Nazis in Berlin by the story's end. Schulz is a proletarian. Yet the reader never learns his first name or what specific profession Schulz has. Bade, in this sense, did not develop nuanced characters. The omnipotent narrator stays mostly with Schulz, but at instances also switches perspective and narrates the story of another character, such as, for instance, Horst Wessel.[35]

In this book, just like in the three films, the Brown Shirt is an extremely important representational item to the fascists. Schulz, an unemployed veteran, first meets the Nazi Karl Schindler on a walk through the city. The words of the fascist impress the proletarian, and Schulz then seeks out the Nazis. He finds the SA man Schindler and three other men in their small and sparsely furnished two-room Nazi Party office. Schindler is frustrated with the slow progress of the Nazi cause in the city and has just donned his Brown Shirt when he runs into Schulz. Schindler takes this second meeting as an opportunity to recruit Schulz, feeling assured that the proletarian will join. He points to his old and well-worn Brown Shirt and predicts that Schulz will be wearing his own Brown Shirt in a matter of weeks.[36] Ultimately, Karl's instinct is correct.

The story returns to Schultz a few months later when Joseph Goebbels arrives in Berlin as *Gauleiter,* appointed by Hitler. During a Nazi meeting in which Goebbels speaks, the Nazi leader of Berlin calls his SA troopers "political soldiers" and, just like Schindler, makes predictions about the growth of the Nazi movement in the city, proclaiming that the six hundred Nazis in Berlin will soon grow to six hundred thousand. The World War I veteran Schulz is enthralled by the fascists and disgusted by the communists, a common theme in these Nazi-era productions, some of whom are in the RFB and wear Russian blouses with red Soviet stars. His bad impression of the left-wing radicals is only hardened when he takes part in another Nazi meeting. Again, Goebbels is the main speaker, and again he is protected by tall and uniformed SA. The troopers impress Schulz when the communists try to stop the meeting with a violent attack against the speaker. During the ensuing brawl, the Brown Shirts remind Schulz of a well-organized military machine. He signs up with Karl Schindler and becomes an SA man amid the shattered glass and broken furniture in the immediate aftermath of the fight.[37]

As a political soldier himself, Schulz partakes enthusiastically in politicized violence. The actions of the SA are depicted by Bade as soldierly deeds (despite the peacetime domestic setting in which the SA acted at the time). Like soldiers behind enemy lines, the SA shed their uniforms to work clandestinely as listening sentries, patrolling alone or in pairs. Like soldiers, wearing their Brown Shirts and their swastika armbands, the SA protect their leader, Joseph Goebbels, during brawls with communists in meetings and rallies. The author attributes the rising numbers of Nazi Party memberships (from six hundred to three thousand) to the actions of these political soldiers. Ultimately, Karl Schindler and Schulz find a cellar to rent and open Berlin's first SA home that they furnish with homemade furniture and donated equipment. Schulz moves into the cellar to be able to take in orders from the leadership in Munich in a timely manner and to guard their secret stash of rubber truncheons. Schulz feels like a soldier once again. He has a uniform, headquarters, and armory. In the proletarian neighborhood they are in, he feels like the commander of a bunker. Ever vigilant, he sometimes warns his troops to stay inside at night.[38] For the young men under the charge of Schulz, the uniform, while worn with pride, is also a source of danger.

With the growing membership of the SA by the spring of 1927, strength in numbers allowed the SA to wear their uniforms openly in the streets. Still, in the story, Schulz tells his men to cover up their uniforms on their way to and from their stronghold due to continuing hostilities among some of the urban population. Only when the Stormtroopers march into the surrounding countryside do they encounter sympathies from the general population. When they march by their leaders, Goebbels and Daluege, in a small town in March 1927, the peasants raided their greenhouses to shower the Brown Shirted columns of the SA with flowers.[39]

Because in the city the SA is not showered with flowers, but sometimes with rocks and flowerpots, the omnipotent narrator relates how the SA march in the streets without disturbances by the communists. The SA apply a technique they themselves call "cotton wool," or padding. While the main body of uniformed SA march in ordered columns in the streets, SA in civilian clothes flank the main body of uniformed troopers on both sidewalks. These men are called "cotton wool" because they assault individuals on the sidewalks who are preparing to attack the more conspicuous marchers in the street. Hence, their padding protects the marchers like cotton wool by absorbing and cushioning them from attacks.[40]

When the Brown Shirts are made illegal in Berlin, the fascists lose their most important publicity tool. Even during the time of the uniform ban, however, the men of the SA continue to wear their Brown Shirts, not the complete uniforms, just the shirt without matching trousers, cap, or armband, in defiance of the law. This in turn causes the police to confiscate the Brown Shirts and arrest Schulz and his men. Schulz takes the Iron Cross off his Brown Shirt, reaches into his military-issue riding pants, and pulls out a bandage with which he secures his war decoration on his bare chest as a spectacle.[41] Schulz and his men not only lose their uniforms in Bade's narrative but also lose their cellar stronghold during the ban on the SA.

As the story unfolds, the now homeless group of SA men around Schulz find "father Mehl," a widowed older man who lost one son in the war and whose other son emigrated to Canada. Miraculously, the seven SA men and their new father figure strike an immediate friendship in a distillery, and it becomes clear rather quickly that father Mehl will also become an SA man—just as soon as the SA prohibition is lifted. Before that time comes, the men of the Berlin SA plan on attending the Nazi Party rally in Nuremberg, where the Brown Shirts are perfectly legal. To do so, they complete their outfits. When Schulz cannot scrape together the money for the train, Mehl sacrifices his savings for his SA boys. In preparation for the trip, Schulz and his men attach new storm numbers to the black collar tabs of their Brown Shirts. They must cover them up, however, on the way to the train station. They wear civilian coats to hide their illicit uniforms. Of course, after safely arriving, the party rally is a success. On the way home to Berlin, however, the SA of the city is arrested, and their Brown Shirts, trousers, and SA caps are confiscated.[42]

Nonetheless, after his diligent work for the movement, Schulz is promoted to *Sturmführer* and receives the newly formed Storm 24 in Berlin. At this point, the narrator shifts to fictionalizing historical events. According to the novel, Joseph Goebbels married his fiancée wearing his Brown Shirt.[43] Historical photographs, however, show that this was an embellishment. The Brown Shirt was illegal at the time of the wedding. In photographs Goebbels is wearing a collared shirt, and perhaps it is an authentic Brown Shirt, but as he also wore a black suit coat and a black tie, the garment in question is effectively covered up. The SA troopers forming an honor guard on both sides of the wedding procession, however, wore white prohibition shirts rather than their Brown Shirts.[44] The actual 1930 prohibition of the SA and the encompassing renewal of the Brown Shirt prohibition, however, is in Schulz's view only one last-ditch effort of the dysfunctional Weimar state to fight the rising tide of Nazism. As soon as the ban is lifted, Berlin's SA rushes home to put on their uniforms and revel in their public display.[45]

The final months before and after the Nazi seizure of power are depicted by Bade as a desperate defensive battle against the communists. Schulz even finds written orders outlining preparations for a civil war that supposedly belong to the communists. Ultimately, the novel provides fictionalized "proof" that the fire that destroyed the German Reichstag and allowed Hitler to suspend democracy in Germany was the signal for a communist uprising against the Nazi-led state—incendiary words to describe the most memorable act of arson in the Nazi seizure of power. Having persuaded readers that the communists remain a danger, the book closes with the communists' incarceration behind barbed wire in concentration camps. Schulz has done his duty and is overjoyed at the prospect of continuing his "good" work in the Third Reich.[46] The end of this novel, as well as all three films, presents a rather formulaic conclusion where communists either reform and become Nazified or are taken into custody as criminal elements.

Similar to this book and the films discussed above, *Männer im Braunhemd: Vom Kampf und Sieg der SA,* by *Sturmhaubtführer* Karl W. H. Koch, is dedicated to the "unknown SA man" and was published in 1936, a few years later in the Nazi period. The book includes a register of all *Gruppenführer* with portraits and a personal note from each of these SA leaders. The book is an uncritical yet comprehensive history of the SA written by an SA leader for the general public in Nazi Germany. The book is thus a reflective look back by the old fighters for the movement who were confessed fascists years before the Nazis came to power from a victorious position. This coffee-table version of an SA history includes numerous illustrations. The stories and the visual depictions of the SA include recollections of Stormtrooper activities during the Weimar era and demonstrate the mythical importance the Nazis themselves lent their Brown Shirts.[47]

For example, chapter 5 is titled "Von der Windjacke zum Braunhemd" (From the trench coat to the Brown Shirt) and describes the switch in purpose from clandestine army to propaganda troop in 1924. According to this Nazi publication, this was connected to the new purpose of the SA. The first SA unit to be used in election propaganda worked during Bavarian state elections in 1924, although they did not have uniforms or even matching outfits. The Nazis connected myths and reality when it came to the introduction of the Brown Shirt. For instance, the author claims that the men of Rossbach's bicycle detachment first wore Brown Shirts on the occasion of a celebration on April 5, 1925, at the Bismarck tower in Starnberg. Yet, as discussed in chapter 2, Rossbach himself explained these men wore Lettow Shirts, not Brown Shirts. The introduction of the Brown Shirt to all men of the SA is dated later that month, on April 30, 1925. Koch connected this occasion to the election of Hindenburg as the president of the Weimar Republic, although Koch calls him president of the German Empire. Both dates are connected to larger events in the history of the movement and appear to have given these events greater importance. Koch does not fail to mention that the men of the Reichsbanner only wear trench coats, whereas the SA has a proper uniform shirt.[48]

The importance and cost of the uniform are depicted in the following chapter, titled "Der Gang zur SA" (The path to the SA). This chapter contains a collection of fictional stories that seem to combine the stories of several different men into one thread. Hence, the plots and the characters are underdeveloped. For instance, the reader never learns the names of the characters finding their way to the Stormtroopers. The reader learns only their profession. In a way, this allows many of the intended readership, specifically former SA men and SA men in Hitler's Germany, to identify with the characters. One of these composite characters described in this chapter is a failed German colonizer who lost his coffee plantation in Africa due to no fault of his own. This "African," as the narrator refers to the main protagonist, is earning some money by giving lectures on his experiences on the Dark Continent. When he joins the SA on a Saturday evening, he does not lose much time thinking about how to procure a complete Stormtrooper uniform. "On Sunday morning the African is out and about getting store owners out of bed, or just out of their homes. He succeeds in procuring clothing, boots and equipment, and reports to SA duty in the early afternoon."[49] The reader does not learn if the "African" is paying for the uniform or if the store owners, who had to open up their shops for him on a day when most stores are closed, sold to him on credit. The uniform is so important, however, that the act of getting a complete uniform, with boots and equipment right away, cannot wait until the stores open on Monday.

In chapter 15, dealing with the last period of illegality for the SA, the author, Koch, dates the introduction of the shoulder strap to September 1929. Although no historical turning point is attached to that date as in the others, there is evidence suggesting that the shoulder strap was worn by some SA men well before that date. Koch does claim, however, that the milestones of the party rallies in Weimar in 1926, Nuremberg in 1927 and 1929, and Braunschweig in 1931 show the dynamic growth of the movement since the introduction of the Brown Shirt. Koch ends this chapter with the same assertions made by Bade about the end of the Nazi prohibition on June 16, 1932. Just as Bade claims that Berlin was swarming with Brown Shirts hours after the uniform was decriminalized, Koch contends that only one hour after the proclamation, Brown Shirted SA men appeared all over the country. Not only that, according to Koch: the Brown Shirt was also generally greeted with joyful jubilations in the streets. Koch claims that even non-Nazis instinctively recognized the SA as the vanguard of a new era in Germany.[50]

According to this book, the mythical impact of the Brown Shirt does not only affect adults. One of the almost comical descriptions of the Brown Shirt's impact revolves around the description of an SA storm taking a trip to the countryside in the chapter "Ein Sturm fährt aufs Land." As in the other stories, the trip from the city to the countryside is a positive experience for the troopers. The rural populations are always depicted as friendly to the Nazi cause. Peasants support the SA in large numbers, in stark contrast to the daily hostilities in the cities. In this chapter, an SA storm travels to a village and integrates itself into the village community. The day after their arrival, the men in their Brown Shirts help with chores and thank their hosts in this way for room and board. One of the SA men, who helps a farmer's wife watch her children, cradles a crying infant in his arms. The child calms and stops crying when this SA man takes the infant, according to Koch, because of the "unfamiliar impression of the Brown Shirt."[51] Although the toddler never saw a Brown Shirt before, this story suggests that the child instinctively knew the shirt represented safety.

CONCLUSION

The Nazis spun myths around themselves immediately after consolidating power in Germany. They believed that the Nazis in the Weimar era stood for bravery, strength, and hypermasculinity as well as for order and unity. Clearly, from their standpoint, this affinity was not common to all Germans. Because of that, early in the Nazi period, the Nazis depicted the Weimar era as a time of struggle. They portrayed themselves as surrounded by foes and at times persecuted and even martyred for their beliefs. The brown uniforms made the men of the

SA and the boys of the Hitler Youth stand out. Nazi filmmakers and authors glorified this ominous situation in hindsight. The Brown Shirt was interwoven within these myths in two important ways. First, it was a source of pride connected to the myth of heroism and military values. Second, it facilitated the crossing of class lines as well as the rural-urban divide, allowing for the German people to unite.

During the Nazi era, fascist authors and directors likened the actions of the Hitler Youth and SA taking part in election campaigns to warfare. Marches and handing out leaflets were part of election battles in which the Nazi combatants performed with bravery and discipline. Ultimately, the uniform aided in this process through its signal function. Only brave men and boys wore their uniform, despite the danger of being easily recognized. This danger of being targeted by political opponents, however, was also a source of pride. It was a symbol of hypermasculinity. Heini Völker, for example, does not let himself be intimidated, despite his youth. Knowing all too well how dangerous it is, he still begs his leader to be allowed to put himself in harm's way. The SA men Brand and Westmar also seek out danger in their respective depictions. They not only proudly wear their provocative uniforms in proletarian neighborhoods but also recruit ever-larger numbers of followers. When they lead these troops through communist quarters, they are easily recognized and targeted by their opponents. The imminent danger to their lives through the signal function of their Brown Shirts is a mark of pride. They live dangerously by provoking the communists on their home turf and are proud of their bravery.

Another factor contributing to a sense of pride when wearing the Brown Shirt is the depiction of the SA in rural areas and in urban areas immediately after Hitler comes to power. The Nazis changed, cleaned up, and glorified real individuals to create the myth of clean-cut National Socialists in a struggle against the republic represented as chaotic. Ultimately, marches in villages and the countryside are occasions when the Brown Shirt inspires observers to cheer the Nazis. This can be attributed to the association of the brown uniform with military values such as discipline, order, and cleanliness. This association was deliberate and functioned well in conservative circles and rural areas. Heini's leader, Kass, for instance, reminds the Hitler Youth that he needs to follow orders when wearing his Brown Shirt. The final victory parades in the city are important elements in all the fictional stories discussed above. There, the successful fighters for the movement are celebrated by the population at large rather than in rural areas alone. In these stories, all Germans ultimately adopt military values.

One last reason for the uniform being a source of pride is connected to class. Not everyone can have a Brown Shirt right away. One must save up, like Erich Lohner's mother, or one must earn it through dedication and sacrifice, like Heini. Still, as the films and books show, poor Germans found ways to obtain a uniform. More important, social elites who can easily afford fine clothes do not wear them but rather opt for the Brown Shirt. The second function of the uniform as seen in film and literature is therefore related to class. The fact that Ulla and Fritz give a complete uniform to the proletarian Heini, who earned his uniform with a heroic deed, is significant.

Nazis wear their uniforms instead of clothing that would identify them as members of specific social classes. The Nazis in these stories therefore cross class lines with ease and with pride or, viewed in another light, subsume class identity beneath their adopted political and social identity as Nazis. Hans Westmar, like Fritz and Ulla Dörries, comes from a middle-class background. The siblings are the children of a doctor. Westmar is a university student in a prestigious dueling fraternity. Bade's character Karl Schindler, who gets Schulz to join the SA, is also a university student. All belong to a well-off elite. They, nevertheless, are convinced of the National Socialist ideal of a classless society within the German people's community. All four seek out proletarians, associate with them, and ultimately guide them into the Nazi fold.

The myths about heroism and the crossing of class boundaries became solidified over time. The film *SA-Mann Brand* is not based on a real character. The director had even more freedom to further develop and strengthen myths with the help of the Brown Shirts. The two books demonstrate that trend further. Although Bade uses real individuals like Goebbels and Wessel as bases for some of his characters, his protagonist, Schulz, like the characters in Koch's book, is intentionally kept one-dimensional. One never learns Schulz's first name or his profession. In Koch's book, published three years after the Nazis came to power, the characters do not even have proper last names. This is intentional. It allows broad sections of Nazi society to identify with these fictional characters. Accordingly, the plots are simple, and the characters are flat. Rounded characters that develop in the plotline acquire affinities only for Nazism, a tactic that humanizes the Nazis and make them approachable, while keeping communists and suspect others at arm's length. Once they put on the Brown Shirt or develop sympathies for the fascists, they exude heroism, like the real Horst Wessel and Herbert Norkus.

To the Nazis themselves, their uniforms were of the utmost importance because they highlighted positive attributes of the Nazi movement. The hero-myth created by the Nazis about themselves, however, cannot be accepted without critical evaluation. A thorough study of the impact of the Brown Shirt during the Weimar years must also rest on research focusing on non-Nazi sources. The following chapter will provide a case study of a specific city. This case study is based on the history of the SA in Hamburg and includes Nazi, liberal, conservative, and communist accounts of the history of the SA. As will be seen, each of these accounts reinforces the thesis of this book about the use and the impact of the SA uniform.

Chapter Seven

HAMBURG, 1921–1933, A CASE STUDY

A case study for the city of Hamburg is ideal for an argument about the SA's successful dual-image construction process in the 1920s. On the surface, Hamburg with its republican traditions seemed unlikely to fall to Nazism.[1] Yet Hamburg's unique long-term social, political, and cultural developments over the centuries, in addition to the financial crisis during the Weimar years, caused fascist ideas to fall on fertile ground just like in other parts of Weimar Germany. The city was traditionally ruled by a financial oligarchy from the Middles Ages to 1871, when the city became part of the German Empire.[2] According to Andrew Wackerfuss, after the elites lost their nominal political hegemony during the Weimar era, the bourgeois press continued to shape the city's mainstream political orientation. Therefore, large parts of Hamburg's citizenry considered the radical Left dangerous. Hence, sharply drawn class lines were in part responsible for Nazi success.[3] Yet this line of argumentation also leaves inroads to further historical investigation. Why, for instance, did Hamburg's elites vote for the Nazis in large numbers rather than other conservative parties? Why was the SA able to carry Hitler to power in Hamburg?

For instance, the *Hamburger Nachrichten,* a conservative bourgeois newspaper for the business and shipping elites of the city, originally affiliated itself with the conservative and Volkish Right.[4] Still, from 1928 onward, the editors of this paper began to transition to positive language when describing Hitler and the Nazis.[5] They argued that the Nazis stood for conservative values and that they were able to unite the splintered German Right.[6] By 1930 the editors still proclaimed conservative values, yet they also increasingly published positive articles about the radical Nazis.[7] This coverage included notes on the SA, as the one organization that actively fought the communists in the streets and in their own neighborhoods. This reporting also included stories of extreme violence in which the editors depicted the SA, nevertheless, as victims of communist aggression.[8] When Hitler became chancellor on January 30, 1933, the editors of the *Hamburger Nachrichten* welcomed the Hitler regime as the only government able to unite all conservative Germans, demonstrating their complete embrace of fascism.[9]

This case study will show that the SA used their uniforms in the manner outlined in the previous chapters to help win votes for Hitler. A close reading of the *Hamburger Nachrichten* and of the *Hamburger Volkszeitung,* the main communist newspaper of Hamburg, demonstrates that the Stormtroopers used the signal function of the Brown Shirt to trigger clash violence with the Left. The bourgeois elites then repeatedly reinterpreted these instances of violence as acts that defended conservative norms. This worked well because the SA additionally used propaganda marches and SA festivities to shape the fascist image in positive ways. The SA in Hamburg represented, in this sense, a duality.

This case study builds on the research findings on Hamburg's bourgeois elites by Anthony McElligott and the insights of Andrew Wackerfuss on Hamburg's SA. In addition to these fine secondary sources, my argument is also supported by a collection of primary sources documenting the rise of Nazism in Hamburg compiled and edited by Werner Jochmann.[10] Of course, my argument is further supplemented by evidence drawn from several other primary-source types. The unpublished memoirs of Alfred Conn, one of Hamburg's bourgeois SA officers from the holdings of the Research Center for History in Hamburg, are especially valuable. Arguably, Conn's memoirs need to be viewed with a critical eye. Conn was excluded from the Nazi Party during the Weimar years. He survived both the Nazi dictatorship and World War II. He then penned his memoirs during the decade after 1945.

His unpublished manuscript may therefore be an attempt to distance himself from his own Nazi past. Undeniably, this may have an impact on Alfred Conn's credibility as a witness. Yet Conn's text does provide an unbiased window into the attitudes of bourgeois Hamburg citizens in the 1920s and early 1930s. It retraces the attraction, growth, and actions of the SA in Hamburg and specifically illustrates the use of the uniform. There are, of course, less problematic primary sources that can help confirm Conn's narrative. The German Federal Archive in Berlin, the City Archives of Hamburg, and the Research Center in Hamburg provide documentary evidence from the files of the Hamburg SA. Finally, evidence from additional Hamburg newspapers, the *Hamburger Anzeiger* and the *Hamburger Fremdenblatt,* reinforces the present work's overall argument.

For such a case study, the wider economic, political, and social context is very important. Hamburg's unique, or exceptional, status during the Weimar years was shaped by several factors. First is a consideration of Hamburg's history. Located at the confluence of the rivers Alster and Elbe, which connect it to the Baltic Sea, the North Sea, and the Atlantic Ocean, the city developed into a leading northern European shipping center. During the Middle Ages, merchants made the city affluent and independent. Hamburg was governed by its own elites as a free imperial city in the Holy Roman Empire. On the surface, Hamburg's political history appeared to be a liberal deviation from the German norm. The bourgeois elites of the city formed a cosmopolitan and liberal class of overseas merchants constituting a special type of social category. This unique social circle ruled independently of church, imperial, and princely influences. These factors, then, contributed to Hamburg's more liberal tendencies than other German cities.[11]

A closer look at the historical development of Hamburg's ruling elites, however, shows a more nuanced picture. Modern political liberalism grew in importance in the nineteenth century. The history of Hamburg's bourgeois ruling elite during this time period is not the history of liberalism and political participation of broad sections of the city's citizens. Indeed, this history is not the history of a city republic. Rather, from the Middle Ages up until the nineteenth century, Hamburg's ruling structure remained oligarchic. A comparatively small group of social elites ruled the wealthy city. This exclusive assembly dominated the city's senate and consequently pushed broad sections of Hamburg's citizens into a paternalistic form of social and economic guardianship. These traditionally developed oligarchic power structures, additionally, kept large sections of Hamburg's society out of the political decision-making process. Hamburg's elites, therefore, did not foster the development of political liberalism.[12]

During the nineteenth century, nevertheless, political liberalism found inroads into the city's political environment. Still, the liberal reform movement in Hamburg during the mid-nineteenth century did not follow the goal of widening political participation to the lower classes. Instead, the bourgeois elites liberalized their views without giving up their claims to leadership. These social elites backed up their claims to political hegemony through ensuring the city's economic success and the establishment and maintenance of welfare programs based on Christian traditions and institutions. The liberal movement in Hamburg was therefore characterized by republican traditions, an elitist leadership structure, and a paternalistic mode of political rule emphasizing social control. Liberal reformers in the city were largely unsuccessful because their interests diverged. These traditions placed a wedge between Hamburg's elites and its disenfranchised masses.[13] Ultimately, despite a broad liberal reform movement during the middle of the nineteenth century, Hamburg's oligarchs remained in power.

HAMBURG IN THE 1920S

The industrial age and especially the introduction of the democratic Weimar constitution further intensified class-based conflict in the city. With industrialization, both Hamburg and its working class grew dramatically. During the early years of the Weimar Republic, this working class, many of whom organized in Hamburg's industries, voted heavily for the Communist Party of Germany (Kommunisitsche Partei Deutschlands [KPD]). The Social Democratic Party (Sozialdemokratische Partei Deutschlands [SPD]), nevertheless, had twice as many seats in the city senate, representing the largest party in the city.[14] Hence, the moderate Left had strong support. The combined leftist vote in the city had grown by the early Weimar period, representing approximately 40 percent. This alone may not have been problematic, but it did leave the two parties open to attack. A longstanding tendency among bourgeois voters often collapsed the KPD and SPD into one amorphous, and purportedly dangerous, leftist mass.[15]

The historian Anthony McElligott clearly demonstrates where the allegiances of Hamburg's elite citizens lay during the final two years of the Weimar Republic. After the SA established a tavern in the middle-class section of the Altstadt (Old Town), the communists attacked the Nazi stronghold. Both parties used handguns in the attack. In the cross fire, a twelve-year-old boy was killed. Two days later, the KPD and the SPD called for a school strike until the Nazi tavern was closed. The police quickly shut down the strike. "For the middle-class parents . . . the SPD and KPD were the ones who posed the real moral and physical danger to the children of the Altstadt, not the SA. . . . The two workers' parties were the real 'disturbers of the peace.'"[16] To Hamburg's bourgeois citizens, the perception of Marxist ideologies or political approaches, such as strikes, carried dangerous connotations.

This attitude came in large part from the collective memory of the (failed) communist attempt to seize power in 1923. The communist uprising in Hamburg was not a spontaneous action undertaken by German communists and workers. Rather, it was meticulously planned and directly supervised by a Soviet military committee that had ultimately misinterpreted developments in Germany. The occupation of the Ruhr region by France in 1923 caused economic chaos and forced inflation. This in turn caused widespread disapproval among the working class. In response, workers in Berlin organized a general strike. This strike movement subsequently spread throughout Germany, forcing the abdication of the government under Wilhelm Cuno. The Soviet military advisers in Hamburg mistook these developments as a clear sign of the strength of the German working class and decided that Germany was ready for a communist revolution. Time was of the essence, and after some initial confusion the communists decided to initiate the uprising in Hamburg. Yet they were unable to spark a Bolshevik-style revolution. The proletariat in Hamburg, as it turned out, did not support a civil war. Widespread strikes in support of the uprising did not manifest, and the authorities quickly crushed the isolated pockets of violence in the city.[17] While anticlimactic, this was not the last proletarian uprising during the Weimar era.

The Great Depression only intensified the moderate and bourgeois fear of the communists. The violence from the radical Left did not stop but flared up again, this time in response to rising pressure from the SA. Between May 25 and May 27, 1932, intense communist rioting shook the city. The extremists turned over cars, smashed shop windows, and took control of the Alsterpavillon, a fine restaurant in the exclusive city center.[18] This reinforced the city elites' alarm surrounding the communists.

The Great Depression also contributed to the collapse of the political center in Hamburg over the course of the final years of the republic. Voters from the upper- and upper-middle-class sections of the city instead showed increasing support for the Nazis. In 1928 the Nazis garnered only 2.15 percent compared to 35.94 percent of the Social Democrats and 16.65 percent for the Communists. In the wake of the economic and social crisis, the Nazis celebrated their first true electoral victory in Hamburg on April 24, 1932. For the first time, the Nazis, with 31.2 percent of Hamburg's total votes, gained more votes than the Social Democrats, whose proportion declined to only 30.2 percent. Their margin in this election represented nearly twice as much as the Communists, who held relatively stable with 16 percent. The Nazis, consequently, gained a plurality in a city council that still included sizable contingents of Social Democrats and Communists. As Richard Hamilton has shown, the bourgeois conservative parties of the center-Right lost many votes to the Nazis in the national elections from 1930 to 1932.[19]

THE SA IN HAMBURG

As these electoral shifts occurred, more and more men flocked to the SA. The most dramatic growth in numbers within the Hamburg SA occurred in 1929, the year the stock market collapsed. The Depression severely affected the city's economy since it depended on international trade. The compromised economy helped to swell the ranks of Hamburg's SA. The organization grew almost fourfold in membership from around four hundred members in 1929 to fifteen hundred men in 1931. This growing Stormtrooper community was more autonomous than most. It provided close emotional bonds between the men and a sense of purpose and social relevance in an era of economic dislocation. The SA homes served especially as a haven from the Depression and provided a sense of community to men facing financial hardship.[20]

Still, this special character of the SA in Hamburg also leaves inroads for further research. As will be seen, the Nazis in Hamburg relied heavily on SA units that were temporarily bused in from the surrounding countryside and other communities. Even within the city, the SA leadership transported units as needed from one city district to the other. The SA that acted in Hamburg then did not exclusively belong to the city's distinctive community of local SA. The success of the SA in Hamburg cannot be attributed only to the fact that Hamburg's Stormtroopers were more autonomous than others. Instead, one needs to investigate how, when, and why SA were bused in from the surrounding regions.

A second important facet of this research concerns the issue of SA violence. The SA's violent actions against the Left initially seemed counterproductive, since the bourgeois elites valued order and security. This specific situation seems, at first glance, paradoxical.[21] A focus on violence alone cannot explain why Hamburg's elites favored the Nazis. Yet if one considers the duality of the SA image and applies a dual analytical focus on violence that was framed as defensive, on the one hand, and disciplined and appealing behavior, on the other, the alleged paradox becomes explicable. The key to this explanation is resting on the positive image the SA built with the aid of their uniforms.

Hamburg's unique history and the special circumstances of Hamburg's SA are thus important to put the following case study into the correct historical context. To begin with, Hamburg's SA was initially insignificant. During the early years of National Socialism and in the period after the Beer Hall Putsch, Adolf Hitler had minimal support in Hamburg. National Socialism in the north of the Weimar Republic was initially dominated by Gregor Strasser.[22] The Nazis in the city pledged their undivided support to Hitler only in late March 1925.[23] Still, it was even later, namely, after 1926 and the introduction of the Brown Shirt, that the SA became a visual element in the city. The signal effect of the uniform was important. It showed that the Nazis operated in the city and helped to trigger clash violence. The uniform also visibly united Strasser followers and Hitler supporters. Finally, the use of the uniform enabled positive image construction. It enhanced the intangible virtues of strength, discipline, and aggressiveness among its wearers. Equipped with this tool, Hitler's SA set out to conquer the Weimar Republic's German North.

Due to these dynamics, organized NSDAP and SA activity in the city developed slowly. When Hamburg's Nazis met in the capital of the neighboring province of Mecklenburg-Schwerin to listen to a speech by Hitler in 1926, the bourgeois newspaper *Hamburger Nachrichten* reported in a critical yet not unsympathetic manner. According to the editors, "Hitler looks very fresh, and, in reality, much better than the distorted image that makes its rounds. . . . So, it is mostly the way that he delivers his speeches and not what the corporal says that gives him his unsurpassed success."[24] The tone of the article is almost patronizing. It shows that to an educated audience, Hitler was a mere corporal who had mastered the techniques of public speaking and image construction.

When Hitler was given permission to speak in Hamburg proper in 1927, one of the bourgeois listeners, Albrecht Erich Günther, noted that Hitler brought passion to politics yet failed to convince through logic. According to Günther, the faces of Hitler's uniformed bodyguards showed the fanaticism of youths who had problems following their leader's theoretical excursions. Günther did not truly understand Hitler's success and concluded that the uneducated and the proletariat needed, even thrived on, dogma and intolerance. Hence, Hitler, as a man of the people, was "an educator towards healthy instincts." Günther's words showed contempt for the demagogue yet appreciation for the man who led the proletariat away from international Marxism and back into the nationalist fold. The uniformed and disciplined proletarian SA made the right impression on Günther.[25]

ALFRED CONN: THE EX-OFFICER AND ORGANIZER

Like Günther, one of Hamburg's SA officers, Alfred Conn, was born into a middle-class Hamburg family. Both belonged to the bourgeois elite. In 1914, like many other young men of his social class and his generation, he joined the German Army enthusiastically and served as an infantry officer from 1914 to the end of the war in 1918. He was wounded yet served the full four years. After the German capitulation, Conn returned home. He hated the republic and detested everyone he considered to be enemies of his German fatherland. He also served in an armed citizens' militia from 1919 to 1920.[26] Following this initial contact with right-wing paramilitary activism, Conn started to leap from one organization to the other. Among these associations were the Wehrwolf and the SA.

As a young veteran, Conn believed it to be his duty to continue the fight. Yet it was difficult for him to find a group that he considered a good ideological fit and included men that engaged in this struggle with the same zeal as himself. He wanted a "state of frontline veterans, a greater German national people's state of a national socialist character."[27] Conn dedicated his time and energies to this endeavor.

Although Alfred Conn never shied away from violence, he was an ideological moderate and an intelligent individual who did not avoid debate with political opponents. Indeed, he could hold his own in public debates with left-wing intellectual heavyweights such as Willi Bredel, a Hamburg-born communist.[28] Conn met Bredel when he attended a public debate with communists in 1924. Conn valued Bredel's intellect and attended the meeting because he did not want to "debate about Marxism, but with the Marxists." Conn claimed that the two men struck up a friendship that night and that they maintained friendly relations thereafter for years to come. Conn also tried to convince his enemies with arguments rather than with brute force alone.[29]

Yet, as an officer in the Wehrwolf, Conn partook in paramilitary training and was ready for violence. The Wehrwolf was a large paramilitary defense association. Nationally organized, like a shadow military, it included tens of thousands of members who were unable to maintain careers in the German military due to the restrictions on the size of the German Army established in the Treaty of Versailles. On Easter weekend of 1925, Alfred Conn took part in the regional *Wehrwolftag* in Hohenweststedt, a town eighty kilometers north of

Hamburg. He and his fellow northern German paramilitaries stayed in makeshift free quarters and participated in field exercises, cross-country marches, and even individualized training. He identified as a soldier and kept in shape. Within the Wehrwolf, former soldiers and Free Corps men maintained connections with each other and former superiors. During a subsequent meeting, for instance, the men listened to a speech given by the former quartermaster-general and World War I hero Erich Ludendorff.[30]

Conn first met Paul Ellerhusen through his work in the paramilitary defense leagues and joined his group. It was Ellerhusen who transferred his men, Conn among them, to the SA.[31] Nevertheless, it was Conn's choice to remain with Ellerhusen. During this time, a constant exchange between personnel of differing political and paramilitary organizations was not uncommon. Conn's final decision to become an officer in Hitler's SA can be attributed to the signal function of the uniform of the Nazis.

Conn remembered exactly when the SA first presented themselves publicly in the Brown Shirt in Hamburg. He witnessed the first propaganda march of the SA on June 12, 1927. Arthur Böckenhauer led the small detachment. The SA impressed Conn because they wore their brown uniforms proudly through the communist neighborhood of the Reeperbahn in the red-light district. They not only wore their highly conspicuous uniforms but also sang marching songs accompanied by a brass band. This public spectacle aimed at triggering clash violence and was thus not without dangers. Conn did not reject violence against the communists. Therefore, this view made a lasting impression on him. Only a short time later, he accepted Ellerhusen's offer to become an officer with the rank of *Sturmführer* in charge of Hamburg's Sturm 2.[32]

The newly appointed *Sturmführer* soon bought his own Brown Shirt, SA cap, and SA tie. For Conn, his uniform was a source of pride. When the city senate banned the uniform, the police temporarily arrested Conn. Conn remembered the police interview clearly because it involved his outfit. Hence, his recollections allow for a detailed description of his personal SA uniform. Although he was a middle-class ex-officer, he did not own a perfectly matching uniform bought at a Brown Store. When asked about his brown corduroy riding breeches, because they appeared to be part of the forbidden brown uniform, Conn argued that his brown breeches with red infantry piping were a present that his father sent to the front during the war. His belt was army issue. The buckle was not a proper SA belt buckle with insignia.

Instead, Conn wore a buckle with a *Wolfsangel,* a symbol widely used by volkish groups that would later be affiliated with some SS units. Conn claimed in the interview that he had won the buckle at a raffle during his time with the defense leagues.[33]

He vividly recalled his first marches in the new uniform into the countryside surrounding the city. Unlike marching through red districts, this SA action was unlikely to cause violence. The same was true for a tour of the bicycle detachment on January 8, 1928, and a regional SA march on January 15. In this context, marching with military-like discipline was very important. Conn noted the differences to the defense leagues as well. During SA outings on the weekends, they did not practice military skills. The SA was meant to look sharp but not necessarily to be a fighting force. Hence, Conn and his Sturm did not practice field exercises but "consistently drilled, especially marching and greeting exercises as preparation for advertisement marches."[34] Conn and his men practiced looking appropriate when marching in public. One of their tasks was to collectively represent the movement in Hamburg's streets. This mission and his uniform were so important to Conn, in fact, that he risked his day job.

In preparation of the city senate elections on February 19, 1928, the SA staged a series of marches through all parts of the city. Alfred Conn had previously secured a job at Carl Meyer and Co., located on the Alster River island Peute. Conn was an anti-Semite, but Carl Meyer was Jewish. His employer's ethnic identity became an embarrassing detail for him. The subsequent loss of his job did not appear to bother Conn. During an advertisement march through the bourgeois neighborhood of Bergedorf on February 12, 1928, he was spotted leading his Sturm in full uniform. This was a large-scale march of all regional Stormtroopers. Conn did not dwell on the fact in his memoirs. According to his recollections, "The march through Bergedorf cost me my position." He continued, "And as [a] conclusion [to the election campaigns for February 19] Hitler spoke at the large ballroom at Sagebiel on February 16. This time and from now on more and more often the SA appeared in uniform." The most important memory of this period that Conn included in his memoirs was his first personal meeting with Adolf Hitler. Ellerhusen introduced his SA officers to Hitler in a small room at Sagebiel. Four days after Conn became unemployed, Hitler shook his hand and exchanged a few words with him. The movement was by this time more important to him than a job at (and income from) a Jewish-owned company.[35]

The editors of the *Hamburger Nachrichten* reported the following day on Hitler's speech. They encouraged their readers to vote for one of the larger conservative bourgeois parties, as opposed to splinter parties in one article.[36] Notwithstanding, they published a second article on the same page in which they praised the Nazis. To them, the Nazis were in a unique position to rally all bourgeois conservative forces. Like Conn, the conservative editors were impressed with the Nazi leader. They summarized Hitler's speech highlighting the argument that democracy is not a fitting form of government for the German people. According to Hitler, democracy gives a platform to pacifists and Marxists. It furthermore weakens the German people because they divide themselves along party lines. Hitler therefore called for a uniting of all conservative forces under the banner of fascism. The editors ended the article with the observation that the meeting was conducted with "exemplary order. Hitler was interrupted several times by strong applause and celebrated enthusiastically in the street even after the meeting ended."[37]

Still, the Nazis in Hamburg did not all act with such resolve. Above all, they could not agree on their leader. Since this situation did not allow for growth, the aimless Hamburg chapter became a concern for the national leadership in Munich. Ultimately, Franz Pfeffer von Salomon, the highest SA leader himself, traveled to Hamburg to arbitrate on April 21, 1928. Yet the infighting did not stop. On April 24, 1928, Böckenhauer temporarily lost his position, and Paul Ellerhusen became the new leader of Hamburg's SA. Ellerhusen was more moderate. Conn subsequently rose in the hierarchy under the protection of Ellerhusen.[38]

Nevertheless, Conn and his Sturm 2 numbered only forty-six men in addition to the two *Truppführer,* Dels and Bisshopinck, and the three *Gruppenführer,* Möller, Wandrey, and Trzebiatowsky. For this district of the city and "in view of our enemies," according to Conn, "this was a tiny number." Yet Conn resolved to make up for that with "heightened activity."[39] One specific form of action was traveling to combine numbers with other units as a show of force.

On Saturday, September 22, 1928, Conn traveled with the entire Hamburg SA to the town of Mölln, approximately fifty kilometers east of Hamburg. Nazi activists there gave them a place to sleep and fed them. In exchange, the Hamburg Brown Shirts combined numbers with the local Brown Shirts for a uniformed propaganda march through town the following day. In this way, they helped the small Nazi groups in the surrounding towns to make a name for themselves.[40] These activities can be seen as nonviolent propaganda in small towns with a population that did not contain as many communists as the city of Hamburg. The signal function of the SA uniform not only served to make the Nazis visible to supporters. Alfred Conn also led his Brown Shirted troopers to the lower-class neighborhoods of his own city in deliberate attempts to cause clash violence.

One of his men, Hans Lühr, lived on Marktstrasse in the district of Nord–St. Pauli. This neighborhood voted predominantly Social Democratic. The neighbors knew of Lühr's political affiliation and bullied him. To make sure that no Brown Shirted trooper would be attacked on his way home, Conn made it a habit to march the entire Sturm home. Sturm 2 escorted those men who did not feel safe. Again, Conn remembered one evening that included an episode of planned clash violence quite vividly. To lure the Social Democratic activists into a trap, he walked with Lühr and another trooper about two hundred meters ahead of the rest of his Sturm. The streets were crowded, and the people "were extremely astonished" when the three men in their SA uniforms "marched on nonchalantly."[41] The young men of the neighborhood struck the supposedly easy targets. The ensuing fight was bloody.

During the following trial, the city authorities resolved that the SA man Hans Lühr would from then on be protected by a police detachment on his way home rather than a troop of uniformed SA.[42] Conn specifically stated in his recollections that he acted aggressively only when others displayed aggression toward him. According to his memoirs, he engaged in violence to defend his men. He did not apply violence when he was not provoked. Luring the other side into attacking a seemingly small group of men, however, was not as defensive as he wanted to make it sound. This episode clearly shows how the SA in Hamburg used the uniformed troopers to trigger violence. This particular episode caused a public trial, where the bourgeois judges of the city sided with the Nazis. The trap set by Conn had won the Nazis a public victory.

Indeed, Alfred Conn, a decorated former officer, proceeded to take the fight into the parts of the city dominated by the Left to provoke clash violence with his troopers. In one instance, Conn recollected a cold winter morning in February 1929. He marched his troop, which had by then grown considerably, through the snowy streets toward Friedrich Street. As he remembered, "The narrow street covered deeply in snow echoed with our marching band's military march 'Prussia's

Glory.' This is the home of the Commune. Curses echo from doorways and windows. Nobody had dared this before. Nobody but us alone can, and will, dare doing this. Soon snowballs, flowerpots and pieces of coal are flying. Quickly, a few SA men jump into the doorways and force the enemy to retreat."[43] The police detachment, which was specifically intended to hinder the SA from engaging in violence, could not get into formation in the narrow street. Conn thus found the perfect place to start his assault on the communists' territory. The narrowness of the street allowed the SA to literally occupy the streets with their uniformed bodies and hold this position for a while. The concentrated Nazi force could not be beaten back by the few Nazi opponents. The SA symbolically invaded proletarian territory with a uniformed formation. The brass band made the presence of the Nazis even more obvious. Naturally, clash violence was the result. Yet this time the ex-officer Conn could tactically control the situation and claim victory for him and his troopers without resorting to the courts.

An important tool for the Nazis in strengthening their power base in the North was deliberately triggered clash violence. The role of the uniform in this was apparent. Yet this functioned best when the violence could be controlled and the Nazis at least saw a chance of winning. Conn's recollections clearly show that if this was not a given, his superior officer, Ellerhusen, was flexible. For example, Ellerhusen allowed his men to travel to large meetings in disguise. When he ordered all of Hamburg's SA men to protect Nazi speakers in the Sagebiel ballroom in the summer of 1930, he added the qualifier that his officers were responsible to advise everyone that "SA men who come by themselves to the meeting will use sufficient disguises."[44] These men were strongly advised to wear an overcoat or to change into their full uniform on site.

The uniform functioned in important ways, both violent and non-violent, but it did not work without widespread use. Thus, Conn and Ellerhusen ordered their men to buy their uniforms. When Pfeffer von Salomon visited Hamburg in April 1928 to attend a general meeting of Hamburg's Nazis, Alfred Conn ordered his men of Sturm 2 to come to the meeting in uniform.[45] When the SA was supposed to protect a Bavarian speaker in March 1929, the Hamburg SA was told by the leadership in Munich that Bavarian speakers "are accustomed to the SA attending meetings in uniforms."[46] Ellerhusen, Conn, and their SA men introduced Bavarian Nazi customs in the form of the Brown Shirt to Hamburg.

If one of Conn's men did not own a uniform, Ellerhusen noted it, as, for example, in the case of SA man Schrotzenberger. Ellerhusen inquired why Schrotzenberger did not own a Brown Shirt after becoming an SA man. According to his group leader, Hans Lühr, SA man Schrotzenberger had always dutifully attended meeting security service in civilian clothes, but unfortunately did not own a uniform.[47] He needed to save his money until he could afford to buy his official Brown Shirt. Only a newly appointed SA man in possession of a Brown Shirt could serve the movement in public. As a result, Schrotzenberger was not allowed to march in formation while he still lacked a uniform. Until he had saved the money, Schrotzenberger could take part only in activities that did not call for public appearances. Schrotzenberger was not, however, punished for the lack of uniform, because Lühr made sure to give him a good reference when Ellerhusen chastised him.

The uniform itself, as has been discussed in earlier chapters, functioned as a tool of social control within the SA. This worked especially well with SA men, as, for instance, with Schrotzenberger, who showed an incredible amount of personal agency and desperately wanted to be seen in his uniform. For men who wanted to be publicly affiliated with the Nazis, a typical punishment included temporarily taking away uniform privileges. Ellerhusen, for example, reprimanded one of his troop leaders on February 26, 1929. He ordered that "the troop leader Stein is punished with uniform prohibition for 8 weeks because of breaches in discipline."[48] Even troop leaders, like Stein, were punished by their superiors through the revoking of the privilege to wear the uniform.

The shirt allowed for the control of the individual trooper, which made concentrating larger SA units from different regions more effective. Yet such tasks became more complicated as the numbers of Hamburg's SA grew. Supplying enough food for the men also became an issue. Conn's men of Sturm 2 therefore practiced traveling with the other Hamburg units during small trips in order to become accustomed to this practice efficiently. They undertook weekend outings in which they prepared food on the go to train for the national Nazi *Reichsparteitag* in Nuremberg in 1929. Conn remembered that "an advertisement march through the Elbe River parishes with lunch united all of Hamburg's SA on May 12, followed by a hike starting at Friedrichsruh on May 25. Those were practices for the coming *Reichsparteitag* in Nuremberg." The men practiced travel on a larger scale to make it a routine prior to such special events. This was necessary because by 1929, due in large parts to the Depression, Conn's Sturm 2 had grown to eighty-two men. The handling of a larger number of troopers presented more difficulties for the officers.[49] Conn, however, could rely on help from Nazi sympathizers. One of these sympathizers lived in a Baltic Sea resort. Conn saw the opportunity to impress bourgeois bathing guests with his brown propaganda troopers.

One of the men of Sturm 2, SA man Ihde, a shop clerk at a large department store, had scouted out an opportunity on a trip to the resort town of Haffkrug, located about eighty-five kilometers from Hamburg on the Baltic coast. Ihde approached Conn in the spring of 1929 and informed him about a farmer and Nazi Party member named Omtjes. Farmer Omtjes had invited the Hamburg SA through Ihde to stay in his barn during the summer. Conn took Ihde and a few other men to Lübeck. From there, like true soldiers, they hiked the twenty-five remaining kilometers to Haffkrug in a forced night march. The men talked to the farmer, checked the accommodations, and agreed to a trip to Haffkrug during the coming bathing season. Omtjes promised to organize a free field-kitchen meal with the help of other Haffkrug residents.[50]

To make the most of this trip, Conn communicated with *Sturmführer* Kosegarten of Sturm 1 Lübeck, in addition to *Sturmführer* and attorney Dr. Böhmker of Sturm 30 Eutin. Taken together, the three units comprised approximately 120 men. Conn made sure that he borrowed the marching band from a Hamburg Sturm. The Lübeck SA brought their own brass band. On Saturday, August 6, the men of the Hamburg SA boarded party member Hermann Ey's truck with a trailer. The men completed the trip from Hamburg to Haffkrug and made themselves comfortable in Omtjes's barn. The following morning, while the men prepared and ate breakfast and then bathed in the Baltic Sea, the truck and trailer went to the train station in Timmendorf to pick up the men from Lübeck. The Eutin SA arrived with their own truck.

This sizable SA detachment then marched in their uniforms accompanied by their two marching bands through the beach resort and the surrounding villages. "The marching bands from Hamburg and Lübeck took turns, and without pause the old Prussian military marches belted out." Conn recollected that they "made a visible impression on the resort guests." That was not enough, however. Even the trip home became an impromptu SA propaganda event. After the small group of Eutin SA drove off in their truck, the Hamburg unit accompanied the Lübeck SA home. That evening they marched through Lübeck together, before driving home at dusk. Since this massing of troopers was a spectacular success for the Nazis, they all agreed to get together the following year to repeat the event.[51]

This regional trip was an opportune exercise for the national Nazi rally at Nuremberg. Massing uniformed SA was a very important propaganda tool for the Nazis. During these mass meetings, the uniform functioned as a symbolic unifier. The uniform visually united SA men of different regions and even men who had diverging ideas of fascism, as, for instance, the followers of Hitler and Strasser. This perceived unity of a group that was not truly monolithic made a deep impression on Conn himself. Again, uniforms and equipment were of the utmost importance in his recollections. The party rally of 1929 was therefore a special occasion for Conn. According to his memoirs, "The party rally was held in Nuremberg . . . from the first until the fourth of August. We had been preparing feverishly for some time. Uniforms and equipment were completed, partly donated by party members, [and] the money for the fare was saved up and collected during meetings. Everybody wanted to come along. Everybody, if possible, was supposed to come." Conn's Sturm 2 by this point had grown to 92 men. Waiting to embark, the train station in Hamburg was crowded. "The platform was swarming with Brown Shirts, and party comrades [that] had come to see us off; it was a joyfully aroused mass."[52] Hamburg's SA was thus prepared to go to the big rally.

On arrival in Nuremberg, Conn wandered the streets of the city in amazement. Music and singing filled the warm air. The Brown Shirts had taken over the entire city. Unlike in Hamburg where the SA could not move freely in all districts, Nuremberg seemed to welcome the masses of SA congregated there. The *Sturmführer* witnessed the arrival of more and more troopers who formed into battalions in the several train stations of the city. The SA columns "steadily streamed" into Nuremberg. Seeing all of them together in one location was truly striking to Conn. "On the early morning of August 4, we all moved to the general assembly of the entire greater German SA. The vast field was full of the endless brown columns."[53] The march of all of these men past their leader was an experience that Conn cherished. He had never seen that many Brown Shirts in one location. This experience was invigorating. Conn drew strength and confidence since the uniform obscured ideological differences. All fascists in Nuremberg looked united. Hence, this massing of people left deep impressions.

Invigorated after the rally, Alfred Conn wanted to see more nonviolent propaganda activity. Marches were not enough. He therefore started to actively court the middle class of the city. He accomplished this task by transforming SA festivities from rough-and-tumble evenings among Nazis that involved alcohol and singing into a form that was more palatable for other audiences. Conn devised Sunday-afternoon dances with music from an SA band and refreshments. The city's middle-class citizens embraced these bourgeois-style tea dances wholeheartedly. According to Conn, these advertised dances also earned considerable revenues for the Nazis. He remembered, "In order to obtain financial means for the Sturm, I held on [October 5, 1929] . . . my first SA festival in the great hall of the *Kolloseum* in the *Hoheluftchaussee*." In this large venue, he combined conservative elements with Nazi propaganda. According to Conn, "The band of the SA brigade played the old army marches. . . . *Gauleiter* Kaufmann [NSDAP leader of Hamburg] gave a speech, the [men of the] *Sturm* entertained with physical sports activities, and finally the SA men performed a play that I wrote myself . . . and then there was a dance."[54] Their efforts to appeal to a broad audience paid off handsomely.

According to Conn's recollections, "The revenue was a couple hundred marks. I held several of such festivities, always with the same success." Clearly, the bourgeois ex-officer knew how to attract a bourgeois audience. Entertainment, a speech by the highest-ranking Nazi of Hamburg, and a dance on a Sunday afternoon were more respectable than an evening at a tavern. The SA in their neat uniforms appeared to be good hosts, and the events were free of any form of violence. Conn remembered that only a few months later, "Our SA festivals had become famous in our section [of Hamburg]. Party members and business owners tried to outdo each other with money donations and with prizes for the raffle."[55] A door charge, refreshments, and raffle tickets, sold to bourgeois dancers and proletarian SA rank and file alike, earned the movement a considerable amount of money. Additionally, Conn established friendly connections between Hamburg's Nazis and its bourgeois elites.

The connections to middle-class citizens allowed Conn to travel comfortably in the service of the SA. Even before the formation of the NSKK, or the motor SA, Hamburg's SA featured a motor section. In fact, Conn had a personal driver. When Conn accompanied SA marches, he usually provided his own intelligence by scouting out the route as the march progressed. He followed the marching columns' planned route, at times watching ahead and at other times following the main body of men. In this way, he tried to spot suspicious activity from anyone trying to engage the SA in unplanned clash violence. Conn, who was injured during the war, could not possibly run up and down the route himself. Therefore, he sat on the pillion seat of party comrade Häfker's private motorcycle. Häfker was a party member but did not belong to the SA. He was a veteran of the army and of the Schlageter Free Corps. He would ultimately become the Nazi Party leader of the city district of St. Pauli. Before the Nazis took power in Hamburg, Häfker acted occasionally as Conn's chauffeur.[56]

When Ellerhusen and Conn planned to travel to Hannover for an SA officers' meeting in January 1930, they were not required to use public transportation. Instead, they sat comfortably in the backseat of party comrade Bonde's private car. Bonde was a well-off master confectioner who also ran a pub on Eifelstrasse. His pub served as *Sturmlokal* for SA Sturm 6. Bonde was a true Nazi activist who offered up his car and his business for the cause. Yet that was not enough. The SA leadership attempted to visually mark the taverns owned by Nazi sympathizers, such as Bonde's. On July 17, 1930, Pfeffer von Salomon ordered his troopers to run an advertising campaign for the owners of establishments frequented by the SA. "If the owners are party members, or would like to keep our business," they were required to purchase a black and white plaque with an SA logo to mark their establishment.[57] In this way, the SA put mild pressure on bar owners to clearly identify their property as Nazi establishments. Party comrade Bonde, however, gladly opened his pub to Sturm 6 and personally drove Hamburg's two highest-ranking SA officers to their meeting in Hannover. He did not require coercion.

In June 1930 Conn again used the help of his party comrades Ey and Omtjes. He took his own Sturm and the men of the Hamburg SS to Haffkrug to repeat the propaganda march of the previous year. Again, they used Ey's truck and trailer, as well as the lodgings supplied by Omtjes. The organization was smooth, and the large SA and SS detachments with two marching bands astonished the bourgeois bathers on the beaches of Haffkrug, Scharbeutz, Timmendorf, and Niendorf. Conn recalled the impact on the spectators. "The beach was full of holiday guests whose numbers were increased by hundreds of families from Hamburg who escaped the city over the weekend." The bands took turns, and their "marches belted electrifyingly, the red flags with the swastikas fluttered glowingly and hundreds of surprised people streamed together and bordered our path." The uniformed men received more than spectator attention. When the police protested, Conn ordered his men to disperse. Yet his men saturated the masses at the resort.[58] *Sturmführer* Conn, however, was a master of propaganda and staged an even more spectacular show centered on their uniforms.

After the march through the beach resorts, Conn took his men to Lübeck, where the SA was still not a common sight. Again, the marchers attracted droves of spectators, and this time Conn came up with a clever propaganda stunt. When the men climbed on their vehicles to start the return journey to Hamburg, the *Sturmführer* used the opportunity to give an impromptu speech. Conn directed attention to their uniforms and proclaimed loudly and sarcastically that "the Brown Shirt we are wearing is dangerous. A state could easily crumble upon the sight of it. Therefore, the shirt is prohibited in Prussia since 6/11. Because we are crossing Prussian territory on our way home, we are forced to undress publicly here and now." Conn sassily "begged all present females to turn their backs to the men temporarily."[59] The stunt led to amusement within the crowd, and the men drove off to the sounds of hearty laughter.

This rather unusual use of the uniform in a staged public protest was a success, and Conn repeated it. The absence of the uniform made the SA a comical and even absurd spectacle that the men actively exaggerated. On August 31, 1930, the legal situation was reversed. The Brown Shirt was illegal in Lübeck, yet legal again in Prussia. The Lübeck police wanted to make sure that no SA uniform was visible, and thus Conn gave his Brown-Shirted troopers the "order to dismount and strip." A large crowd of people watched as the SA switched into outfits that included top hats, bare chests, and a sleeveless red shirt complete with a large swastika on the chest. "The men in their 'civilian outfits' resembled a carnival procession."[60] Conn exaggerated the effect and showed the public that the wearing of the uniform promoted a disciplined and orderly image.

Still, despite the spectacle, Alfred Conn also displayed tactical talent when dealing with the police. When the SA marched in uniform with a brass band, they usually did so in a closed column in the street. In Hamburg marching in a closed column blocked traffic. Thus, every propaganda march had to be approved by the police, who often obliged. If the police did not give permission, Alfred Conn simply changed the way the SA marched. In those cases, the SA appeared without the brass band and occupied both sidewalks in loose order. In order to avoid congestion among pedestrians, troopers had a timetable and a list of streets they had to cover. According to Conn, "For that nobody needed police permission." Conn himself was chauffeured by motorcycle and continuously checked the timing. According to his memoirs, "In that way, I was able to concentrate the entire Sturm in the spots in which dangerous situations might occur."[61] Using this strategy, Conn saturated the sidewalks of Hamburg in a coherent manner without breaking traffic laws. He also made sure that the risk of uncontrolled clash violence was low by maintaining strength in numbers.

This boldness provoked one of the most dramatic outbursts of clash violence in Hamburg on September 7, 1930. Hitler gave a speech in Hamburg the day before on Saturday, September 6, in preparation of the upcoming Reichstag elections. The bourgeois editors of the *Hamburger Nachrichten* covered the speech on their front page. According to them, one hour before the event started the venue was full, and masses of people congregated in the streets. When Hitler entered the podium, thousands cheered and gave standing ovations. The predominantly young followers were carried away by enthusiasm caused by the "impression of unity and exemplary discipline" given by the Nazis. The editors also noted that it was not so much *what* Hitler said but rather how he said it that mattered, and they likened the speech to a thrilling movie. During the speech Hitler argued that Germany was divided into two large ideological camps, Marxism and bourgeois nationalism. According to Hitler, both ideologies were engaged in a battle with each other, yet both lacked the strength for final victory. The speech ended by Hitler noting that the division among the nationalists was responsible for their weakness. Neither pacifism nor democracy, only the Nazis, could save Germany. The speech was repeatedly interrupted by shouts of "*Heil!*" and ended with the singing of the national anthem.[62] Hitler and his call for unity among bourgeois circles made a profound impact among conservatives. This was not true, however, for all of Hamburg's citizens. Accordingly, violence erupted.

THE BATTLE OF STERNSCHANZE

Only one week before the Reichstag elections that proved to be the Nazi electoral breakthrough (Sunday, September 14) and only one day after the Hamburg Hitler speech on September 6, Paul Ellerhusen ordered a march of Hamburg's entire SA brigade through the proletarian neighborhoods. He thought this was a fitting demonstration of strength, especially the day after Hitler's speech in his city. The tactician in his officer Conn, however, rebelled. Conn argued that a mass of one thousand men in a drawn-out column could not possibly be controlled or expected to move quickly enough if attacked on either end. The police prohibited closed columns in the streets that day. The SA was forced to walk on the sidewalk in a loose formation, which made supervising the men even more difficult. The fact that Hamburg's newly created motor SA was out on field exercises that morning robbed Conn of the possibility to scout out the streets effectively. Conn only had Häfker and his motorcycle at his personal disposal.[63] Ellerhusen did not heed Conn's advice and ordered the march to proceed. Conn, ever the soldier, obeyed his orders and went about the task like a true officer. He called up Häfker and ordered him to get his motorcycle. Conn rode on the pillion seat and ordered his driver to ride up and down the planned route. With the information he gained from this reconnaissance, Conn hoped to avoid an uncontrolled confrontation and keep all his men as closely together as possible.

However, according to Conn, the two long, drawn-out columns, like tapeworms made of Brown Shirts, ran directly into several truckloads of communist fighters of the RFB. When it came to the street fight, the SA were broken up, and a wild brawl with knives and brass knuckles followed. The numerically stronger communists taught the SA a lesson that day. After the fight, Conn and Häfker rode around to find and regroup his men, yet they had taken flight. The battle was lost. One SA man died after receiving several knife wounds. Several others received stitches from the SA doctor, who was wounded himself. The episode was excessively violent. For the city council, the violence was too much. The following day the council announced that the SA uniform, the most important propaganda tool in the SA arsenal, was prohibited in Hamburg—just one week prior to the national elections.[64]

The communists, of course, shared this sentiment. For them, the incident was an act of self-defense that followed a Nazi attack on a communist propaganda motorcade. According to the editors of the *Hamburger Volkszeitung,* the communists amassed trucks decorated with red signs and flags from all city districts in preparation for the Reichstag elections. On the afternoon of September 7, about three hundred bicyclists, a few dozen motorcyclists, and more than sixty trucks carrying activists assembled for a propaganda motorcade through all parts of the city. Two trucks carried propaganda materials. One additional truck carried a speaker system that broadcast recorded speeches and music. According to the editors, this large force ran into a group of about five hundred uniformed SA that marched in closed formation in the street. The SA first attacked two of the communist motorcyclists. The workers then dismounted from their trucks and defended themselves against the Nazis, who used knifes, brass knuckles, clubs, shoulder straps with lead weights, and revolvers. The fascists lost one SA man, and one policeman was stabbed in the neck by a Nazi. The editors stressed, however, that the police and the Nazis worked together.[65] A worker-correspondent for the *Hamburger Volkszeitung* additionally witnessed the SA attack innocent bystanders, including women and children. One SA man allegedly fired his revolver into a group of onlookers.[66]

To the communists, the SA was outnumbered and marched in parts of the city that they considered their own. Furthermore, the SA acted illegally by marching in closed formations. This unlawful action, however, was not stopped by the police. Even worse, the police protected the aggressive Nazis, who used lethal force against communist activists and bystanders alike. The communists also noted that the Nazis were responsible for wounding policemen. Even though the communists had amassed an overwhelming force for their election propaganda, the small group of aggressive and highly organized Nazis attacked them with unnecessary brutality under police protection. The SA and the police acted like invaders in proletarian neighborhoods.

Hamburg's bourgeois elites, however, viewed this violent incident differently. According to the editors of the *Hamburger Nachrichten*, the communists had murdered yet again. Fully uniformed members of the communist Red Front-Fighters League used daggers and batons to attack National Socialists and the police that left one dead, eleven severely wounded, and twenty-five lightly wounded victims.[67] The Marxists had stabbed forty-eight-year-old *Truppführer* Dreckmann in the heart. Dreckmann died later in the hospital and left a wife and adolescent daughter.[68]

In an almost contradictory fashion, an eyewitness account from the *Hamburger Nachrichten* places blame on the communists for acting with extreme brutality. According to their reporting, a group of Nazis, some in Brown Shirts and some in regular clothes, marched in loose order on the sidewalk. This group was attacked by twenty truckloads of communists in full Red Front-Fighters League uniforms. This force outnumbered and outflanked the SA, attacking them from three sides.

This caused the SA leaders Dettmann and Andree to order the strategic withdrawal into the Sternschanze train station. The communists then chased the retreating Nazis with knives, batons, and bottles.[69]

Yet another eyewitness account printed in the *Hamburger Nachrichten* claimed that the communists ambushed the Nazis. They had waited on trucks behind a police cordon for the end of the Nazi marchers. Once the end of the procession passed the police, who formed a barrier between the antagonistic groups, the communists attacked both the police and the SA. According to this witness, the Marxist fighters surrounded the police, who were rescued by SA men who came to their aid. This witness ends his account by arguing, "A bigger bloodshed was avoided only thanks to the iron discipline of the Brown Shirts." The SA, in this account, protected the police who defended themselves against overwhelming numbers of communists. The Left prepared with strategic attacks for civil war and revolution. According to this article, the Nazis were the only ones who were willing and able to lead the German people away from Marxism by confronting it in the streets.[70]

Not surprisingly, another article in the same issue of the *Hamburger Nachrichten* voiced irritation at the decision of the Hamburg senate to outlaw the Brown Shirt. The editors cited the police, who defended the decision with the argument that the police could not protect all Nazis acting aggressively. This article ended with the biting comment that the uniforms of the republican Reichsbanner were not illegal and that the behavior of the Red Front-Fighters was worse than that of the SA. The editor predicted that the Nazis would survive this new period of illegality in the city, as it had in previous ones.[71]

In the wake of the street battle, the elites of the city showed a lack of concern about the realities of the violent encounter. The police and the bourgeoisie were caught between two highly polarized and radicalized groups. Both sides accused the other of using uniformed formations and illegal or improvised weapons. Both sides blamed the attack on their opponents, and both sides accused each other of extreme brutality, even against innocent bystanders and the police. Still, the bourgeois editors picked their champions and celebrated a moral victory even though Hamburg's SA had been defeated. The bourgeois editors noted that the SA men in their Brown Shirts were attacked and that they saved themselves—and the police—from organized communist terror. Sixty communist trucks with a loudspeaker brought the fear of revolution to the elite circles of the city. Clash violence in this case played into the hands of the fascists because conservatives portrayed Brown Shirted Nazis as heroic defenders of law and order.

In 1930 the citizens' league for Hamburg, Altona, and Wandsbek published a pamphlet that reflected the bourgeois fears that communism evoked. It also showed that the elites did not differentiate between social democrats and communists. In the first paragraph of the pamphlet, the citizens' league voiced their opinion that social democracy and communism were two political directions born out of the same ideology based on class antagonism. "The idea of class struggle and the elimination of private property and the establishment of a common economy to this day create the foundation of the Communist as well as the Social Democratic Party." The bourgeois citizens' league expressed its contempt for the Social Democrats, a party that, according to them, only thinly veiled its ties to the Bolsheviks. The Soviet Communists, however, were the real enemy. "While the International only exists on paper within the Social Democratic Party . . . the Communist Party not only has the International in their program, but is a homogeneous Communist World Party, with its center in Moscow whose sub-organizations, like the Communist Party of Germany, only follow the orders given out by the central commission in Moscow."[72] The economic crisis of the early 1930s thus widened the gap between Hamburg's elites and Hamburg's proletariat.

Hamburg's elites viewed the real enemy as the ones on their left, as a list of the citizens' league's pamphlet shows. Table 1 shows the number of alleged communist-led attacks in the city between July and December 1929.

TABLE 1. COMMUNIST ATTACKS AND WOUNDED, JULY–DECEMBER 1929

	JULY	AUGUST	SEPTEMBER	OCTOBER	NOVEMBER	DECEMBER
ATTACKS	11	29	69	79	86	69
WOUNDED	14	47	102	134	127	92

Data from *Der Bürgerbund für Hamburg , Altona, Wandsbek e. V.:* "Die Bolschewistische Gefahr, Politik der Buergerlichen Sammlung," in Jochmann, *Nationalsozialismus und Revolution,* 301.

The number of violent clashes in 1929 rose steadily until its peak in November, when the situation cooled. The latent civil war in the city, for bourgeois elites at least, was real. Fear of communism pushed elites into the arms of the Nazis. This did not occur in spite of violence but rather because of the fascist violence against the Left, successfully provoked and reframed as initiated by the communists.

Considering these circumstances, it is not surprising that this particularly violent episode did not interrupt the increase in Nazi voters in Hamburg's elections only a few days later. The SA leadership in Munich, nevertheless, punished Conn's superior, Ellerhusen, by revoking his command. The lost battle thus brought Conn a promotion. He became the leader of the entire SA brigade of Hamburg. As such, Conn also introduced changes. He learned from previous mistakes and applied his expertise, leading to a thorough militarization of SA operations. Despite the prohibition of the uniform, he gave out new orders for the national election on Sunday, September 14, 1930. The order demonstrates that Conn used his military expertise to enhance security for his men. No one could take the day off, due to the threat of additional communist attacks. Conn assigned specific city districts and officers to his troops and told the men which taverns to congregate in while awaiting updated orders. Ideally, the taverns would also serve the men food. To avoid chaos through prank calls in the headquarters, Conn also established code numbers for each of his officers and for two of his intelligence-hub telephone lines.[73] Conn used his SA like a civil war army in an election campaign.

As Hamburg's highest SA man, Conn implemented more initiatives. If his men chose to fight for him and the movement, then he would take good care of them. If his men united to visually represent the movement, then he would ensure that his men were always well groomed. He therefore ensured that his men, and especially the unemployed, had the opportunity to clean their uniforms regularly by establishing a laundry service. However, both labor and detergent were expensive. Initially, the men were supposed to pay at least for the laundry detergent. To save expenses for labor, Conn recruited the women of Hamburg's National Socialist Women's League. The women reacted enthusiastically. One of them, Carla Voss, allowed Conn's SA the use of her own laundry facilities in her basement in the Rothenbaumchausee.[74]

Despite this initial display of enthusiasm, however, some of the women were not willing to give up their own expensive equipment. When Conn asked if the Women's League activists would allow the SA to use their washing machines, most women replied that they needed the machines themselves. Therefore, Conn used the revenue from his SA festivities to purchase his own washing machines. In the face of this resolve, the Nazi Women's League again exhibited willingness to help and agreed to oversee their maintenance and operation. Nevertheless, with his own facilities and machines, Conn determined to run his operation independently of the Women's League, if not right away, then over time. This news caused many of the women to change their minds. Again, Carla Voss leaped into action. She contacted the youth group of the German Women's Order under the leadership of Olly Krispin. However, even with the combined efforts of thirty girls working in shifts, the task was daunting. Conn resolved to purchase even more washing machines in the future to save labor and time.[75]

Obviously, to the bourgeois SA officer, cleanliness was of the utmost importance. This was not the case for some of his troopers. Some men needed to be reminded to keep a clean appearance, even though laundry services were scheduled every Saturday. For instance, Conn specifically mentioned on October 30, 1930, that he "expect[s] storm 19 to use the laundry services the following Saturday more enthusiastically than the previous Saturday." Some men of Sturm 19 had not washed their uniforms in almost two weeks. To avoid traffic jams, he scheduled his men to have their laundry done storm by storm. Thus, the men of Sturm 20 "will use the laundry facilities on the Saturday in two weeks without waiting for any special orders."[76] It seems as if the men were resistant to maintaining the level of hygiene that their commanding officer would have preferred.

Yet Alfred Conn went beyond simply ensuring the cleanliness of his troopers. He knew that the image of the SA also rested on numbers and the strength that a large group of uniformed men suggested. Once he made sure that all his men looked neat and well groomed, Conn took the concept of shelter, from the *Sturmlokal,* to the next level. He established an SA home as a dormitory for men without jobs, men who wanted to move out of their parents' homes, and men who were forced to leave their homes because of their Nazi affiliations. Since many of the unemployed SA men were skilled tradesmen, Conn was able to rent a large rundown apartment on Heinrich Barth Street cheaply. Unemployed carpenters, bricklayers, plumbers, and electricians fixed up the apartment. Conn was able to purchase "a number of former submarine beds" through a contact with a major named Enneccerus.[77] The bunk beds lined the walls of several bedrooms. The men utilized a shared kitchen and bathroom. Conn also relocated his laundry service to this location. Conn's *Sturmführer* Paschke became the house father of the new SA home and came to occupy a small, private room.

This cost cutting allowed Hamburg's SA leader to make a real home for his men. According to Conn, "The rent, divided among all would be so low that every unemployed SA man could pay it easily with his dole." The SA home, once up and running, actually earned money. The officer in charge of finances, *Truppführer* Mollenhauer, regularly checked the flow of revenue. In this capacity, Mollenhauer learned that Paschke had begun to use his position for personal gains. Unauthorized fund-raisers and the embezzlement of sixty-two Marks and eighty-two Pfennings forced Conn to fire Paschke and in his place put a *Gruppenführer* named Schorman of Sturm 19 in charge of the Heinrich Barth Strasse SA home.[78]

Overall, the new SA home presented a double benefit. It both was popular among the men and generated funds for the SA. Soon after it opened, it was at capacity. Conn had given his men shelter, communal meals, and the feeling of barracks life. Yet they not only functioned as residences for the unemployed. According to Peter Longerich, the SA homes worked in a twofold manner. The second function was practical, by enabling SA leadership to keep their shock troops ready for action around the clock.[79]

Conn's actions did not go unnoticed. Even high-ranking Nazis recognized his zeal. This in turn caused Conn to document the finances of his SA home in detail. Nazi Party member Theodor Wessenmeier penned an article about the project that appeared in the Nazi newspaper *Völkisher Beobachter*. The supplemental publication *Der SA Mann* from December 18, 1930, brought Conn's actions to the attention of northern Nazi leader Gregor Strasser. Strasser asked for details, and Conn obliged, giving the information in a letter to Strasser.[80] A passage of this letter is worth quoting in full since it illustrates the financial situation of the unemployed SA in Hamburg well. It also shows the financial challenges faced by the SA men and the fact that despite these challenges, the laundry had become a fixed part of the SA budget.

> As support an SA man receives a weekly amount of 10 Marks. With this he lives in the home in a way that ensures he is free of sorrows, he lives among comrades and not in loneliness, and that he is easily available to the leadership. We calculated that rent, electricity, heating, simply cooked common meals, and washing and ironing of his laundry together make up about 7 Marks weekly, while 3 Marks remain to him for SA service and his personal needs. Of course, it is unavoidable that life

> remains barren, yet in this way he is carefree and is surrounded by cheerful camaraderie at all times. Nowadays, an employed head of a family has no ampler endowed life.[81]

Thus, a clever leader like Conn built a very successful operation. Under Conn, the numbers of Hamburg's SA grew steadily. The men lived modestly but comfortably and even had about a third of their weekly welfare allowance remaining after paying room and board. These resources could be spent on SA activities and membership dues. Thriftiness and communal living arrangements allowed Conn to squeeze financial reserves even out of the unemployed SA troopers. This won him the praise and approval of his superiors. Nevertheless, he did not keep his position for long.

After a short but restless period of total dedication to the movement, Conn was informed that he would have to give up command of the SA brigade Hamburg to Arthur Böckenhauer in November 1930. Böckenhauer had talked his way back into the party and the SA. Conn was convinced that this decision came about due to intrigues within the higher leadership ranks. Conn hated Böckenhauer and only reluctantly gave up the brigade of about one thousand men to his rival. According to Conn, Hitler thought a man with qualities such as Böckenhauer was safer in the ranks of the SA than working against them. When Conn found that he had lost command of his brigade to Böckenhauer, he quit both the SA and the Nazi Party.[82]

Although Conn made no mention of this in his memoirs, documentary evidence suggests that he lost his position due to a very specific reason beyond the actions of Böckenhauer. Alfred Conn lost his favor with the leadership in Munich because of his relation to Walter Stennes. The Berlin SA leader Stennes had led two revolts among the Berlin SA. Stennes was expelled from the party in 1931.[83] Immediately after Stennes's expulsion, Conn published a pamphlet in which he expressed his reasoning for leaving the SA. According to Conn, the party leadership compromised with established elites when it came to religion and capitalism rather than clinging to their radical beliefs. Conn then appealed to his men to join the fight for an unaltered National Socialism. This was perhaps the primary reason for his break with the SA and the party.[84] Although a third theory claims that Conn lost his position because of his pagan beliefs, the documentary evidence available for this case study did not support this theory.[85]

There may have been a combination of factors leading to Conn's decisions to disassociate himself from the Nazis. Whatever the reasons may be, decades later Alfred Conn recorded the modest beginnings and the ultimate triumph of the SA in his memoirs. Conn was present when the second SA formed, when the Brown Shirt was first introduced to the city streets, and when the SA had its most dramatic period of growth, in part thanks to his ingenuity. Conn's memoirs demonstrate how the developments outlined in the preceding chapters played out on the ground in a specific location. First and foremost, Conn shows that the Brown Shirt was of utmost importance to him personally. He liked to wear his Brown Shirt in public, and he emphasized that repeatedly. Second, his memoirs confirm that the Brown Shirt was essential not only to him but also on a larger scale. He used his Brown Shirted men to trigger clash violence against the Left, claiming to defend the interests of the middle class. He also used his uniformed men in positive image construction as opposed to intimidation. More practically, he ensured that his men had shelter, food, and access to laundry services. He then used his neat troopers to entertain conservative citizens during tea dances. Finally, his memoirs demonstrate that Conn actively amplified the positive effects of the Brown Shirt by massing the men through travel and creative combinations of troopers. Conn used motorcycles, trucks, and cars owned by party activists and introduced his SA to the conservative elites of Hamburg.

ARTHUR BÖCKENHAUER: THE EX-POLICEMAN AND PROPAGANDIST

Under Böckenhauer's revived SA leadership, the Hamburg SA brigade was now experienced in travel and exchange of troopers, they had mastered the arts of military drill and style, and they marched with their own brass bands. Conn was an astute organizer and strategist who established a coherent, disciplined, and uniformed SA in the city. Nevertheless, Böckenhauer did not disappoint his superiors. He took what Conn established and expanded the entire organization. He was a master at logistics and massed his SA in repeated propaganda marches. His work also expanded to include SA-provided protection of Nazi activists who handed out flyers. This also involved the shuffling of troopers from one end of the city to the other. During this kind of work, the Brown Shirts again had a signal function, which can be seen through the example of a communist sympathizer in Hamburg-Eppendorf.

On August 4, 1931, the Nazi Party section from the Hamburg district of Eppendorf complained to the party propaganda section in Hamburg proper that about twenty-five hundred flyers, made in response to a current speech by Stalin, had not been handed out because no SA security attachment was available. The Eppendorfers asked for protection, since "without such the section cannot hand out fliers in *Niendorferstrasse, Kegelhof,* and *Frickstrasse.*" The reason they gave was that "the communist rabble lives in these streets and is always there in great numbers when we show up." Specifically, "In *Niendorferstrasse,* for instance, there lives a Negro who, especially on Sunday mornings, is always watching out for us and as soon as he spots us calls together the bandits." Because of that, "A handing out of flyers is impossible, because a flyer troop of 10 to 12 men is in a few minutes facing 50 to 100 communists. Work here is only possible under large-scale SA protection."[86] The signal function of the uniform seemed to play into the hands of Nazi opponents. Yet at this point, the SA had enough men to protect Nazi activists handing out flyers.

When SA leaders in neighboring districts needed protection, Böckenhauer sent his men to back them up. A constant borrowing of SA units for specific election campaigns was normal. For instance, on May 8, 1931, the Hamburg SA traveled to Oldenburg to participate in an election rally. The large number of men called for logistical considerations. The men were told where and how to stand in line for their food on arrival in Oldenburg. The meeting spot in town was marked by a green flag.[87] By 1931 the Hamburg SA had become a considerable force.

Hamburg's new SA leader also contributed to a streamlining of SA culture. Marchers that included a brass band were much more useful for propaganda marches. Music was particularly important. When Böckenhauer heard about the new "Horst Wessel Song," the song that would eventually become the hallmark of the Nazi movement, he immediately wrote a short note to the SA headquarters in Berlin. Horst Wessel had belonged to the Berlin SA and died there in a shooting with communists. The talented propaganda chief Joseph Goebbels immediately made a martyr out of Wessel. The march he wrote became the official SA march.[88] In August 1931, Böckenhauer wrote his letter to Berlin stating, "[The SA in] Hamburg would like to ask for information as to where one can purchase the Horst Wessel march for brass band . . . and for how much one could purchase it."[89] Hamburg's SA thus played the new SA march shortly after it came out. Conn's band always played the old army marches. Böckenhauer's men added the brand-new "Horst Wessel Song" into their repertoire.

This growing SA force, singing their propaganda songs in the streets, effectively triggered more clash violence with Hamburg's communists. Over the spring of 1932, tensions continuously heightened. The communists saw themselves pushed into a corner and acted aggressively when Nazis, who handed out flyers under the protection of the SA, invaded proletarian territory and even attacked an inn stronghold. As in the battle of Sternschanze, the attack on a communist tavern on the morning of Sunday, February 14, 1932, ended with a dead Stormtrooper. Again, the communist newspaper and the bourgeois press did not agree on what happened. The difference was that this time, the Nazis did not run into the communists by accident. The police report, cited by several of Hamburg's newspapers, confirmed as much. Still, in the press, many additional facts were hotly disputed.

According to the communist editors of the *Hamburger Volkszeitung,* the Nazis provoked the proletarian inhabitants of the city center. At around nine thirty in the morning, the fascists marched by the tavern Ezinger. At ten thirty, the Nazis returned and stormed the bar without warning. As patrons started to leave, to avoid being caught in the brawl, a group of fifty to sixty fascists reinforced the attackers and smashed the windows. The innkeeper tried to alarm a nearby police patrol car, yet the police refused to act and advised the innkeeper to notify his local police department. It was a full two hours later that the local authorities sent a police detachment to the besieged inn. Ultimately, the police then closed the bar for two weeks because the communists had planned attacks on the Nazis at this location.[90]

According to a news-service report printed in the communist paper, one Nazi died during the brawl. Although the Nazis and the bourgeois press claimed that the communists initiated the attack, it was the Nazis who attacked first. According to the *Nordischer Nachrichtendients* (Nordic news service), the Nazis lied when they claimed that the communists had hurled bottles and glasses at them from inside the inn. This report closed noting that all fascists who had been arrested spent only a short amount of time in police custody.[91]

An eyewitness, who spoke to the *Hamburger Volkszeitung,* purportedly encountered a group of sixty to seventy Nazis who tried to storm the Ezinger bar and smashed the windows. Shots also rang out. In the general melee of the attack, the Nazis pulled out revolvers and started shooting wildly. During this shoot-out, the witness described how one Nazi was about to pull his trigger, while another fascist ran into the line of fire. The shot rang out, and one man collapsed to the ground. According to additional witnesses, the closing of the Ezinger inn and the claim that violence erupted from there are clear indications that the SA was being systematically ordered into proletarian quarters to distract them from the nefarious and secret dealings of their own leaders during election campaigns.[92]

The editors of the *Hamburger Anzeiger,* one of Hamburg's most popular newspapers, on the other hand, did not agree with that interpretation of events. The *Anzeiger* claimed that the communist Wilhelm Hans Karl Schlieper had killed the twenty-three-year-old SA man Heinrich Heissinger. The article elaborated that the Nazis had started the lawful distribution of flyers early, at about eight thirty in the morning. A group of Hamburg's SA protected the men distributing the propaganda material. This was necessary because the communist inhabitants of Hamburg's Gängeviertel harassed the Nazis. When the Nazis had no flyers left to hand out, the communists attacked the Nazis because of their natural superiority in their own neighborhood. At first the brawlers used sticks, belts, and other blunt instruments. At one point, however, the communists cleared a line of fire, and Schlieper shot a few rounds with his pistol into the group of Nazis. Heissinger was killed by a head shot from about fifty meters. The communists then fled to the Ezinger tavern, pursued by the Nazis. Only the arriving police stopped the chaos and arrested thirty of the brawlers. According to the police investigation, the communist Schlieper was in all probability the perpetrator. The twenty-four-year-old did not return to his lodgings. He supposedly left the inn through the back door before the police arrived and was attempting to flee to Russia by ship.[93]

The bourgeois writers of the *Hamburger Nachrichten* agreed with their colleagues. To them, the occurrences of February 14 represented another blatant act of communist terror in the city. The communists had followed the Nazis handing out flyers for quite some time and finally, under the leadership of a known member of the "Young Anti-Fascist Guards," opened the attack with revolvers.[94] Also citing the police report, the *Hamburger Nachrichten* confirms that Heinrich Heissinger, a butcher born on July 28, 1909, was shot in the head during the brawl.[95] Regarding the suspected murderer, the bourgeois account continued, "Urgently suspected of murdering Heissinger is Wilhelm Hans Karl Schlieper, born October 13, 1907 in Mühlheim."

The police report provided Schlieper's full address and noted that he was likely attempting to escape abroad. The police promised that informants with information regarding the suspect's whereabouts would be guaranteed full protection.[96]

The *Hamburger Nachrichten* went one step further than the mainstream *Anzeiger,* however, by allowing the Nazis to present their own version of the story to their bourgeois readers. A statement provided by Hamburg's Nazi Party office reported that section Neustadt of the NSDAP conducted a flyer handout on Sunday morning. Because this particular district of the city was a communist stronghold, each of the men handing out flyers had protection in the form of two to three SA men. The communists harassed the Nazi Party members and allegedly fired ten to twelve shots without warning. After Heissinger was mortally wounded, the Nazi Party members chased the murderers into the tavern and were attacked from the inside with bottles and glasses.[97]

Overall, the communist story paints a picture of an aggressive Nazi paramilitary that protected Nazi activists and aggressively attacked a communist inn located deep within a proletarian part of the city. The violence was therefore justified. Their mouthpiece, the *Hamburger Volkszeitung,* acknowledged that a Nazi died, yet they provided conflicting details about who was responsible for his death, ultimately asserting that the victim died by friendly fire. Moreover, the editors claimed, conspiratorially, that the Stormtroopers were ordered to engage in violence to distract the men from the actions of their own leaders. The true purpose of this action, however, was to bring terror into a proletarian safe haven. The *Hamburger Anzeiger* not only named the dead Nazi, acknowledging his victimhood, but also gave specific details about the young communist who allegedly pulled the trigger. Identifying the name and known whereabouts of the suspected perpetrator without corroborating evidence represented a bold assertion. The communists alone represented the events of February 14, 1932, as an act of self-defense. To many other citizens of Hamburg, however, the incident was framed as just another episode of communist terror.

To the organized communists of Hamburg, however, the incident embodied one of many cases in which the SA invaded their neighborhoods and spread terror. In the spring of 1932, the threat of invasion and intimidation tactics became more permanent. The editors of Hamburg's communist paper committed the entire front page of their weekend issue of April 1–2, 1932, to the problem of SA homes.[98]

According to one of the front-page articles, the makeup and location of SA strongholds in the city gave clues as to what the Nazis wanted to accomplish. The editors noted that the name "SA home," as used by the Nazis, was misleading, since larger establishments functioned like army barracks. The men lived and slept in the strongholds and maintained constant vigilance. Factory buildings, large inns, and boardinghouses were used as SA barracks that held several SA storms each. More modest establishments, featuring accommodations for ten to thirty SA men, could be found in smaller inns, business spaces, and private homes. These strongholds of various sizes should not be confused with SA taverns that functioned only as meeting places during the day. Rather, these strongholds were the bases from which the Nazis harassed Hamburg's working-class citizens.[99]

The SA strongholds, according to the article, not only served to prepare the fascists politically for a civil war but also played concrete strategic and tactical roles. The SA barracks, located close to bridgeheads and other strategically important points, provided the Nazis advantages against proletarian citizens or even against the regular military during an armed Nazi uprising. The SA barracks at the hotel Schlesischer Hof, for instance, housed two SA storms of about two hundred men and allowed the Nazis to control the central train station and main post office. Additionally, the SA strongholds served a political purpose. The Nazis pushed their barracks outward from predominantly bourgeois neighborhoods and into proletarian-dominated parts of the city. This could be particularly threatening, from the communist perspective, when the fascists put large barracks at the periphery of red districts. From these locations, they distributed propaganda and collected intelligence on the communists' organizations. Since this was typically accomplished only through SA terror, these barracks became the epicenters of street-level fascist resistance to communist ideology.[100] The editors of the *Hamburger Volkszeitung*, however, refused to become mere victims. They went on the offensive and published locations and key details about all SA strongholds in Hamburg's red districts of Eppendorf, Winterhude, Barmbeck, Elmsbüttel, and Altona. In one article, the paper included four detailed maps showing communist neighborhoods and exact addresses of all SA homes. The comprehensive list that accompanied the maps included names of individuals and businesses that harbored SA units.[101]

Over the course of 1932, the *Hamburger Volkszeitung* dedicated four more articles to the growing problem of SA homes in and around the city.[102] All of these articles point toward the fact that the SA continued to press into their territory, gaining even more strongholds for their murderous troops. The communists clearly recognized the growing threat of terror. They also recognized that the Nazis represented an increasing danger not only to organized labor but also to the Weimar Republic itself. What the communists did not understand, however, is that their active resistance to the invasion of their districts by the SA played into the hands of the fascists. The Nazis did not want a civil war against the republic. Instead, they initiated a civil war with the communists. This was designed to win over the bourgeois elites of the city. That this worked quite well can be seen in the Hamburg press's reactions to the events surrounding the Reichstag elections on April 10, 1932.

On election Sunday, communists and Nazis alike took to the streets in support of their respective parties' campaigns. During the day, several groups of communists and SA clashed. During one ensuing brawl, revolver shots rang out, killing two Nazis and wounding two others. Like the events surrounding the deaths of SA men Dreckmann and Heissinger, the press discussed this renewed outbreak of violence extensively. Of course, the Nazis also wounded several communists that day. Hamburg's bourgeois press, nevertheless, took the side of the fascists.

According to the *Hamburger Volkszeitung*'s reporting, the rabble-rousing Nazis triggered the violence. The SA concentrated a large number of armed SA in their barracks, which were protected by the police. These armed SA troopers systematically harassed Hamburg's working-class citizens from there. The police supported the SA in these efforts. The Marxists, nevertheless, showed a united front that included both communists and social democrats who successfully defeated Nazi aggressors.[103] In a second article detailing the violent election afternoon, the communist editors reported about a second incident. A group of about thirty Marxists was attacked by an overwhelming force of two separate SA groups numbering between eighty and one hundred men. They outflanked the communists and subsequently assaulted them from two sides. The editors cited the police report, noting that the men of one SA troop fired shots and accidentally killed twenty-seven-year-old SA man H. Brands and twenty-six-year-old SA man H. Hahn, who had attacked the Marxists. The editors recounted several more instances in which Nazis assaulted and wounded Marxists.[104]

The *Hamburger Nachrichten* also noted the violence. They did not, however, celebrate Marxist unity but criticized the Left for systematically hunting down SA men. They cited several incidents from the election weekend in which the communists were the perpetrators. According to their reporting on Saturday, April 9, a mob of about fifty communists attacked two bicyclists, beat them, and stole their bicycles. One of the cyclists, however, pulled a revolver and wounded two of the attackers. In a separate incident on Saturday, the police were notified of a wounded SA man in the SA bar in Sophienallee. Twenty-year-old SA man Carl Zierener suffered a shot to the stomach and injuries to the face. In a third episode reported by the *Hamburger Nachrichten*, communists stabbed the twenty-five-year-old SA man Artur Thiez in the neck. Although the report ended with a note about the number of arrested Nazis that weekend, the editors asked their readers if it was open season on the men of the SA. To them, the communists acted overly aggressive toward the Nazis, not the other way around.[105]

The editors of the communist paper, on the other hand, claimed that the two dead SA men, Brands and Hahn, were shot by their own people. While this is entirely possible, it is also unlikely. The *Volkszeitung* editors voiced their concern about the growing Nazi threat and made sure to note that the Nazis attacked communists and Reichsbanner men. To them, answering violence with violence was an appropriate reaction. The editors of the *Hamburger Nachrichten* abhorred the violence. Yet, at the same time, they argued that this violence was initiated by the Marxists. They propagated the theory that the communists terrorized the SA because they represented the only force able and willing to pay the communists back in kind. Thus, because the bourgeois press chose the SA as the champions of Hamburg's conservative citizens, violence again played into the hands of the Nazis.

In the meantime, Hamburg's SA grew and perfected their logistics, allowing them to transport men into the city to impress and intimidate with ever-larger numbers of marching SA men. On Hitler's birthday, April 20, 1932, Böckenhauer mobilized twenty-six hundred SA men for a march through the city without difficulty.[106] The SA marched with more than five thousand men through the city center during the propaganda marches for the April 1932 city council elections.[107] These were the first elections in which the Nazis won more votes than the Social Democrats, with 31.2 percent versus 30.2 percent, respectively.[108]

Hamburg's Left noted not only the larger numbers but also the intended changes to the SA uniform, as outlined in chapter 5. The communists paid attention to the uniform of their SA opponents. The *Hamburger Volkszeitung* noted and discussed the fascists' plans to professionalize the SA's look by giving them an overcoat and a cap based on military models.[109] Interestingly, the communist press knew of the anticipated changes on June 8, 1932, almost a full month before SA chief of staff Ernst Röhm actually announced the expected modifications in an SA internal order on July 7.[110]

The June 8 article of the *Hamburger Volkszeiung* revealed astonishing details about the new uniform of the SA. Citing the paper *Hamburgischer Correspondent* as a source of information, the article notified readers that the new Nazi uniform regulations came in tandem with the reorganization after the period of illegality had lapsed. Due to expedience, the new uniforms would incorporate several updated items. Whereas the SA had worn the Brown Shirt and brown breeches, they would transition to a tunic in the style of the British military. The article described the material, color, and cut in minute detail. In addition to the new tunic, the editors also claimed that the SA troopers would exchange their older tall lace-up boots with riding boots. The boots, as well as the other leather equipment, would retain their characteristic brown color. This article finally reported that the decision to give the typical SA cap the shape of a German military cap had not been made yet and that the colors of the long new overcoats for the winter would be of a darker-hued brown.[111]

Yet the Left's attention was not only focused on the details of the new SA uniform. They were also interested in who would foot the bill. While the actual SA order indicated that only those officers and men who could afford the new items would have the opportunity to buy them, the communist editors of the *Volkszeitung* presumed a connection between the fascist paramilitary and capitalist business interests.[112] On June 13, 1932, the *Hamburger Volkszeitung* included an article asking *who* would be paying for the new SA uniforms. According to the editors, the British paper *Daily Express* reported that the preparations for the uniforms were in such a heightened state that thousands of tailors in Berlin were busy trying to keep up with the large number of Nazi orders. They followed this claim with a price calculation. One uniform of the new type would cost no less than 150 Marks. If Hitler's claims that the SA had four hundred thousand men was true, then the new uniforms for the entire organization would cost about 60 million Marks. The communists asked who would pay this large sum, considering that the Nazi Party had troubles paying their bills to several different debtors, and one of the perks of SA homes was particularly aimed at unemployed SA men receiving welfare payments. According to the editors, there were only two logical conclusions as to where the Nazis could possibly obtain such funds. Either capitalist "exploiters" had channeled the money to Hitler, or the Nazis appropriated government funds. The editors demanded answers in the name of Hamburg's working-class citizens.[113]

The communists thought they had uncovered a scandalous connection. The Left, apparently, did not know that the men of the SA had to purchase their own uniforms, or perhaps they believed it was more opportunistic to suggest that big business was involved. Nevertheless, they popularized this notion in public to discredit the SA as puppets of the bourgeoisie. By this reasoning, the workers in the SA were not true proletarians because they served the class enemy for the price of a chic new militaristic uniform. Interestingly, the Communist Party member Kasper, then in the Prussian parliament, attempted to make this connection in a public debate, which the *Hamburger Volkszeitung* reported on in their weekend edition for June 18–19, 1932. As Kasper characterized the SA as servants of big capital, an opportunely timed interjector shouted that the Nazi paramilitary was scheduled to receive new uniforms. Kasper answered with the catchy slogan "Der SA der Nazis Goldene Tressen und dem Volke nichts zu fressen," meaning "Golden trimmings for the Nazi SA and nothing to eat for the people."[114] To the Left, it seemed obvious that the men of the SA could not pay for their extravagant new uniforms themselves. If the National Socialists, however, received money from German and international capitalist corporations or the antiproletarian government, they could not be true socialists at all.

In all, the communists had gathered information about the changes to the SA uniform and scandalized this plan in their paper by connecting the new coat and cap to the military and to capitalist exploiters. The Marxists showed a keen interest in the changes, as they reported on them widely the month before the SA leadership themselves notified their men. The communists and their sympathizers reading the *Volkszeitung* effectively knew about the coming changes before the official announcement from the leadership reached the SA rank and file. The Left also noted the intent. The SA intended to look more like the military. To them, that made the SA a militaristic fascist band in the hands of bourgeois conservative elements—a clear threat. Hamburg's SA, under Röhm's national leadership, endeavored to look more respectable in the eyes of Hamburg's bourgeoisie. To Hamburg's capitalist elites, the SA indeed embodied the military virtues of order, discipline, and bravery. Due to these varying perceptions among the city's political factions, even incidents of extreme violence involving the SA did not deter the conservatives from championing the Nazis. Indeed, only a few days after the communists and the Nazis had discussed the changes to the SA uniform, violence broke out again.

ALTONA'S BLOODY SUNDAY

On Sunday, July 17, 1932, the SA marched through the proletarian district of Altona, ultimately leaving eighteen dead and many more wounded. According to Wackerfuss, the SA amassed "around 7,000 uniformed storm troopers. . . . Most had been driven in from across northern Germany, including Hamburg itself, but also the rural towns and cities of Schleswig-Holstein and Lower Saxony."[115] While this number is in line with communist reporting, according to the bourgeois newspaper *Hamburger Nachrichten,* the number of uniformed SA was about eleven thousand.[116] The real number may have been somewhere between the seven and eleven thousand estimated men when the Nazis and communists clashed. This time, however, the police observed and protected the SA. The press sources do not give a clear picture as to who started the shooting. One will likely never know for sure, but what is confirmed is that the police and the organized communists of Altona exchanged extended gunfire. SA men, bystanders, and even citizens of Altona who were inside their homes became collateral damage, with some getting shot and killed.[117]

To the communists, this bloodbath was a result of the aggressive Nazi invasion. The *Hamburger Volkszeitung* claimed the following Monday in a large front-page article titled "Blood Sunday in Altona" that the Nazis and the police had invaded their neighborhood. According to the editors, the police aggressively used machine guns, rifles, tear gas, and two armored cars to battle "massive red self-defense." The communists blamed the outbreak of violence on the SA, who came heavily armed with revolvers and batons along with the police, under their social democratic chief. The *Volkszeitung*'s editors immediately called the police report and the bourgeois press who reported on the event liars. The conservative press suggested that communist snipers attacked the marching SA from rooftop windows.

The truth, according to the Marxists, was that the SA had opened fire on bystanders and into windows from within the marching column. The police then started to clear the streets with massive force, shielding the Stormtroopers while they ran to safety. The senseless fire from two armored police cars killed and wounded many innocent bystanders. The building of two barricades protected the workers from this murderous fire. In this telling of events, the communist editors employed a triumphant tone when they reported that the SA column was torn apart in three locations, the SA march had to be canceled in the retreat, and the Stormtroopers were chased out of Altona.[118]

The *Hamburger Volkszeitung* also included a section with eyewitness accounts.[119] According to this section's reporting, the Nazis had originally planned to concentrate between fifteen and eighteen thousand men yet could muster only five thousand from Hamburg and the surrounding areas. When this smaller than anticipated group entered the proletarian quarters of the city, the SA leaders ordered their men to draw their revolvers.[120] Mounted police, also armed with drawn revolvers and tear-gas grenades, rode ahead of the Nazis and supported the fascists. When the Nazis fell out to shoot bystanders, the proletarians fought back and were consequently met with police fire that emptied the streets.[121] The police then cordoned off street after street, forced the workers into the buildings, and did not stop shooting. The police cover fire allowed the Nazis to retreat, according to this eyewitness report. It is important to note that his report, like most "eyewitness" stories from this era, remained unverified.[122]

The reporting of the *Hamburger Nachrichten* on that Monday was drastically different. Their front-page headline read "Civil War in Altona."[123] According to one of the paper's articles on the events of July 17, the communist attack on the SA was ordered and directed by Soviet "civil war bandits."[124] These coordinated attacks aimed at spreading terror. This terror was meant to turn into a civil war against the conservative and bourgeois sections of German society. According to the bourgeois editors, on July 17 the Marxists chose Altona as a battlefield for their civil war. The eleven thousand assembled National Socialists conducted an election propaganda march with exemplary discipline through the district of Altona when they were provoked and ultimately ambushed.[125]

A second front-page article in the bourgeois paper specified that when the Brown Shirts marched through the district of Ottensen, the assembled bystanders showered the men of the SA with flowers.

In Altona communists first tried to attack and disrupt the marching column. The Brown Shirts' cautious and disciplined behavior, however, was exemplary from their viewpoint. Yet the communist press had called for violence against the Nazis, inciting snipers to attack the SA from rooftop windows. At this moment, the police started to shoot back and tried to clear the streets of the Marxists. The well-prepared attackers, however, erected barricades to disrupt both the marching Nazis and the police. In some sections of Altona, the ensuing firefight lasted about an hour. The editors also pointed to the fact that wounded Marxists were ushered to safety by waiting motor vehicles, which further strengthened their thesis of a well-planned attack. The SA proceeded with their march even in the face of cross fire and chaos. Not only that, but after they returned to the safety of Ottensen, they also held a propaganda rally with speakers who decried the communist violence and called for the election of Hitler to return to stable social conditions.[126]

An eyewitness account printed in the *Hamburger Nachrichten* supports this version of the story. According to the witnesses, the communists started shooting the peaceful marchers of the SA as well as the assembled Nazi sympathizers along the route from well-hidden positions. Two of the Brown Shirts, SA men Koch and Büttig, and ten others received mortal wounds. The communists even fired a machine gun from a rooftop window at the marchers and bystanders.[127] The edition of the *Hamburger Nachrichten* also included two photographs taken on the day of the confrontation. Under the headline "Victims of the Red Murderers," the photos showed one troop of Hamburg's Sturm 2/31, with two dead, as well as SA man Koch with his troop of Hamburg's Sturm 2/31.[128]

The bourgeois paper presented a story of red revolution and chaos navigated by the SA, who upheld conservative values like discipline, which validated National Socialist myths about themselves. The *Hamburger Nachrichten,* nevertheless, went further and echoed the Nazi myth of death and resurrection for the movement. According to the editors, "There is nothing that can weaken national socialist strength." Their dead "are not extinguished from the columns of fighters for nationalism, since their spirit lives on in the ones who fill their gap in the ranks. From the blood of the fallen grow ever new fighters for Hitler's idea."[129] Even though the Nazis provoked the violence with a march of eleven thousand Stormtroopers through the proletarian district, in all probability they did not fire first in the immediate presence of the police. The actual shoot-out occurred between organized Marxists and the police. Because of that, the SA continued marching—or running—into the safety of a neighboring bourgeois neighborhood. The *Hamburger Nachrichten* picked the Nazis as their champions and repeated their myths. The SA tactic of provoking violence and then acting like they were attacked had worked out quite well again.

Throughout 1932 the party kept Böckenhauer and his growing SA busy with constant propaganda and security activity for their respective districts of the city. He shuffled his men back and forth according to the needs of the party. For instance, on January 2, 1932, the SA was ordered by the Nazi Party to send an entire storm to protect a group distributing flyers at the gates of the communist-dominated docks and the harbor.[130] On Saturday, April 9, fifty of Hamburg's SA men protected a propaganda event in the inner city.[131] Since the party had come by a quantity of flyers, the party needed more SA to make sure that all available flyers were handed out. Ultimately, the party requested 50 more men from Böckenhauer.[132] On July 22, the party asked for the protection of 100 men in two separate shifts, one in the morning and one at night, for an entire week.[133] On October 5, the party apologized for the late request for men. They assured Böckenhauer that they would also avoid problems with the food supply for the men in the future. Immediately following their apology, they asked for another 150 SA men to protect yet another flyer-distribution event.[134] The daily report for the Hamburg SA for February 1932 shows that the heightened activity did not cease but only intensified the following year. From February 26 to March 3, the SA did not protect but rather marched in large numbers during six different days in six different districts throughout Hamburg.[135]

Böckenhauer was not only a talented organizer but also an enthusiastic follower of new techniques regarding Nazi propaganda. He fervently embraced the new medium of film to bring images of his SA to interested audiences. On October 9, 1932, Hamburg's entire SA came together for a rally. Böckenhauer not only invited the general inspector of the SA to show off his troopers but also hired a cameraman working for the private film company of Friedrich Bruhn. The cameraman filmed the entire gathering in order to make a movie about the rally. On October 26, 1932, after enough time had lapsed to allow the Bruhn Company to develop the film and show the uncut material to Böckenhauer, the SA leader sent exhaustive instructions as to how the movie was to be edited. He sent a seven-page letter in which he prearranged the entire film, complete with cutting instructions, title, and captioning. Böckenhauer left nothing to chance and allowed no room for artistic freedom among the professionals. The SA was to be shown only in the way that he envisioned it. Böckenhauer wanted the results quickly as well, leaving production staff only two days to have the film ready for another prerelease viewing.

Böckenhauer dictated that no running messengers, no horses, and no images of officers and SA musicians wearing coats over their Brown Shirts were to be shown. Everything needed to look disciplined, and everybody needed to appear uniform. Only tight ranks, not men in the process of forming ranks, could remain in the final cut.[136] The end result was a propaganda film that suggested power in numbers, discipline, and SA uniformity. This film was shown to some audiences who had never seen an SA rally. The SA earned revenue through the sale of tickets, and, most important, the rally was shown repeatedly, even if the SA uniform was forbidden in Hamburg at the time of the viewing. If the SA could not march, they could always show a film containing a highly idealized picture of themselves and even make money while gaining exposure in the process.

The film showed citizens an idealized image. To enhance the image of live marchers, Böckenhauer went beyond the forming of SA bands and also rented bands. He even referred other northern German SA leaders to an especially friendly professional band from his city. During a train ride back north after an SA meeting, Böckenhauer talked to the leader of Hanover's SA. Because they changed the subject, Böckenhauer could not give enough information and decided to send a follow-up letter to Hanover. Böckenhauer had learned that marching music was important and thus advised the fellow SA officer, "It was my intention to give you a few hints regarding the *Kapelle Boss*." This brass band "plays well and is especially suitable to play military marches. In addition, his musicians are young and therefore able to march." Böckenhauer then went on to tell the Hanover SA that the neighboring SA in Schleswig-Holstein always rented the same band. This band had a bus and rode from village to village, only actually marching in the communities. In this way, the band never tired and always sounded good.[137] Böckenhauer had learned to adopt from others what worked and was quick to give others advice regarding successful strategies.

The SA in Hamburg applied these strategies masterfully during election campaigns. On April 24, 1932, the Nazis won fifty-one seats in the city council and thus for the first time two seats more than the Social Democrats.[138] In the subsequent national elections, the last free national elections during the Weimar period on November 6, 1932, the Nazis garnered 33.1 percent of all votes. These results prompted conservative elites to persuade President Hindenburg to appoint Hitler as the new chancellor on January 30, 1933.[139] The editors of the *Hamburger Nachrichten* rejoiced, arguing that Hitler would bring a nationalist-conservative German government that would erase all mistakes, weakness, and chaos of the Weimar era. Hamburg's bourgeois elites anticipated Hitler uniting all conservative elements of German society and welcomed a conservative coalition government under Hitler as chancellor. The editors argued that they had demanded such a government for months. Now that this demand had become a reality, the path for a stronger Germany was paved.[140]

According to Hamburg's Nazis and their SA leader, Böckenhauer, this path to a stronger Germany led straight through the red district of Altona. Even before the German fascists were able to fully consolidate power and eliminate democracy altogether, they demonstrated their strength. On Sunday, February 26, 1933, Böckenhauer ordered his men to march through Altona again. This time the police arrested communist leaders beforehand. Marxist resistance was effectively crushed before the SA started marching. This time there was only sporadic shooting, and there were no SA martyrs. The SA celebrated their anticipated total victory not only by marching through Altona but also by holding a concert there and decorating parts of the district with swastika flags. For the communists of Hamburg, the Nazi takeover of their strongest district had begun.

The bourgeois editors of the *Hamburger Nachrichten* rejoiced at this prospect of final Marxist defeat and gleefully reported on the SA marches through Hamburg and Altona.[141] The paper also reported on several police raids that uncovered a communist plot. According to this article, the Nazi marches of 10,000 men in Hamburg and at least the same number of men in Altona resulted only in 10 to 15 wounded, because the police arrested hundreds of organized communists on the morning of the marches. The police foiled the planning of terror attacks on the SA marchers when they closed a secret meeting of about 150 communists in the communist inn Holsteinischer Hof in the early morning hours of the march (February 26). The police confiscated papers and flyers. They also raided other communist bars and kept known leaders locked up for most of that Sunday. The relatively low number of attacks including firearms resulted in fewer wounded and no dead, when compared to earlier incidents, and represented only a small fraction of what the communists had originally planned as a counterattack.[142]

The *Hamburger Nachrichten*'s reporting on the march in Hamburg, led by Böckenhauer himself, showed that in the city proper no extra security measures were necessary. Many thousands of sympathetic onlookers cheered the 10,000 Nazis who assembled at the snow-covered Moorweide field with flags and marching bands. At nine thirty in the morning, Böckenhauer himself gave final instructions to his officers, and the Nazis marched off at twenty minutes to ten. The column made up of four standards and three police units escorting the marchers then paraded through the city for three and a half hours. Every step of the way, bystanders cheered them on. The bourgeois editors noted that the column's discipline did not allow hecklers to disturb the slow and resolute march. According to the conservative press, the marching bands, the singing of patriotic songs, the sounds of drums and pipes, and the sight of fluttering flags made a deep impression on the citizens who observed the spectacle. After the end of this orderly march, parts of Hamburg's SA went to reinforce the SA marchers in Altona.[143]

This additional security measure was, in hindsight, not necessary. As the editors of the *Hamburger Nachrichten* reported, the concert of Altona's police band and the SA march through the red district remained undisturbed. Although unthinkable only a few weeks prior, the band's pavilion was decorated with swastika flags, and an SA band lined up next to the performing policemen. Thousands of bystanders applauded the joint impromptu concert. During the performance, SA troopers who had marched through Hamburg earlier arrived by train and truck. Nazi motorists circled the playing bands and onlookers, attracting the attention of the audience. Indicating their preparedness and showing their allegiances, a police escort wearing steel helmets and a large swastika flag led the Nazi marchers. The column started on their way through Altona at two in the afternoon and marched all the way to the district of Ottensen and then returned. After the march, one of Hamburg's Nazi Party leaders, Emil Heinrich Brix, reminded the assembled audience of Altona's bloody Sunday and proclaimed that the two fallen SA men had marched in spirit with them. Their comrades had left their spaces open when in their formed ranks. Ultimately, Brix also noted that many policemen, who were now able to openly show their Nazi allegiances, had volunteered to accompany the SA marchers, and the SA men welcomed them into the ranks of the National Socialists. The *Hamburger Nachrichten* illustrated their dedication to conservative unity by adding that the men of the Stahlhelm, albeit separate from the SA, also marched through Altona. Together, the Stahlhelm, the SA, and the police dominated the proletarians in their own neighborhood.[144]

The editors of the *Hamburger Volkszeitung* reported on the SA marches in a defiant front-page article that contradicted the version of events as portrayed by the conservatives. The Monday, February 27, 1933, edition was the first new edition in two weeks. The paper came back after a brief ban aimed to keep communist organizing efforts at a minimum prior to the elections. The headline announced that the communists were there to stay. Four weeks into a Nazi-led coalition government had shown the proletariat that only the communists could save them, they claimed.[145] Another front-page article titled "SA March through Occupied Territory" reported on the SA march through Hamburg. The communist paper claimed that the Nazi march remained mostly undisturbed because the route led primarily through bourgeois quarters of the city. The workers lining the streets of Weidenstrasse and Barmbeckerstrasse, nevertheless, voiced their discontent through jeering. When the marching columns reached Altona, they faced icy rejection from the assembled workers in this take on events. The police actions in Altona, therefore, resembled the actions of occupiers in enemy territory. The Altona policemen giving the concert even wore swastika armbands on their police uniforms. Yet only a few Nazi sympathizers were there, they claimed, to listen. The arrival of Hamburg's SA to reinforce the occupiers' march through Altona showed blind obedience and militarism. While the SA marched, the police, using trucks and armored cars and armed with machine guns and hand grenades, applied brute force. They dominated Altona, broke into communist offices, and confiscated propaganda material. Mounted police and police foot patrols swept the streets of red flags before the SA marchers came through. Ultimately, the editors argued, only a very strong police force allowed the SA to march through Altona. The citizens of the district neither cheered nor watched the spectacle.[146] Hence, the *Hamburger Volkszeitung* printed a story radically different from the one found in the *Hamburger Nachrichten*. To the communists, only the use of force by government authorities—sporting Nazi flags, no less—enabled this to occur. The article's tone was defiant, yet this defiance was to no avail. Shortly thereafter, the new Nazi authorities of the city shut down the paper for the remainder of the Nazi period.

As this example demonstrates, the communist press expressed their shock at the turn of events through the denial of Nazi strength. They likened Altona to territory that had been invaded by an enemy. Bourgeois reporting showed that trouble was anticipated, large police escorts protected the Brown Shirts, and the police acted aggressively even before the Marxists had a chance to assemble for the defense of their own district. In fact, some people, including two SA men, received injuries during violent clashes that day.[147] Still, the bourgeois press's reporting also showed relief that their champions marched in Altona by forcing organized Marxist resistance to their knees. This time it happened with the full power of the state represented by the police. Yet the Nazis did not dominate the entire city, or the Weimar state, quite yet.

Since January 30, 1933, the Nazis held important positions in the coalition government. Yet they did not want to share power or function within the confines of parliamentary democracy. Ultimately, it took the fascists only a few months to dismantle democracy and the Weimar Republic after these critical developments. SA terror, especially, forced the election result of 43.9 percent on March 5, 1933, solidifying Hitler's hold on power.[148] Hamburg's citizens lost the ability to vote in free elections until after the end of the Nazi dictatorship.

CONCLUSION

After the Nazis came to power, Hamburg's fascists immediately started to rewrite their own history. In an article published on Hitler's birthday on April 20, 1933, in the *Hamburger Nachrichten,* the editors claimed that after Hitler's aborted coup d'état on November 9, 1923, the Hamburg SA kept business going as usual.[149] They acted as if the few SA in Hamburg, without uniforms or organizational structures, kept active while underground. However, the handful of Nazis in the predominantly red city had no such presence in 1923. Hamburg's Nazis had no chance without the initial protection of the SA. Only much later did the SA represent the movement in the streets.

As this chapter has shown, the real beginnings of the Hamburg SA were much humbler. Before 1926 the SA was barely visible and only one among many right-wing political organizations. This changed with the introduction of the Brown Shirt in 1926. This is when Conn, for instance, first saw the uniformed SA that made such an impact on him that he decided to leave the Wehrwolf and join the Nazi Stormtroopers.[150] This also worked for other young Nazi sympathizers. The SA in Hamburg, for example, used expensive SA uniforms as raffle prizes to draw young men into Nazi meetings by 1927. For instance, Hamburg's Sturm 2 invited young men by flyer to join their SA evening on April 30, 1927. The flyer invited all party members, SA men, and their friends to listen to music and a speech and, in addition, to drink beer and take part in a raffle. For the price of a ticket, a young man could win a complete uniform with all the extras.[151]

The SA made an impact in the city at large after 1929. This occurred only after the introduction of the brown uniform that made the men of the SA stand out from other Weimar paramilitaries. By 1933 the SA saturated the city during large propaganda marches. After the SA became a visible part of city life, it served as a constant source of political friction with the Left. Yet despite and indeed because of this friction, the SA carried Hitler to power. Anthony McElligott argues that, during the final years of the republic, Hamburg's elites voted for the Nazis because of their fear of communism and their attraction to the Nazi image specifically based on their Brown Shirts. He suggests that the young, unemployed communists "appeared in the public imagination as uncouth, undisciplined, workless lay-abouts." In contrast, "The SA members most usually appeared in uniform, in small, disciplined groups. . . . [T]hey presented a picture akin to positive, military order."[152] Bourgeois elites favored the Stormtroopers because of their militarized and forceful image. They acted aggressively against the Left and courted the conservative elites. Hamburg's SA officers carefully constructed this duality.

As the evidence presented in this chapter shows, the uniform served as a crucial device in this endeavor. It triggered clash violence against opponents. The uniform aided in setting traps for opposing street fighters, as the case of SA man Lühr showed. This case also demonstrated that bourgeois elites reinterpreted these incidents as heroic endeavors. Conn claimed to have acted only in self-defense. The conservative judges of the city sided with Conn and Lühr.[153] The tactic worked, and the uniform functioned perfectly in this manner. Additionally, during incidents of violence, the uniform may have hidden protective skullcaps.[154] The SA troopers could consequently act even more self-assured and aggressive with this added protection. The uniform thus contributed further to the heroic image that the SA cultivated.

That this drew in other Nazi sympathizers is best illustrated through Alfred Conn. As discussed above, he was impressed when he saw SA troopers march through a proletarian neighborhood and switched his allegiance from the Wehrwolf to the SA.[155]

The uniform also served a second function intended for a different audience. The marching columns of the SA looked aesthetically pleasing to conservative and bourgeois audiences longing for order. Conn, for instance, ensured that the uniforms of his men were always clean and ironed. He established a laundry service and made sure that his men, through communal living arrangements in SA homes, had enough money for these services. The men drilled in marching and in military greetings to make their movements resemble a legitimate and disciplined propaganda army.[156] The uniform also functioned as a tool for social control. The men liked to wear the uniform. SA man Stein, for instance, was not allowed to wear his uniform for two months as punishment for breaches of discipline. His commanding officer, Ellerhusen, successfully used the right to wear the uniform as a tool to control his men.[157]

Bourgeois elites in Hamburg also valued unity among themselves. The diary of Luise Solmitz, for instance, shows this clearly. Solmitz wished for a volkish, classless community that she thought she had found among the Nazis.[158] Particularly, large numbers of uniformed SA made the desired impression on her. Conn's logistical talent allowed for the massing of SA in the city to create this effect. This was due in part to his work establishing group homes with limited financial resources. This in turn allowed for larger concentrations of SA in safe locations. It was the mastering of logistics and travel as well as constant borrowing from other SA units, however, that allowed the Stormtroopers to amass truly impressive numbers. Conn, for instance, routinely traveled with his men to support other troops in nearby towns and beach resorts.[159] This also made the desired impact among bourgeois audiences. The large SA march on February 6, 1933, specifically, left Solmitz with the positive impression of unified masses she recorded in her diary. The uniform veiled differences among the Nazis and made them appear as a monolithic bloc. Therefore, the SA exemplified the right-wing unity she, and others, desired.[160] Solmitz did not represent all conservative citizens, yet as this chapter confirms, the *Hamburger Nachrichten,* Hamburg's conservative newspaper, had expressed sympathetic views for years when reporting on the Nazis.[161]

The SA in Hamburg courted conservative elites without violence and in smaller and more intimate settings as well. Conn's SA band entertained these audiences. Hosting concerts, plays performed by SA men, and the organization of afternoon dances also belonged to the duties of Hamburg's Stormtroopers. As Conn recalled, this light entertainment aimed at conservative audiences became very popular. Some businessmen of the city attended these dances regularly and even donated money for the fascist cause.[162] The Brown Shirts in Hamburg lived a duality. They were simultaneously brutal fighters against the Left and polite hosts to the right-wing citizens. This duality helps to explain why Hamburg's elites sided with the Nazis.

Conclusion

WEIMAR CULTURE AND THE END OF WEIMAR DEMOCRACY

This book has provided cultural historical evidence to support the argument that the SA constructed a positive dual image, reconciling the dichotomy between violence and discipline. The image-construction process rested heavily on the uniform. It served two important functions. First, the brown uniforms had a signal function that triggered violence. During clash violence, the uniform made the men look intimidating and provided hidden protection. Second, the uniform manipulated the male body in positive ways. It made the men look fit, tall, neat, and disciplined to potential supporters. Additionally, it provided uniformity and thus the illusion of a monolithic fascist bloc, suggesting strength in numbers. Both functions of the uniform helped to establish a positive SA image among bourgeois elites and within conservative circles. This image reflected the myth that the SA acted as militant defenders of order and discipline, while their opponents represented either public disorder and criminality or just weakness in the face of chaos.

A cultural history of the SA uniform thus contributes to our current understanding of the Nazi seizure of power. This contribution is framed by three points. First, a cultural history of the Brown Shirt, and thus an approach based on affective male gender construction, reveals a connection between fashion and politics. The uniform developed from the bottom up. It originated in a specific SA troop brought into the Nazi fold from the defense leagues and developed into the main uniform of the SA and eventually the entire Nazi movement during the Weimar era. The uniform of the SA, the organization that publicly symbolized the Nazi movement, overlapped with general cultural preferences. The Nazis looked youthful, clean, and disciplined in a republic that they themselves decried as decrepit, weak, and failed.

Second, the bottom-up approach to establish a party uniform undertaken by the SA leadership highlights inroads for individual agency. The officers who introduced the original Brown Shirt and the men who purchased the name-brand Brown products acted voluntarily in efforts to lend the SA an attractive image. No one handed out Brown Shirts for free. Therefore, the Nazis established a positive image partially through approaches based on Stormtrooper consumption and consumerism and thus from the bottom up, rather than from the top down.

Third, these two factors add to a nuanced understanding of rising Nazi popularity during the final years of the Weimar Republic. Admittedly, the Great Depression was an important factor that Hitler exploited for his purposes. Leading up to Hitler's final elections in March 1933, the Nazis created a climate of constant aggression and latent civil war against their political opponents. These elections took place after the elimination of civil rights and the deputization of the SA as police. The SA actively attacked, murdered, and arrested leading communist and socialist leaders in the run-up to the final round of elections. At the same time, coordinated SA marches in the streets offered a message designed to threaten potential voters while also convincing the middle class that a civil war loomed. Nazi violence drew in bourgeois and conservative elements of society because they feared Marxists of all orientations, implicitly justifying Nazi violence.

Nevertheless, that is only half of the story. There was an additional factor drawing in support that reflected the second half of the SA's dual character. This half's importance is demonstrated by the fact that the Nazis did not develop in a vacuum. Hitler established the NSDAP as one of the largest mass movements in the splintered political world of the Weimar Republic. The elections leading up to March 1933 brought Hitler into a position of power, a power that conservative elites tried to harness, yet Hitler never let go of until his death. The fact that Hitler was able to create a mass movement between the years 1921 and 1933 shows that many Germans did not need to be scared into submission. They voted in ever-growing numbers for the Nazis rather than the other conservative nationalist parties. In order to fully understand how the Nazis became a popular mass movement, one must also consider the successful Nazi efforts to establish a positive image. This image rested in the duality of the SA and was deeply rooted in the political culture of the Weimar Republic.

Weimar culture was never perfect; rather, it was deeply flawed. Key aspects of the political culture of the republic originated in the German Empire and were adopted and modified first by the elites of the Weimar government and then by the leaders of the Nazi state. During the Weimar years, this political culture was already permeated with militarist ideals that influenced the politics of all political parties. Hitler did not invent political spectacle. He just gave it an antidemocratic and fascist spin. He ultimately also enlarged its dimension using the resources of the German state during the years of the Nazi dictatorship. Before the Nazis could commandeer these vast government resources, however, they perfected their own image between 1920 and 1933. The Nazis, then, originated and developed *within* Weimar political culture. They did not stand outside of Weimar society. Rather, they were an integral part of it. The cultural history of Hitler's Brown Shirt thus expands our understanding of Weimar culture. This culture was vibrant and forward looking at times, yet also marked by antidemocratic tendencies that paved Hitler's way to power.

Hitler and his Nazis came to power in the first half of the twentieth century. In the first half of the twenty-first century, neo-Nazis in Germany not only have emerged but are changing their image. Sturdy, trendy sports and outdoor clothing belongs to this new Nazi look. Companies like Thor Steinar produce cutting-edge, fashion-forward outdoor clothing that an ideological outsider would never recognize as having a fascist underpinning. The neo-Nazi looks fashionable in today's context, yet those who subscribe to this ideology still follow the old xenophobic and aggressive fascist theories. They, like their predecessors, attract young people with this attractive image. After they make initial contact with the help of a chic new look, right-wing parties deliver their xenophobic message.[1] Today's neo-Nazis do what the original Nazis did in 1926. They introduced a reworked and positive image based on fashionable, clean-cut, and sporty clothing.

This investigation into the origin and use of the Nazi uniform thus bears insights that are valuable in the present. It is important to remember that democracy is not always stable. It is based on mutual respect, dialogue, and compromise. Accordingly, it sometimes appears messy or chaotic. During prolonged periods of crisis caused by political, social, or economic unrest, democratic institutions are at their weakest. It is during these times that voters look for simple solutions offered by radical, charismatic voices at both ends of the political spectrum. At its worst, this can cause a political polarization. In this kind of situation, fascists appeal to the emotions of voters. They play on fears among the voting public of chaos and present themselves as stable, the force of order. If they do that successfully, as the Nazis did, they are able to dismantle democracy from the inside once in power. A shift in focus from logic to emotions sets such developments in motion. The key to understanding this critical shift is a thorough recognition of how fascists use culture, including material culture, to achieve their political ends.

NOTES

INTRODUCTION: HITLER AND HIS STORMTROOPERS

1. Chris McNab, *Hitler's Master Plan, 1933–1945: The Essential Facts and Figures for Hitler's Germany* (London: Amber Books, 2011), 142.
2. Peter Longerich, *Die Braunen Bataillone: Geschichte der SA* (Munich: Verlag C. H. Beck, 1989), 96, 121.
3. Andrew Wackerfuss, *Stormtrooper Families: Homosexuality and Community in the Early Nazi Movement* (New York: Harrington Park Press, 2015), 57.
4. Longerich, *Die Braunen Bataillone,* 97, 100.
5. Thomas Balistier, *Gewalt und Ordnung: Kalkül und Faszination der SA* (Münster: Verlag Westfälisches Dampfboot, 1989), 65. On this critique of Balistier, see Michael Walter, review of *Gewalt und Ordnung: Kalkül und Faszination der SA,* by Thomas Balistier, *Medienwissenschaft: Rezensionen* 7, no. 3 (1990).
6. Daniel Siemens, *Stormtroopers: A New History of Hitler's Brownshirts* (New Haven, CT: Yale University Press, 2017).
7. Wackerfuss, *Stormtrooper Families.*
8. Irene Guenther, *Nazi Chic? Fashioning Women in the Third Reich* (New York: Berg, 2004).
9. See Hartmut Berghoff and Thomas Kühne, eds., *Globalizing Beauty: Consumerism and Body Aesthetics in the Twentieth Century* (New York: Palgrave Macmillan, 2013), particularly the chapters by Ulrike Thoms, "Consuming Bodies: The Commodification and Technification of Slenderness in the Twentieth Century," 42–43; Hartmut Berghoff and Thomas Kühne, "'It Makes Princes of Those Who Have It': Beauty and Consumerism in the Twentieth Century," 3; and Michael R. Müller and Anne Sonnenmoser, "Medial Beauty: Three Sociological Lenses on Late Modern Body Aesthetic," 66–68.
10. Kathleen Canning, "The Politics of Symbols, Semantics, and Sentiments in the Weimar Republic," *Central European History* 43, no. 4 (2010): 579; Julia Sneeringer, "The Shopper as Voter: Women, Advertising, and Politics in Post-inflation Germany," *German Studies Review* 27, no. 3 (2004): 486.
11. On modern consumer culture and its relation to liberal democracy, see Molly Loberg, *The Struggle for the Streets of Berlin: Politics, Consumption, and Urban Space, 1914–1945* (Cambridge: Cambridge University Press, 2018), 7. On communism and consumerism, see Sneeringer, "Shopper as Voter," 490–91. On Nazism and consumerism, see Loberg, *Struggle for the Streets of Berlin,* 205; and Siemens, *Stormtroopers,* 97–102.
12. Barbara Caine and Glenda Sluga, *Gendering European History* (New York: Leicester University Press, 2000).
13. Jennifer Craik, *Uniforms Exposed: From Conformity to Transgression* (New York: Berg, 2005), 29.
14. Nathan Joseph, *Uniforms and Nonuniforms: Communication through Clothing* (New York: Greenwood Press, 1986), 65–84.
15. Joan Nunn, *Fashion in Costume, 1200–2000* (Chicago: New Amsterdam Books, 2000).
16. Jennifer Craik, "Uniforms and Men's Fashion: Tailoring Masculinity to Fit," in *Men's Fashion Reader,* edited by Andrew Reilly and Sarah Cosby (New York: Fairchild Books, 2008), 429–44.

17. Jochen Hung, "'Bad' Politics and 'Good' Culture: New Approaches to the History of the Weimar Republic," *Central European History* 49 (2016): 441–53.
18. Anthony McElligott, *Rethinking the Weimar Republic: Authority and Authoritarianism, 1916–1936* (London: Bloomsbury Press, 2014), 16, 209, 155, 5.
19. Nadine Rossol, *Performing the Nation in Interwar Germany: Sport, Spectacle and Political Symbolism, 1926–36* (London: Palgrave Macmillan, 2010), 3.
20. Hung, "'Bad' Politics and 'Good' Culture," 453.
21. Dirk Schumann, *Political Violence in the Weimar Republic, 1918–1933: Fight for the Streets and Fear of Civil War* (New York: Berghahn Books, 2009), 87, 187; Eve Rosenhaft, *Beating the Fascists? The German Communists and Political Violence, 1929–1933* (Cambridge: Cambridge University Press, 1983), 2–3.
22. Pamela Swett, *Neighbors and Enemies: The Culture of Radicalism in Berlin, 1929–1933* (Cambridge: Cambridge University Press, 2004), 234.
23. Gerhard Botz coined the term in *Gewalt in der Politik: Attentate, Zusammenstösse, Putschversuche, Unruhen in Östereich, 1918 bis 1934* (Munich: Wilhelm Fink Verlag, 1976).
24. Rosenhaft, *Beating the Fascists?*, 3.
25. Peter Longerich, *Die Geschichte der SA* (Munich: C. H. Beck, 2003), 65.
26. James M. Diehl, *Paramilitary Politics in Weimar Germany* (Bloomington: Indiana University Press, 1977), 111; Schuman, *Political Violence in the Weimar Republic*, 310.
27. Peter Merkel, *The Making of a Stormtrooper* (Princeton, NJ: Princeton University Press, 1980), 100; Longerich, *Die Geschichte der SA*, 65.
28. Diehl, *Paramilitary Politics in Weimar Germany*, 176.
29. Schuman, *Political Violence in the Weimar Republic*, 309.
30. Longerich, *Die Geschichte der SA*, 275; Schuman, *Political Violence in the Weimar Republic*, 310.
31. Rosenhaft, *Beating the Fascists?*, 8.
32. Longerich, *Die Geschichte der SA*, 60.
33. Rosenhaft, *Beating the Fascists?*, 208; Schuman, *Political Violence in the Weimar Republic*, 309, 311.
34. Petra Maria Schulz, *Ästhetisierung von Gewalt in der Weimarer Republik* (Münster: Westfälishes Dampfboot, 2004), 12; Diehl, *Paramilitary Politics in Weimar Germany*, 153; Longerich, *Die Geschichte der SA*, 275–77.
35. Werner Jochmann, *Nationalsozialismus und Revolution: Ursprung und Geschichte der NSDAP in Hamburg, 1922–1933, Dokumente* (Frankfurt am Main: Europaische Verlagsanstalt, 1963).

CHAPTER ONE: THE MILITARIZATION OF POLITICAL CULTURE IN WEIMAR GERMANY, 1918–1933

1. Detlef Peukert, *The Weimar Republic: The Crisis of Classical Modernity* (New York: Hill and Wang, 1987), 16.
2. Ibid., 16–18.
3. Michael Wildt, *Generation des Unbedingten: Das Fuehrungskorps des Reichssicherheitshauptamtes* (Hamburg: Hamburger Edition, 2003), 45.
4. Eve Rosenhaft, *Beating the Fascists? The German Communists and Political Violence, 1929–1933* (Cambridge: Cambridge University Press, 1983), 3.
5. Dirk Schumann, *Political Violence in the Weimar Republic, 1918–1933* (New York: Berghahn Books, 2009), 97; Larry Eugene Jones, "The German Right in the Weimar Republic: New Directions, New Insights, New Challenges," in *The German Right in the Weimar Republic: Studies*

in the History of German Conservatism, Nationalism, and Antisemitism, edited by Larry Eugene Jones (New York: Berghahn Books, 2014), 9.

6. Rosenhaft, *Beating the Fascists?,* 3; Schumann, *Political Violence in the Weimar Republic,* 187; Nadine Rossol, *Performing the Nation in Interwar Germany: Sports, Spectacle and Political Symbolism, 1926–1936* (New York: Palgrave Macmillan, 2010), 18; Kathleen Canning, "The Politics of Symbols, Semantics, and Sentiments in the Weimar Republic," *Central European History* 43, no. 4 (2010): 579; Jennifer Craik, "Uniforms and Men's Fashion: Tailoring Masculinity to Fit," in *Men's Fashion Reader,* edited by Andrew Reilly and Sarah Cosby (New York: Fairchild Books, 2008), 429–44.
7. Photograph of SA in generic uniforms and in SA uniforms, July 1926, Ca 331, NSDAP-50, Sturmabteilungen der NSDAP (SA), Bundesarchiv, Koblenz, Germany; photograph of Stahlhelm men in generic uniforms and in Stahlhelm uniforms, March 1931, Ca 332, STAHL, Der Stahlhelm Bund der Frontsoldaten e.V. (BdF), Bundesarchiv, Koblenz, Germany; photgraph of men of the Roter Frontkämpferbund in generic uniforms and in Roter Frontkämpferbund uniforms, January 1927, Ca 350, Demonstrationen, Bundesarchiv, Koblenz, Germany.
8. Jane Tynan, "Military Dress and Men's Outdoor Leisurewear: Burberry's Trench Coat in First World War Britain," *Journal of Design History* 24, no. 2 (2011): 140, 144, 139.
9. Ibid., 146.
10. Windbreaker, Deutsches Historisches Museum, Weimar Uniformen Sammlung, Archiv des Deutschen Historischen Museums, Berlin.
11. Tynan, "Military Dress and Men's Outdoor Leisurewear," 144.
12. Joan Nunn, *Fashion in Costume, 1200–2000* (Chicago: New Amsterdam Books, 2000), 142, 180.
13. See, for instance, illustrations for men's outdoor and work wear in the American Bellas Hess & Co. spring and summer 1925 catalog as well as the Charles William Stores, Inc., spring and summer 1927 catalog. See also breeches and boots in Tina Skinner and Lindy McCord, *Flapper Era Fashion from the Roaring '20s* (Atglen, PA: Schiffer, 2004), 115.
14. Nunn, *Fashion in Costume,* 180.
15. Chris McNab, *Military Uniforms: Visual Encyclopedia* (London: Amber Books, 2011), 438; Tynan, "Military Dress and Men's Outdoor Leisurewear," 142; Boris Mollo, *The Indian Army* (Aylesbury: Blandford Press, 1981), 158.
16. Samuel T. Williamson, "Sam Browne—His Belt," *New York Times,* November 9, 1941.
17. Daniel Guerin, *The Brown Plague: Travels in Weimar and Early Nazi Germany* (Durham, NC: Duke University Press, 1996), 53, 99.
18. Volker R. Berghahn, *Der Stahlhelm Bund der Frontsoldaten, 1918–1935* (Düsseldorf: Droste Verlag, 1966), 14, 19; James M. Diehl, *Paramilitary Politics in Weimar Germany* (Bloomington: Indiana University Press, 1977), 96–97; Berghahn, *Der Stahlhelm Bund der Frontsoldaten,* 286.
19. Stahlhelm cap, Deutsches Historisches Museum, Weimar Uniformen Sammlung, Archiv des Deutschen Historischen Museums, Berlin.
20. Daniel Siemens, *Stormtroopers: A New History of Hitler's Brownshirts* (New Haven, CT: Yale University Press, 2017), 43; Eric Weitz, *Weimar Germany* (Princeton, NJ: Princeton University Press, 2007), 114–15.
21. Stahlhelm jacket, Deutsches Historisches Museum, Weimar Uniformen Sammlung, Archiv des Deutschen Historischen Museums, Berlin.
22. Floyd R. Tubbs and Robert W. Clawson, *Stahlhelm: Evolution of the German Steel Helmet,* rev. ed. (1971; reprint, Kent, OH: Kent State University Press, 2000), 10–11, 21.

23. Ibid., 7.
24. Stahlhelm cap, Deutsches Historisches Museum, Weimar Uniformen Sammlung, Archiv des Deutschen Historischen Museums, Berlin; Stahlhelm belt buckle, ibid.
25. Berghahn, *Der Stahlhelm Bund der Frontsoldaten,* 27; Mathias Sprenger, *Landsknechte auf dem Weg ins Dritte Reich?* (Munich: Ferdinand Schöningh), 209–12.
26. Tynan, "Military Dress and Men's Outdoor Leisurewear," 144.
27. Stahlhelm jacket, Deutsches Historisches Museum, Weimar Uniformen Sammlung, Archiv des Deutschen Historischen Museums, Berlin; Windbreaker, ibid.
28. Tynan, "Military Dress and Men's Outdoor Leisurewear," 144; Siemens, *Stormtroopers,* 43.
29. Diehl, *Paramilitary Politics in Weimar Germany,* 176–77, 179.
30. Reichsbanner cap, Deutsches Historisches Museum, Weimar Uniformen Sammlung, Archiv des Deutschen Historischen Museums, Berlin.
31. Siemens, *Stormtroopers,* 43.
32. Photograph of Reichsbanner men in generic uniforms, May 1928, Ca 332 REICH, Reichsbanner Schwarz-Rot-Gold, Bundesarchiv, Koblenz, Germany.
33. Photograph of Reichsbanner men in generic uniforms, ibid.
34. Donna Harsch, *German Social Democracy and the Rise of Fascism* (Chapel Hill: University of North Carolina Press, 1993), 23–25.
35. Siemens, *Stormtroopers,* 43.
36. Reichsbanner belt buckle, Deutsches Historisches Museum, Weimar Uniformen Sammlung, Archiv des Deutschen Historischen Museums, Berlin.
37. Photograph of Reichsbanner men in generic uniforms, May 1928, Ca 332 REICH Reichsbanner Schwarz-Rot-Gold, Bundesarchiv, Koblenz, Germany.
38. Diehl, *Paramilitary Politics in Weimar Germany,* 178.
39. Carsten Voigt, *Kampfbünde der Arbeiterbewegung: Das Reichsbanner Schwarz-Rot-Gold und der Rote Frontkämpferbund in Sachsen, 1924–1933* (Cologne: Böhlau Verlag, 2009), 268, 166; Peukert, *Weimar Republic,* 16–18; Wildt, *Generation des Unbedingten,* 45.
40. Vernon L. Lidtke, *The Alternative Culture: Socialist Labor in Imperial Germany* (New York: Oxford University Press, 1985), 76–77; Rossol, *Performing the Nation in Interwar Germany,* 30–31, 18–25; Diehl, *Paramilitary Politics in Weimar Germany,* 131.
41. Diehl, *Paramilitary Politics in Weimar Germany,* 189, 184–85, 189; Pierre Aycoberry, *The Social History of the Third Reich, 1933–1945* (New York: New Press, 1998), 19.
42. Voigt, *Kampfbünde der Arbeiterbewegung,* 272.
43. Siemens, *Stormtroopers,* 43.
44. RFB cap, Deutsches Historisches Museum, Weimar Uniformen Sammlung, Archiv des Deutschen Historischen Museums, Berlin.
45. RFB shirt, ibid.
46. RFB belt buckle, ibid.
47. RFB cap, ibid.; RFB armband, Deutsches Historisches Museum, Weimar Uniformen Ausstellung, Berlin.
48. Rosenhaft, *Beating the Fascists?,* 30–33.
49. Diehl, *Paramilitary Politics in Weimar Germany,* 187.
50. Voigt, *Kampfbünde der Arbeiterbewegung,* 272; Peukert, *Weimar Republic,* 16–18; Wildt, *Generation des Unbedingten,* 45.
51. Voigt, *Kampfbünde der Arbeiterbewegung,* 272–73.

CHAPTER TWO: FROM A TROPICAL TUNIC TO THE BROWN SHIRT

1. Jürgen Herbst, *Requiem for a German Past: A Boyhood among the Nazis* (Madison: University of Wisconsin Press, 1999), 11.
2. Thomas Childers, *The Nazi Voter* (Chapel Hill: University of North Carolina Press, 1983), 43–45.
3. Bruce Campbell, *The SA Generals and the Rise of Nazism* (Lexington: University Press of Kentucky, 1998), 173.
4. Daniel Siemens, *Stormtroopers: A New History of Hitler's Brownshirts* (New Haven, CT: Yale University Press, 2017), 3.
5. Peter Longerich, *Die Braunen Bataillone: Geschichte der SA* (Munich: Verlag C. H. Beck, 1989), 22–24.
6. Siemens, *Stormtroopers,* 8–9.
7. Longerich, *Die Braunen Bataillone,* 24.
8. Michael Miller and Andreas Schulz, *Leaders of the Storm Troops* (Warwick: Helion, 2015), 1:27.
9. Longerich, *Die Braunen Bataillone,* 36; Siemens, *Stormtroopers,* 22.
10. Ian Kershaw, *Hitler, 1889–1936: Hubris* (New York: W. W. Norton, 1998), 167; Gerhard Rossbach, *Mein Weg Durch die Zeit: Erinnerungen und Bekenntnisse* (Weilburg-Lahn: Vereinigte Weilburger Buchdruckereien, 1950), 81.
11. Longerich, *Die Braunen Bataillone,* 43–44.
12. Herman Göring, "Verhalten der Kampfverbände am 1. Mai 1923," July 1923, Bestandssignatur NS 23, Archivnummer 509, Bundesarchiv, Berlin.
13. Photograph of Reichsbanner men in generic uniforms, May 1928, Ca 332, REICH, Reichsbanner Schwarz-Rot-Gold, Bundesarchiv, Koblenz, Germany.
14. Quoted in Siemens, *Stormtroopers,* 21.
15. Herman Göring, "Verhalten der Kampfverbände am 1. Mai 1923," July 1923, Bestandssignatur NS 23, Archivnummer 509, Bundesarchiv, Berlin.
16. Herman Göring, "Allgemeine Richtlinien bei Gründung einer S.A.," July 1923, Bestandssignatur NS 23, Archivnummer 509, Bundesarchiv, Berlin.
17. Chris McNab, *Military Uniforms: Visual Encyclopedia* (London: Amber Books, 2011), 66–67.
18. US War Department, *Technical Manual TM-E 30–451, Handbook on German Military Forces* (Washington, DC: US War Department, 1945), IX-3—IX-4.
19. Herman Göring, "Verhalten der Kampfverbände am 1. Mai 1923," July 1923, Bestandssignatur NS 23, Archivnummer 509, Bundesarchiv, Berlin.
20. Photograph of Reichsbanner men in generic uniforms, May 1928, Ca 332, REICH, Reichsbanner Schwarz-Rot-Gold, Bundesarchiv, Koblenz, Germany.
21. Herman Göring, "Verhalten der Kampfverbände am 1. Mai 1923," July 1923, Bestandssignatur NS 23, Archivnummer 509, Bundesarchiv, Berlin.
22. Adolf Hitler, *Mein Kampf* (New York: Houghton Mifflin, 1971), 494–97.
23. "Herrn. Lutze Elberfeld," August 11, 1925, Bestandssignatur NS 23, Archivnummer 509, Bundesarchiv, Berlin.
24. Ernst Röhm, *Die Geschichte eines Hochverräters* (Munich: Verlag Franz Her Nachfolger G.m.b.H., 1930), 291–92; Rossbach, *Mein Weg Durch die Zeit,* 81.
25. David Jablonsky, *The Nazi Party in Dissolution: Hitler and the Verbotzeit, 1923–1925* (London: Frank Cass, 1989), 90; Röhm, *Die Geschichte eines Hochverräters,* 292.
26. Rossbach, *Mein Weg Durch die Zeit,* 89.
27. John R. Angolia, *Cloth Insignia of the NSDAP and SA* (San Jose, CA: R. James Bender, 1985), 125.

28. Hew Strachan, *The First World War in Africa* (Oxford: Oxford University Press, 2004), 56; McNab, *Military Uniforms: Visual Encyclopedia*, 70.
29. Rossbach, *Mein Weg Durch die Zeit*, 89–90.
30. Ibid., 90.
31. Finanzgruppe Sparkassenverband Niedersachsen, Sparkassengeschichten, Otto Marxer: Die kurze "braune Ära" des Sparkassenverbandes, www.sparkassengeschichten.de/sparkassengeschichten/geschichten/otto-marxer.html.

32. Otto Marxer, "An die Oberste SA Führing," October 23, 1935, Bestandssignatur NS 23, Archivnummer 509, Bundesarchiv, Berlin.

33. Siemens, *Stormtroopers*, 20.
34. Richard Bessel, *Political Violence and the Rise of Nazism* (New Haven, CT: Yale University Press, 1984), 139–41.
35. Rossbach, *Mein Weg Durch die Zeit*, 137.
36. Ibid., 133, 87–88, 176.
37. Karl W. H. Koch, *Männer im Braunhemd: Vom Kampf und Sieg der SA* (Leipzig: Berlin Druck, 1936), 48.
38. "Geschichte der SA, Sonderdruck 4 der Zeitschrift *Die SA*," Munich, June 1941, Bestandssignatur NS 23, Archivnummer 509, Bundesarchiv, Berlin.
39. "SA Befehl 10, Dienstanzug," November 14, 1926, Bestandssignatur NS 23, Archivnummer 509, Bundesarchiv, Berlin.
40. Deutsches Historisches Museum, Lebendiges Museum Online, Bestand, Uniform für einen Scharführer der SA im Sturm 5 (Gruppe Berlin), www.dhm.de/lemo/bestand/objekt/uniform-der-sa-um-1930.html.
41. SA Brown Shirt, Deutsches Historisches Museum, Weimar Uniformen Sammlung, Archiv des Deutschen Historischen Museums, Berlin.
42. Susan B. Kaiser. *The Social Psychology of Clothing* (New York: Fairchild, 1997), 122, 124.
43. Kershaw, *Hitler*, 221.
44. "SA Befehl 1, Brief Adolf Hitlers an Haubtmann von Pfeffer," November 1, 1926, Bestandssignatur NS 23, Archivnummer 509, Bundesarchiv, Berlin.
45. Ibid.
46. "SA Befehl 3, SA und Öffentlichkeit (Propaganda)," November 3, 1926, Bestandssignatur NS 23, Archivnummer 509, Bundesarchiv, Berlin.
47. Nathan Joseph, *Uniforms and Nonuniforms: Communication through Clothing* (New York: Greenwood Press, 1986), 51.
48. Siemens, *Stormtroopers*, 33; Torsten Homberger and Linda Arthur Bradley, "Nazi Dress: Hitler's Storm Troopers and Appearance Management, 1921–1933," *Critical Studies in Men's Fashion* 2, no. 2 (2015): 188.
49. Viktor Lutze, "An die Leitung der N.S.D.A.P.," August 8, 1925, Bestandssignatur NS 23, Archivnummer 509, Bundesarchiv, Berlin.
50. "Herrn. Lutze Elberfeld," August 11, 1925, Bestandssignatur NS 23, Archivnummer 509, Bundesarchiv, Berlin.
51. "SA Befehl 10, Dienstanzug," November 14, 1926, Bestandssignatur NS 23, Archivnummer 509, Bundesarchiv, Berlin.
52. Ibid.
53. Peter Merkl, *The Making of a Stormtrooper* (Princeton, NJ: Princeton University Press, 1980), 3–25.
54. Photograph of Adolf Hitler in a Windbreaker during the 1926 party rally, July 3–4, 1926, Da-225–10 Reichsparteitag 1926, Bundesarchiv, Koblenz, Germany.
55. "SA Befehl 10, Dienstanzug," November 14, 1926, Bestandssignatur NS 23, Archivnummer 509, Bundesarchiv, Berlin.

56. Photograph of Adolf Hitler in a Brown Shirt during the 1927 party rally, August 19–21, 1927, Da-225–10 Reichsparteitag 1927, Bundesarchiv, Koblenz, Germany.
57. Deutsches Historisches Museum, Lebendiges Museum Online, Bestand, Bundestracht des BDM mit Gebietz-Armabzeichen "Südost Oberdonau," www.dhm.de/lemo/bestand/objekt/mi000988.
58. Ibid.
59. Photograph of SA marching in Braunschweig showing the three men leading the column wearing *Kletterwesten*, 1931, Ca 331 NSDAP-50 Sturmabteilungern der NSDAP (SA), Bundesarchiv, Koblenz, Germany.
60. "SA Befehl," August 22, 1927, Bestandssignatur NS 23, Archivnummer 1239, Bundesarchiv, Berlin.
61. "SA Befehl," August 25, 1927, Bestandssignatur NS 23, Archivnummer 1239, Bundesarchiv, Berlin.
62. Photograph of Adolf Hitler wearing an SA cap during the 1927 party rally, August 19–21, 1927, Da-225–10 Reichsparteitag 1927, Bundesarchiv, Koblenz, Germany.
63. Bessel, *Political Violence and the Rise of Nazism*, 75–92.
64. "SA Befehl, Kopfschutz," August 8, 1930, Bestandssignatur NS 26, Archivnummer 305, Bundesarchiv, Berlin.
65. Rossbach, *Mein Weg Durch die Zeit*, 89; Otto Marxer, "An die Oberste SA Führing," October 23, 1935, Bestandssignatur NS 23, Archivnummer 509, Bundesarchiv, Berlin.
66. "SA Befehl," March 25, 1929, Bestandssignatur NS 23, Archivnummer 514, Bundesarchiv, Berlin.
67. "Erlass Nr. 3," February 27, 1931, Bestandssignatur NS 23, Archivnummer 514, Bundesarchiv, Berlin.
68. "Verordnung," March 12, 1931, Bestandssignatur NS 23, Archivnummer 514, Bundesarchiv, Berlin.
69. "Verfügung," April 22, 1931, Bestandssignatur NS 23, Archivnummer 514, Bundesarchiv, Berlin.
70. Peter Fritzsche, *Germans into Nazis* (Cambridge, MA: Harvard University Press, 1998), 223.
71. Richard Hamilton, *Who Voted for Hitler?* (Princeton, NJ: Princeton University Press, 1982), 393; Childers, *The Nazi Voter*, 178; Jürgen Falter, *Hitler's Wähler* (Munich: Verlag C. H. Beck, 1991), 181.
72. Kaiser, *Social Psychology of Clothing*, 374.
73. Paul Fox, *The Image of the Soldier in German Culture, 1871–1933* (London: Bloomsbury Academic, 2018).
74. Luise Solmitz quoted in Werner Jochmann, *Nationalsozialismus und Revolution: Ursprung und Geschichte der NSDAP in Hamburg, 1922–1933, Dokumente* (Frankfurt: Europäische Verlagsgemeinschaft, 1963), 403; Despina Stratigakos, *Hitler at Home* (New Haven, CT: Yale University Press, 2015), 88.

CHAPTER THREE: THE BROWN GARMENT OF HONOR, MATERIAL CULTURE, AND SOCIAL CONTROL

1. Thomas Balistier, *Gewalt und Ordnung: Kalkül und Faszination der SA* (Münster: Verlag Westfälisches Dampfboot, 1989), 65.
2. Jennifer Craig, *Uniforms Exposed* (New York: Berg, 2005), 39.
3. Peter Longerich, *Die Braunen Bataillone: Geschichte der SA* (Munich: Verlag C. H. Beck, 1989), 116–20.
4. Sheryl Kroen, "Historiographical Reviews: A Political History of the Consumer," *Historical Journal* 47, no. 3 (2004): 722; Daniel Siemens,

Stormtroopers: A New History of Hitler's Brownshirts (New Haven, CT: Yale University Press, 2017), 42, 94–95; Molly Loberg, *The Struggle for the Streets of Berlin: Politics, Consumption, and Urban Space, 1914–1945* (Cambridge: Cambridge University Press, 2018), 7.

5. Loberg, *Struggle for the Streets of Berlin,* 205.
6. Nationalsozialistische Deutsche Arbeiterpartei, Reichszeugmeisterei, *SA Preisliste* (Munich: Reichszeugmeisterei), 2–10.
7. Corey Ross, "Mass Culture and Divided Audiences: Cinema and Social Change in Inter-war Germany," *Past and Present* 193 (2006): 195.
8. Siemens, *Stormtroopers,* 94–95; Frank Trentmann, "Beyond Consumerism: New Historical Perspectives on Consumption," *Journal of Contemporary History* 39, no. 3 (2004): 377.
9. Nationalsozialistische Deutsche Arbeiterpartei, Reichszeugmeisterei, *SA Preisliste*; Jan Longman, "Americanization through Credit? Consumer Credit in Germany, 1860s—1960s," *Business History Review* 85 (Autumn 2011): 533.
10. John R. Angolia, *Cloth Insignia of the NSDAP and SA* (San Jose, CA: R. James Bender, 1985), 129.
11. Nationalsozialistische Deutsche Arbeiterpartei, Reichszeugmeisterei, *SA Preisliste,* 1–3.
12. Alfred Conn, *Alfred Conn Nachlass,* 11/C1 SA Gau Hamburg, 112, Forschungsstelle für Zeitgeschichte in Hamburg, Hamburg.
13. "Report," April 23, 1931, Nationalsozialistische Deutsche Arbeiterpartei (NSDAP) B1 SA Hamburg, Gliederung und örtliche Zustandigkeit 1925, 1929–36, 1939–40, Staatsarchiv Hamburg, Hamburg.
14. Siemens, *Stormtroopers,* 94.
15. Schneidhuber, "Richtilinien für die Neuaufstellung von SA-Gruppen," September 1929, Bestandssignatur NS 26, Archivnummer 304, Bundesarchiv, Berlin.
16. "NSDAP Verordnungsblatt der Obersten SA-Führung," February 1, 1933, Bestandssignatur NS 26, Archivnummer 308, Bundesarchiv, Berlin.
17. "NSDAP Verordnungsblatt der Obersten SA-Führung," August 8, 1932, Bestandssignatur NS 26, Archivnummer 307, Bundesarchiv, Berlin.
18. Julia Sneeringer, "The Shopper as Voter: Women, Advertising, and Politics on Post-inflation Germany," *German Studies Review* 27, no. 3 (2004): 478; Yvette Florio Lane, "'No Fertile Soil for Pathogens': Rayon, Advertising, and Biopolitics in Late Weimar Germany," *Journal of Social History* 44, no. 2 (2012): 550, 548.
19. "Sturmbefehl," August 4, 1928, Bestandssignatur NS 23, Archivnummer 1239, Bundesarchiv, Berlin.
20. "SA Befehl 10, Dienstanzug," November 14, 1926, Bestandssignatur NS 23, Archivnummer 509, Bundesarchiv, Berlin.
21. Ibid.
22. "SA Befehl," June 5, 1930, Bestandssignatur NS 23, Archivnummer 1239, Bundesarchiv, Berlin.
23. "SA Befehl," August 1, 1930, Bestandssignatur NS 23, Archivnummer 1239, Bundesarchiv, Berlin.
24. Longerich, *Die Braunen Bataillone,* 100.
25. "Polizei Dortmund, Sonderbefehl Nr. 23," June 17, 1930, Bestandssignatur NS 23, Archivnummer 471, Bundesarchiv, Berlin.
26. Ibid.
27. "SA Befehl," August 1, 1930, Bestandssignatur NS 23, Archivnummer 1239, Bundesarchiv, Berlin.
28. "SA Befehl," June 14, 1930, Bestandssignatur NS 23, Archivnummer 1239, Bundesarchiv, Berlin.

29. "SA Befehl, Weisse Verbotshemden," July 10, 1930, Bestandssignatur NS 23, Archivnummer 471, Bundesarchiv, Berlin.
30. Zörgiebel, Polizeipräsident Berlin, "Rechtsbewegung," June 26, 1930, Bestandssignatur NS 23, Archivnummer 471, Bundesarchiv, Berlin.
31. Siemens, *Stormtroopers,* 45.
32. Der Minister des Innern, Carl Severing, "Beschluss," April 1, 1931, Bestandssignatur NS 23, Archivnummer 471, Bundesarchiv, Berlin.
33. Nathan Joseph, *Uniforms and Nonuniforms: Communication through Clothing* (New York: Greenwood Press, 1986), 80, 69, 66.
34. "Die S.A.-Wirtschaft. 1. Bekleidungswesen," Bestandssignatur NS 23, Archivnummer 509, Bundesarchiv, Berlin.
35. "SA Befehl 7, Disziplin," November 7, 1926, Bestandssignatur NS 23, Archivnummer 509, Bundesarchiv, Berlin.
36. Ibid.
37. Ibid.
38. "SA Befehl 10, Dienstanzug," November 14, 1926, Bestandssignatur NS 23, Archivnummer 509, Bundesarchiv, Berlin.
39. Longerich, *Die Braunen Bataillone,* 86–87.
40. "SA Befehl," August 25, 1927, Bestandssignatur NS 23, Archivnummer 1239, Bundesarchiv, Berlin.
41. "Erfahrungen beim Gen. Appell am 14.5.33," May 16, 1933, Bestandssignatur NS 23, Archivnummer 405, Bundesarchiv, Berlin.
42. Ibid.
43. "SA Befehl 10, Dienstanzug," November 14, 1926, Bestandssignatur NS 23, Archivnummer 509, Bundesarchiv, Berlin.
44. "Besondere Anordnung Nr. 2," August 1, 1931, Bestandssignatur NS 23, Archivnummer 404, Bundesarchiv, Berlin.
45. "SA Befehl 10, Dienstanzug," November 14, 1926, Bestandssignatur NS 23, Archivnummer 509, Bundesarchiv, Berlin.
46. "Betreffend SA Mann Fels," September 22, 1931, Bestandssignatur NS 23, Archivnummer 904, Bundesarchiv, Berlin.
47. "SA Befehl," May 8, 1931, Bestandssignatur NS 23, Archivnummer 904, Bundesarchiv, Berlin.
48. Joseph, *Uniforms and Nonuniforms,* 80.
49. "SA Befehl 1, Brief Adolf Hitlers an Haubtmann von Pfeffer," November 1, 1926, Bestandssignatur NS 23, Archivnummer 509, Bundesarchiv, Berlin; "SA Befehl 3," November 3, 1926, Bestandssignatur NS 23, Archivnummer 509, Bundesarchiv, Berlin; "SA Befehl 7," November 7, 1926, Bestandssignatur NS 23, Archivnummer 509, Bundesarchiv, Berlin.
50. "SA Befehl 10, Dienstanzug," November 14, 1926, Bestandssignatur NS 23, Archivnummer 509, Bundesarchiv, Berlin.
51. Longerich, *Die Braunen Bataillone,* 104, 108, 110.
52. Loberg, *Struggle for the Streets of Berlin,* 188.
53. Siemens, *Stormtroopers,* 95.

CHAPTER FOUR: ASSEMBLING THE TROOPERS—THE LOGISTICS OF MILITARIZATION

1. "SA Befehl 1, Brief Adolf Hitlers an Haubtmann von Pfeffer," November 1, 1926, Bestandssignatur NS 23, Archivnummer 509, Bundesarchiv, Berlin.
2. Andreas Werner, "SA und NSDAP; SA: 'Wehrverband,' 'Parteitruppe' oder 'Revolutionsarmee'?" (PhD diss., University of Erlangen, 1964), 386.
3. Daniel Siemens, *Stormtroopers: A New History of Hitler's Brownshirts* (New Haven, CT: Yale University Press, 23017), 64.
4. Linda Conze, "Die Ordnung des Festes / Die Ordnung des Bildes: Fotografische Blicke auf Festumzüge in Schwaben (1926–1934),"

Zeithistorische Forschungen / Studies in Contemporary History 12 (2015): 234–35, 214.

5. Vernon L. Lidtke, *The Alternative Culture: Socialist Labor in Imperial Germany* (New York: Oxford University Press, 1985), 51.
6. Siemens, *Stormtroopers,* 14.
7. "Betreffend Propagandafahrt der Radfahrer in die Walddörfer," January 19, 1928, Bestandssignatur NS 23, Archivnummer 1239, Bundesarchiv, Berlin.
8. Ibid.
9. Ibid.
10. Sasha Disko, *The Devil's Wheels: Men and Motorcycling in the Weimar Republic* (New York: Berghahn Books, 2016), 34–49, 88, 92.
11. Adelheid Von Saldern, "Cultural Conflicts, Popular Mass Culture, and the Question of Nazi Success: The Eilenriede Motorcycle Races, 1924–39," *German Studies Review* 15, no. 2 (1992): 326, 332.
12. Dirk Schumann, *Political Violence in the Weimar Republic, 1918–1933: Fight for the Streets and Fear of Civil War* (New York: Berghahn Books, 2009), 187; J. A. S. Grenville, *The Jews and the Germans of Hamburg: The Destruction of a Civilization, 1790–1945* (Routledge: New York, 2012), 52.
13. Schumann, *Political Violence in the Weimar Republic,* 187.
14. "Besondere Anordnung," May 27, 1930, Bestandssignatur NS 23, Archivnummer 1239, Bundesarchiv, Berlin.
15. "SA Befehl Motorstürme," April 1, 1930, Bestandssignatur NS 23, Archivnummer 511, Bundesarchiv, Berlin.
16. Disko, *Devil's Wheels,* 140.
17. Ibid., 326.
18. "SA Befehl Motorstürme," April 1, 1930, Bestandssignatur NS 23, Archivnummer 511, Bundesarchiv, Berlin.
19. "Betreffend: Einsatz der Motorstürme im Wahlkampf," February 4, 1932, Bestandssignatur NS 23, Archivnummer 511, Bundesarchiv, Berlin.
20. Disko, *Devil's Wheels,* 326; Siemens, *Stormtroopers,* 65.
21. "Betreffend: Einsatz der Motorstürme im Wahlkampf," February 4, 1932, Bestandssignatur NS 23, Archivnummer 511, Bundesarchiv, Berlin.
22. Siemens, *Stormtroopers,* 65.
23. Schumann, *Political Violence in the Weimar Republic,* 226–27.
24. "NSDAP Verordnungsblatt der Obersten SA-Führung," August 8, 1932, Bestandssignatur NS 26, Archivnummer 307, Bundesarchiv, Berlin.
25. Peter Longerich, *Die Braunen Bataillone: Geschichte der SA* (Munich: Verlag C. H. Beck, 1989), 112–13.
26. "Betrifft: Flugwesen," July 7, 1932, Bestandssignatur NS 26, Archivnummer 307, Bundesarchiv, Berlin.
27. Ibid.
28. Conze, "Die Ordnung des Festes / Die Ordnung des Bildes," 234–35.
29. Schumann, *Political Violence in the Weimar Republic,* 188.
30. Lidtke, *Alternative Culture,* 76–77, 85–86.
31. Eric Weitz, *Weimar Germany* (Princeton, NJ: Princeton University Press, 2007), 114.
32. Schumann, *Political Violence in the Weimar Republic,* 188.
33. Nathan Joseph, *Uniforms and Nonuniforms: Communication through Clothing* (New York: Greenwood Press, 1986), 83, 82.
34. Ibid., 82.
35. Frank Trentmann, "Beyond Consumerism: New Historical Perspectives on Consumption," *Journal of Contemporary History* 39, no. 3 (2004): 377.
36. "SA Befehl Nürnberg," August 15, 1927, Bestandssignatur NS 23, Archivnummer 510, Bundesarchiv, Berlin.

37. Ibid.
38. Longerich, *Die Braunen Bataillone,* 131.
39. "SA Befehl! Massenverpflegung—Allgemeines," June 20, 1929, Bestandssignatur NS 26, Archivnummer 304, Bundesarchiv, Berlin.
40. Ibid.
41. Ibid.
42. "SA Befehl Reichsparteitag 1929 Massenverpflegung," June 25, 1929, Bestandssignatur NS 26, Archivnummer 304, Bundesarchiv, Berlin.
43. Ibid.
44. Alfred Conn, "Alfred Conn Nachlass, Memoiren," 11/C1 SA Gau Hamburg, 71, Forschungsstelle für Zeitgeschichte in Hamburg, Hamburg.
45. "SA Befehl," August 20, 1929, Bestandssignatur NS 26, Archivnummer 304, Bundesarchiv, Berlin.
46. Ibid. (emphasis in the original).
47. Ibid.
48. Conn, "Alfred Conn Nachlass, Memoiren," 11/C1 SA Gau Hamburg, 72, Forschungsstelle für Zeitgeschichte in Hamburg, Hamburg.
49. Longerich, *Die Braunen Bataillone,* 117.
50. Peter D. Stachura, "Der Kritische Wendepunkt? Die NSDAP und die Reichstagswahlen Vom 20. Mai 1928," *Vierteljahreshefte fuer Zeitgeschichte* 26 (1978): 87–88.
51. Stachura, "Der Kritische Wendepunkt?," 87–88.
52. Conn, "Alfred Conn Nachlass, Memoiren," 11/C1 SA Gau Hamburg, 72, Forschungsstelle für Zeitgeschichte in Hamburg, Hamburg.
53. "Befehl von SA Führer an Gruppe Mitte Süd," March 28, 1931, Bestandssignatur NS 23, Archivnummer 510, Bundesarchiv, Berlin.
54. "SA Befehl zum Aufmarsch in Oldenburg am 10.5.31," May 8, 1931, Bestandssignatur NS 23, Archivnummer 904, Bundesarchiv, Berlin.
55. Longerich, *Die Braunen Bataillone,* 86.

CHAPTER FIVE: THE PROFESSIONALIZATION OF A CIVIL WAR ARMY

1. Gerhard Rossbach, *Mein Weg Durch die Zeit: Erinnerungen und Bekenntnisse* (Weilburg-Lahn: Vereinigte Weilburger Buchdruckereien, 1950), 216; Bruce Campbell, *The SA Generals and the Rise of Nazism* (Lexington: University Press of Kentucky, 1998), 90.
2. Peter D. Stachura, "The Political Strategy of the Nazi Party, 1919–1933," *German Studies Review* 3, no. 2 (1980): 270; Campbell, *SA Generals and the Rise of Nazism,* 86.
3. Peter Longerich, *Die Braunen Bataillone: Geschichte der SA* (Munich: Verlag C. H. Beck, 1989), 96, 167.
4. Daniel Siemens, *Stormtroopers: A New History of Hitler's Brownshirts* (New Haven, CT: Yale University Press, 2017), 58.
5. Campbell, *SA Generals and the Rise of Nazism,* 90–91, 93.
6. "Die Organisation der Totschläger," *Vorwärts,* August 26, 1930, Bestandssignatur NS 23, Archivnummer 510, Bundesarchiv, Berlin.
7. Ibid.
8. Ibid.
9. Richard Hamilton, *Who Voted for Hitler?* (Princeton, NJ: Princeton University Press, 1982), 476.
10. "Aus den Mitteilungen des LKA Berlin 5. Uniformen," May 15, 1931, Bestandssignatur NS 23, Archivnummer 471, Bundesarchiv, Berlin.
11. "SA Befehl," August 25, 1927, Bestandssignatur NS 23, Archivnummer 1239, Bundesarchiv, Berlin.
12. "Aus den Mitteilungen des LKA Berlin 5. Uniformen," May 15, 1931, Bestandssignatur NS 23, Archivnummer 471, Bundesarchiv, Berlin.

13. "Leben Wir Schon im Dritten Reich?," *Gross Hagener Stadtnachrichten,* October 19, 1931, Bestandssignatur NS 23, Archivnummer 471, Bundesarchiv, Berlin.
14. Ibid.
15. "Erlass Nr. 5," November 28, 1931, Bestandssignatur NS 23, Archivnummer 514, Bundesarchiv, Berlin.
16. Ibid.

17. Ibid.
18. Campbell, *SA Generals and the Rise of Nazism,* 104–5.
19. "Erlass Nr. 5," November 28, 1931, Bestandssignatur NS 23, Archivnummer 514, Bundesarchiv, Berlin.

20. "Leben Wir Schon im Dritten Reich?"
21. "Betrifft: Bekleidung," July 7, 1932, Bestandssignatur NS 26, Archivnummer 307, Bundesarchiv, Berlin.
22. Ibid.
23. See, for instance, the tunics worn by SA generals in Campbell, *SA Generals and the Rise of Nazism,* 3.
24. "Betrifft: Bekleidung," July 7, 1932, Bestandssignatur NS 26, Archivnummer 307, Bundesarchiv, Berlin.
25. Ibid.
26. Ibid.
27. Ibid.
28. Ibid.
29. Ibid.
30. "Betrifft: Dienstanzug, Verfügung," September 22, 1932, Bestandssignatur NS 26, Archivnummer 307, Bundesarchiv, Berlin.
31. "Lagebericht Polizeidirektion München," October 20, 1932, Bestandssignatur NS 23, Archivnummer 510, Bundesarchiv, Berlin.
32. Ibid.

CHAPTER SIX: CLASSLESS HEROES—THE CENTRALITY OF THE BROWN SHIRT IN MYTHIC NAZI FILM AND LITERATURE

1. *Hans Westmar: Einer von Vielen, Ein Deutsches Schicksal aus dem Jahre 1929,* directed by Franz Wenzler (Siegel-Monopolfilm, 1933); *Hitlerjunge Quex,* directed by Hans Steinhoff (Universum Film AG, 1933); *SA-Mann Brand,* directed by Franz Seitz (Bavaria Film AG, 1933).
2. Eric Rentschler, *The Ministry of Illusion: Nazi Cinema and Its Afterlife* (Cambridge, MA: Harvard University Press, 1996), 56.
3. Jay W. Baird, *To Die for Germany: Heroes in the Nazi Pantheon* (Bloomington: Indiana University Press, 1990), 127, 111.
4. Wilfried Bade, *Die SA Erobert Berlin* (Munich: Verlag Knorr und Hirt München, 1933).
5. Karl W. H. Koch, *Männer im Braunhemd: Vom Kampf und Sieg der SA* (Berlin: Stubenrauch Verlagsbuchandlung, 1936).
6. Baird, *To Die for Germany,* 1, 73, 109.
7. *Hans Westmar.*
8. Ibid., 0:13:24.
9. Ibid., 0:22:13, 0:27:55.
10. Ibid., 0:28:00, 0:32:21.
11. Ibid., 0:35:02.
12. Ibid., 0:42:34–0:45:12.
13. Ibid., 0:51:47.
14. Ibid., 0:52:33, 0:54:34, 1:01:48.
15. Ibid., 1:06:11, 1:12:01–1:13:44.

16. Ibid., 1:18:35, 1:21:02–1:22:54.
17. *Hitlerjunge Quex*.
18. Ibid., 0:17:04.
19. Ibid., 0:22:24, 0:24:19.
20. Ibid., 0:24:52.
21. Ibid., 0:25:35.
22. Ibid., 0:33:25.
23. Ibid., 0:38:59, 0:42:00.
24. Ibid., 0:47:18–0:47: 55.
25. Ibid., 1:02:39, 1:10:57.
26. Ibid., 1:14:04, 1:16:48, 1:20:26.
27. Ibid., 1:20:26, 1:23:34, 1:27:02.
28. *SA-Mann Brand*.
29. Ibid., 0:12:15.
30. Ibid., 0:13:31–0:13:44.
31. Ibid., 0:46:10.
32. Ibid., 0:50:51–0:51:11, 0:53:37.
33. Ibid., 1:14:35–1:14:59.
34. Ibid., 1:34:00.
35. Bade, *Die SA Erobert Berlin*.
36. Ibid., 18.
37. Ibid., 27, 36, 39, 42–43.
38. Ibid., 46, 58, 65, 70.
39. Ibid., 72, 79.
40. Ibid., 87.
41. Ibid., 123, 129.
42. Ibid., 133–34, 137, 139, 147.
43. Ibid., 225–26.
44. Photograph of Goebbels wedding, December 19, 1931, Bild 183-R32860, Bundesarchiv, Koblenz, Germany.
45. Bade, *Die SA Erobert Berlin*, 230, 235.
46. Ibid., 257, 260–61.
47. Koch, *Männer im Braunhemd*.
48. Ibid., 46, 48, 251.
49. Ibid., 68.
50. Ibid., 234, 240, 248.
51. Ibid., 157.

CHAPTER SEVEN: HAMBURG, 1921–1933, A CASE STUDY

1. P. E. Schramm, *Hamburg: Ein Sonderfall in der Geschichte Deutschlands* (Hamburg: Christians, 1964).
2. Andreas Schulz, "Liberalismus in Hamburg und Bremen zwischen Restauration und Reichsgründung (1830–1870)," *Historische Zeitschrift*. Beihefte, n.s., 19, Liberalismus und Region Zur Geschichte des deutschen Liberalismus im 19. Jahrhundert (1995): 159–60.
3. Andrew Wackerfuss, "The Stormtrooper Family: How Sexuality, Spirituality, and Community Shaped the Hamburg SA" (PhD diss., Georgetown University, 2008), 134–35; Anthony McElligott, "Street Politics in Hamburg, 1932–33," *History Workshop* 16 (1983): 88.
4. "Für die Deutschvölkischen: Liste 2," *Hamburger Nachrichten*, February 16, 1928.
5. "Die Störung der Deutschnationalen Sagebiel-Versammlung," *Hamburger Nachrichten*, February 16, 1928.
6. "Hitler Über die Demokratie," *Hamburger Nachrichten*, February 17, 1928.

7. "Eine Rede Hitlers in Hamburg: Riesenversammlung Bei Sagebiel," *Hamburger Nachrichten,* September 7, 1930.
8. "Neuer Mord der Hamburger Kommunisten: Ein Nationalsozialist Ermorder," *Hamburger Nachrichten,* September 8, 1930; "Bürgerkrieg in Altona," *Hamburger Nachrichten,* July 18, 1932.
9. "Hitler ist Reichckanzler," *Hamburger Nachrichten,* January 30, 1933.
10. McElligott, "Street Politics in Hamburg," 88; Wackerfuss, "Stormtrooper Family"; Andrew Wackerfuss, *Stormtrooper Families: Homosexuality and Community in the Early Nazi Movement* (New York: Harrington Park Press, 2015); Werner Jochmann, *Nationalsozialismus und Revolution: Ursprung und Geschichte der NSDAP in Hamburg, 1922–1933, Dokumente* (Frankfurt: Europäische Verlagsgemeinschaft, 1963).
11. For information on the history of Hamburg, see, for instance, Gerd Augner, *Die Kaiserliche Kommission der Jahre 1708–1712: Hamburgs Beziehungen zu Kaiser und Reich zu Anfang des 18. Jahrhunderts* (Hamburg: Verein fuer Hamburgische Geschichte, 1983); Ekkehard Boehm, "Wirtschaft und Politik in Hamburg zur Zeit der Reichsgruendung," *Zeitschrift des Vereins fuer Hamburgische Geschichte* 64 (1978): 31–53; Jan Heitman, *Das Ende des Zweiten Weltkrieges in Hamburg* (Frankfurt: Peter Lang, 1990); Thomas Krause, *Hamburg wird Braun: Der Aufstieg der NSDAP von 1921–1933* (Hamburg: Ergebnisse Verlag, 1987); Detlef Rogosch, *Hamburg im Deutschen Bund, 1859–1866* (Hamburg: Kraemer, 1990); and Schramm, *Hamburg.*
12. Andreas Schulz, "Weltbürger und Geldaristokraten: Hanseatisches Bürgertum im 19. Jahrhundert," *Historische Zeitschrift* 259, no. 3 (1994): 670.
13. Schulz, "Liberalismus in Hamburg und Bremen zwischen Restauration und Reichsgründung," 159–60.
14. *Anlage 5,* in Jochmann, *Nationalsozialismus und Revolution,* 449.
15. McElligott, "Street Politics in Hamburg," 88.
16. Ibid., 87–88.
17. Heinz Habedank, *Zur Geschichte des Hamburger Aufstandes, 1923* (Berlin: Dietz Verlag,1958); Erich Wollenberg, "Der Hamburger Aufstand und die Thälmann-Legende," *Schwarze Protokolle,* no. 6 (1973).
18. Auszüge aus den Tagebüchern von Frau Luise Solmitz, 25.5.32 und 27.5.32, in Jochmann, *Nationalsozialismus und Revolution,* 405–6.
19. Jochmann, *Nationalsozialismus und Revolution,* 449; Richard Hamilton, *Who Voted for Hitler?* (Princeton, NJ: Princeton University Press, 1982), 108.
20. Wackerfuss, *Stormtrooper Families,* 111, 173.
21. Ibid., 57.
22. David Jablonsky, *The Nazi Party in Dissolution: Hitler and the Verbotzeit, 1923–1925* (London: Frank Cass, 1989), 172.
23. Grussbotschaft der Hamburger Nationalsozialisten an Adolf Hitler, March 24, 1925, in Jochmann, *Nationalsozialismus und Revolution,* 206.
24. "Adolf Hitler Sprach," *Hamburger Nachrichten,* May 3, 1926.
25. Albrecht Erich Günther: Bericht Über Hitlers Erste Wahlrede in Hamburg, in Jochmann, *Nationalsozialismus und Revolution,* 269–74.
26. Alfred Conn, "Alfred Conn Nachlass," 11/C1 SA Gau Hamburg, 3–20, Forschungsstelle für Zeitgeschichte in Hamburg, Hamburg.
27. Ibid., 49.
28. Bredel was a gifted poet and novelist who ultimately ended his career as a highly decorated East German state poet. During that later East German

period, many schools bore Bredel's name as a testament to his success and ideological affiliations.

29. Conn, "Alfred Conn Nachlass," 11/C1 SA Gau Hamburg, 35, Forschungsstelle für Zeitgeschichte in Hamburg, Hamburg, 35.
30. Ibid., 44–45.
31. Ibid., 52.
32. Ibid., 56.
33. Ibid, 85.
34. Ibid., 59.
35. Ibid.
36. "Aufruf," *Hamburger Nachrichten,* February 17, 1928.
37. "Hitler Über die Demokratie."
38. Conn, "Alfred Conn Nachlass," 11/C1 SA Gau Hamburg, 35, Forschungsstelle für Zeitgeschichte in Hamburg, Hamburg, 60.
39. Ibid., 61.
40. Ibid., 63.
41. Ibid., 67.
42. Ibid., 68.
43. Ibid., 66.
44. "Brigade Befehl," August 14, 1930, 922 SA Gau Hamburg, Forschungsstelle für Zeitgeschichte in Hamburg, Hamburg.
45. "Befehl für Sturm 2," April 23, 1928, 922 SA Gau Hamburg, Forschungsstelle für Zeitgeschichte in Hamburg, Hamburg.
46. "An Pg. Ellerhusen," March 5, 1929, Bestandssignatur NS 23, Archivnummer 1239, Bundesarchiv, Berlin.
47. "Gruppenbericht," December 3, 1928, 922 SA Gau Hamburg, Forschungsstelle für Zeitgeschichte in Hamburg, Hamburg.
48. "Brigadebefehl," February 26, 1929, 922 SA Gau Hamburg, Forschungsstelle für Zeitgeschichte in Hamburg, Hamburg.
49. Conn, "Alfred Conn Nachlass," 11/C1 SA Gau Hamburg, 69, Forschungsstelle für Zeitgeschichte in Hamburg, Hamburg, 70.
50. Ibid., 70.
51. Ibid., 70.
52. Ibid., 71.
53. Ibid., 71–72.
54. Ibid., 73.
55. Ibid., 73, 82.
56. Ibid., 93.
57. "SA Befehl," July 17, 1930, Bestandssignatur NS 23, Archivnummer 1239, Bundesarchiv, Berlin.
58. Conn, "Alfred Conn Nachlass," 11/C1 SA Gau Hamburg, 83, Forschungsstelle für Zeitgeschichte in Hamburg, Hamburg, 84.
59. Ibid.
60. Ibid., 91–92.
61. Ibid., 77.
62. "Eine Rede Hitlers in Hamburg."
63. Conn, "Alfred Conn Nachlass," 11/C1 SA Gau Hamburg, 83, Forschungsstelle für Zeitgeschichte in Hamburg, Hamburg, 93.
64. Ibid., 93–95, 96.
65. "Blutüberfall der Hitlerbanden an der Sternschanze: Die Mordbanditen Von Arbeitern in die Flucht Geschlagen," *Hamburger Volkszeiting,* September 8, 1930.
66. "Augenzugen Sprechen," *Hamburger Volkszeiting,* September 8, 1930.

67. "Neuer Mord der Hamburger Kommunisten."
68. "Ein Nationalsozialist Ermordet," *Hamburger Nachrichten,* September 8, 1930.
69. "Was die Augenzeugen Sagen: Unglaubliche Roheitsakte," *Hamburger Nachrichten,* September 8, 1930.
70. "Polizisten Von Rotfront Umzingelt," *Hamburger Nachrichten,* September 8, 1930.

71. "Uniformverbot für Die—Braunhemden," *Hamburger Nachrichten,* September 8, 1930.

72. *Der Bürgerbund für Hamburg , Altona, Wandsbek e. V.:* "Die Bolschewistische Gefahr, Politik der Buergerlichen Sammlung," in Jochmann, *Nationalsozialismus und Revolution,* 300–301 (emphasis in the original).
73. "SA Befehl für Wahlsonntag den. 14 Scheiding 1930," 922 SA Gau Hamburg, Forschungsstelle für Zeitgeschichte in Hamburg, Hamburg.
74. Conn, "Alfred Conn Nachlass," 11/C1 SA Gau Hamburg, 110. Forschungsstelle für Zeitgeschichte in Hamburg, Hamburg.
75. Ibid., 111.
76. "Standartenbefehl vom 30. Oktober 1930," 922 SA Gau Hamburg, Forschungsstelle für Zeitgeschichte in Hamburg, Hamburg.
77. Conn, "Alfred Conn Nachlass," 11/C1 SA Gau Hamburg, 111, Forschungsstelle für Zeitgeschichte in Hamburg, Hamburg.
78. Ibid., 112.
79. Peter Longerich, *Die Braunen Bataillone: Geschichte der SA* (Munich: Verlag C. H. Beck, 1989), 128.
80. Conn, "Alfred Conn Nachlass," 11/C1 SA Gau Hamburg, 112, Forschungsstelle für Zeitgeschichte in Hamburg, Hamburg.
81. Ibid., 112.
82. Ibid., 119.
83. Longerich, *Die Braunen Bataillone,* 111.
84. Alfred Conn, *Aufruf and die Hamburger SA,* April 25, 1931, quoted in Jochmann, *Nationalsozialismus und Revolution,* 340.
85. Wackerfuss, *Stormtrooper Families,* 194–96.
86. "Betrifft Flugblattverteilung," August 4, 1931, 614-2-05 A1-A18 B53, Staatsarchiv Hamburg, Hamburg.
87. "SA Befehl zum Aufmarsch in Oldenburg am 10.5.31," May 8, 1931, Bestandssignatur NS 23, Archivnummer 904, Bundesarchiv, Berlin.
88. Jay W. Baird, *To Die for Germany: Heroes in the Nazi Pantheon* (Bloomington: Indiana University Press, 1990), 73–107.
89. "Kapelle Boss Harburg," September 30, 1931, Bestandssignatur NS 23, Archivnummer 904, Bundesarchiv, Berlin.
90. "Nazis Stürmen Arbeiterlokal: Schönfelder-Polizei Schliesst Das Lokal und Behaubted, Dass 'Die Kommunisten Geschossen Haben' Augenzeugen Bestätigen Das Gegeteil," *Hamburger Volkszeitung,* February 15, 1932.
91. Ibid.
92. "Der Bericht eines Augenzeugen," *Hamburger Volkszeitung,* February 15, 1932.
93. "Blutiger Sonntag in Hamburg: Strassenschlacht im Gängeviertel: Ein Nationalsozialistischer Zettelverteiler Von Kommunisten Erschossen," *Hamburger Anzeiger,* February 15, 1932.
94. "Nationalsozialist Ermordet! Kommunisten Überfallen Flugblattverteiler der NSDAP.—:Sammelplatz Kurze Strasse.—Mit Armeepistolen, Steinen, und Flaschen.—Die 'Antifa' Beteiligt," *Hamburger Nachrichten,* February 15, 1932.
95. Ibid.

96. "Der Name des Mörders," *Hamburger Nachrichten,* February 15, 1932.
97. "Der Bericht der Nationalsozialisten," *Hamburger Nachrichten,* February 15, 1932.
98. "Die Mordhöhlen der SA in Gross-Hamburg," *Hamburger Volkszeitung,* April 2–3, 1932.
99. "SA Kasernen die Schlupfwinkel der Mord SA," *Hamburger Volkszeitung,* April 2–3, 1932.
100. "Haubtbahnhof Beherrscht," *Hamburger Volkszeitung,* April 2–3, 1932.
101. "Einfallstore in die Arbeiterviertel; Eppendorf, Winterhude, Barmbeck, Elmsbüttel, Altona," *Hamburger Volkszeitung,* April 2–3, 1932.
102. "SA Mordhöhlen Auch im Roten Barmbeck," *Hamburger Volkszeitung,* April 9–10, 1932; "SA Hausst in der Bismarckstrasse," *Hamburger Volkszeitung,* May 31, 1932; "SA Mordkaserne in Altonaer Arbeiterviertel," *Hamburger Volkszeitung,* September 14, 1932; "Auch in Ottensen eine Neue Nazikaserne," *Hamburger Volkszeitung,* November 30, 1932.
103. "Blutige Naziüberfälle ouf KPD—und Reichsbanner Arbeiter: Überall Schwere Provokationen—Erfolgreiche Gemeinsamen Abwehraktionen Von Kommunisten und Reichsbannerarbeitern," *Hamburger Volkszeitung,* April 11, 1932.
104. "Nazis Erschiessen am Ausschlägerweg Eigene Leute," *Hamburger Volkszeitung,* April 11, 1932.
105. "Sind Nationalsozialisten Freiwild? Jagd auf SA-Leute in Hamburg," *Hamburger Nachrichten,* April 11, 1932.
106. "Werbemarsch, am Mittwoch den 20. April 1932," 614-2-05 A1-A18 B 212, Staatsarchiv Hamburg, Hamburg.
107. Wackerfuss, *Stormtrooper Families,* 306.
108. "Anlage 5, Wahlergebnisse in Hamburg von 1919 bis 1932," in Jochmann, *Nationalsozialismus und Revolution,* 449.
109. "SA Erhält Reischswehrmütze und Uniformrock," *Hamburger Volkszeitung,* June 8, 1932; "Wer Bezahlt die Neuen Uniformen der SA Banditen," *Hamburger Volkszeitung,* June 13, 1932; "Preussennotverordnung Aufgehoben," *Hamburger Volkszeitung,* June 18–19, 1932.
110. "Betrifft: Bekleidung," July 7, 1932, Bestandssignatur NS 26, Archivnummer 307, Bundesarchiv, Berlin.
111. "SA Erhält Reischswehrmütze und Uniformrock."
112. "Betrifft: Bekleidung," July 7, 1932, Bestandssignatur NS 26, Archivnummer 307, Bundesarchiv, Berlin; "Wer Bezahlt die Neuen Uniformen der SA Banditen?"
113. "Wer Bezahlt die Neuen Uniformen der SA Banditen?"
114. "Preussennotverordnung Aufgehoben."
115. Wackerfuss, *Stormtrooper Families,* 312.
116. "Bürgerkrieg in Altona."
117. "Wir Klagen An," *Hamburger Volkszeitung,* July 19, 1932.
118. "Blutsonntag in Altona," *Hamburger Volkszeitung,* July 18, 1932.
119. "Hier Berichten Augenzeugen," *Hamburger Volkszeitung,* July 18, 1932.
120. "18000 Angekündigt—Nur 5000 Kommen," *Hamburger Volkszeitung,* July 18, 1932.
121. "Der Aufmarsch der Mordpest Gesprengt," *Hamburger Volkszeitung,* July 18, 1932.
122. "Panzerwagen und Maschinengewehre gegen Arbeiter," *Hamburger Volkszeitung,* July 18, 1932.
123. "Bürgerkrieg in Altona."
124. "Mordplan Gegen Hitler," *Hamburger Nachrichten,* July 18, 1932.

125. "Bürgerkrieg in Altona."
126. "SA Marschiert in Altona: Polizei Kämpft Gegen Rote Dachschützen," *Hamburger Nachrichten,* July 18, 1932.
127. "Barikaden und Gasbomben: Ein Augenzeuge Melded Uns," *Hamburger Nachrichten,* July 18, 1932.
128. "Opfer der Roten Mörder," *Hamburger Nachrichten,* July 18, 1932.
129. "Mordplan Gegen Hitler."
130. "An die SA Untergruppe Hamburg," January 2, 1932, Bestandssignatur NS 23, Archivnummer 404, Bundesarchiv, Berlin.
131. "An die SA der NSDAP, Untergruppe Hamburg," April 7, 1932, Bestandssignatur NS 23, Archivnummer 404, Bundesarchiv, Berlin.
132. "An die SA Untergruppe Hamburg," April 8, 1932, Bestandssignatur NS 23, Archivnummer 404, Bundesarchiv, Berlin.
133. "An die SA Untergruppe Hamburg," July 22, 1932, Bestandssignatur NS 23, Archivnummer 404, Bundesarchiv, Berlin.
134. "An die SA der NSDAP Untergruppe Hamburg," October 5, 1932, Bestandssignatur NS 23, Archivnummer 404, Bundesarchiv, Berlin.
135. "Der SA Gruppe Nordesee," February 20, 1933, Bestandssignatur NS 23, Archivnummer 405, Bundesarchiv, Berlin.
136. "Anweisung für den Film," October 26, 1932, Bestandssignatur NS 23, Archivnummer 405, Bundesarchiv, Berlin.
137. "Kapelle Boss Harburg," September 30, 1931, Bestandssignatur NS 23, Archivnummer 904, Bundesarchiv, Berlin.
138. "Anlage 5, Wahlergebnisse in Hamburg von 1919 bis 1932," in Jochmann, *Nationalsozialismus und Revolution,* 449.
139. Deutsches Historisches Museum, Lebendiges Museum Online, Zeitstrahl, NS-Regime 1933, Etablierung der NS-Herrschaft, www.dhm.de/lemo/kapitel/ns-regime/etablierung/.
140. "Hitler Ist Reichskanzler: Die Regierung der Harzburger Front: Die Nationale Konzentration," *Hamburger Nachrichten,* July 18, 1932.
141. "Werbemärsche der Nationalsozialisten," *Hamburger Nachrichten,* February 27, 1933.
142. "Verbrecherische Angriffspläne: Kommunistische Terrorgruppe Ausgehoben," *Hamburger Nachrichten,* February 27, 1933.
143. "SA Marschiert in Hamburg," *Hamburger Nachrichten,* February 27, 1933.
144. "SA in Altona," *Hamburger Nachrichten,* February 27, 1933.
145. "Wir Sind Da und Wir Bleiben Da," *Hamburger Volkszeitung,* February 27, 1933.
146. "SA Marsch Durch Besetztes Gebiet," *Hamburger Volkszeitung,* February 27, 1933.
147. "Revolverschüsse auf SA," *Hamburger Nachrichten,* February 27, 1933.
148. Deutsches Historisches Museum, Lebendiges Museum Online, Bestand, Ergebnis der Reichstagswahl am 5. März 1933, www.dhm.de/lemo/bestand/objekt/Reichstagswahl-5-Maerz-1933.
149. *Hamburger Nachrichten,* April 20, 1933, 922 SA Gau Hamburg, Forschungsstelle für Zeitgeschichte in Hamburg, Hamburg.
150. Conn, "Alfred Conn Nachlass," 11/C1 SA Gau Hamburg, 56, Forschungsstelle für Zeitgeschichte in Hamburg, Hamburg.
151. "Stosstrupp Albatross Kameradschaftsabend, " 614–05 A 1-A 18 B 164, Staatsarchiv Hamburg, Hamburg.
152. McElligott, "Street Politics in Hamburg," 88.
153. Conn, "Alfred Conn Nachlass," 11/C1 SA Gau Hamburg, 67, Forschungsstelle für Zeitgeschichte in Hamburg, Hamburg, 68.

154. "SA Befehl, Kopfschutz," August 8, 1930, Bestandssignatur NS 26, Archivnummer 305, Bundesarchiv, Berlin.
155. Conn, "Alfred Conn Nachlass," 11/C1 SA Gau Hamburg, 56, Forschungsstelle für Zeitgeschichte in Hamburg, Hamburg.
156. Ibid., 110–11, 112, 59.
157. "Brigadebefehl," February 26, 1929, 922 SA Gau Hamburg, Forschungsstelle für Zeitgeschichte in Hamburg, Hamburg.
158. "Auszüge aus den Tagebüchern von Frau Luise Solmitz," June 1, 1932, in Jochmann, *Nationalsozialismus und Revolution,* 406.
159. Conn, "Alfred Conn Nachlass," 11/C1 SA Gau Hamburg, 112, Forschungsstelle für Zeitgeschichte in Hamburg, Hamburg, 63, 70, 83.
160. "Auszüge aus den Tagebüchern von Frau Luise Solmitz," February 6, 1933, in Jochmann, *Nationalsozialismus und Revolution,* 422.
161. "Auszüge aus den Tagebüchern von Frau Luise Solmitz," September 4, 1932, in Jochmann, *Nationalsozialismus und Revolution,* 410.
162. Conn, "Alfred Conn Nachlass," 11/C1 SA Gau Hamburg, 82, Forschungsstelle für Zeitgeschichte in Hamburg, Hamburg.

CONCLUSION: WEIMAR CULTURE AND THE END OF WEIMAR DEMOCRACY

1. See, for instance, Rachel Nolan, "Neo-Nazi Fashion: Thor Steinar and the Changing Look of the German Far Right," *Spiegel Online International,* November 20, 2008.

INDEX

Page references in *italics* refer to figures and photos.

age, SA restrictions on, 70–72, 105
airplanes and aviation: flight school plans by Nazis, 104–5; for transporting speakers, 83–84
alcohol prohibition, 72
Altona's Bloody Sunday, 169–77
Andree (SA leader), 153
Angolia, John, 58
anti-Semitism: boycott of Jewish-owned stores, 5; in Hamburg, 140; propaganda films and depiction of, 109–10, 113–14; Shoah and SA crimes, 3
Arbeitsgemeinschaft Rossbach (Working Group Rossbach, Free Corp unit), 40
armbands: early Nazi use of, 34, 36, *36*, 37; of RFB, 29
Austro-Hungarian military, caps of, 36

Bade, Wilfrid, 108, 121–25, 127, 129
Baden, uniform prohibitions in, 65
Baird, Jay W., 108–9
Balistier, Thomas, 2–3
Bavaria: early SA as paramilitary in, 32; lederhosen as part of uniform in, 47–48, *49*; national elections (1928) in, 91; uniform prohibitions in, 65
Beer Hall Putsch (November 9, 1923), 9, 33, 37–38, 44, 137, 177
belts, belt buckles, and shoulder straps: Reichsbanner's belt buckle, 25; SA marketing of, 60–63, *61–63*; Sam Browne belt, 17, 19–20, 23, 25, 28, 29, 34; and SA professionalization, 103; shoulder straps, 1, 17, 19–20, 46, 58–63, 126, 152; Stahlhelm belt buckle, 23
Berlin police, on Nazi professionalization, 97–98
bicycles: and *Lettow Hemden* uniform, 39–41, 125–26; SA rallies and use of, 76–79, 83–84, 92–93, 140, 166
Bisshopinck (Truppführer), 63–64, 141
Bloody Sunday (Altona), 169–77
Böckenhauer, Arthur: demotion and reinstatement of, 141, 158; and election day clash violence (Hamburg, April 10, 1932), 165–69, 173–74; and Ezinger tavern attack, 161–64; SA marches and rallies led by, 71–72, 77, 139, 159–61, 172–75
Böhmker, Dr., 145
Bolsheviks, 28–30, 135, 154
Bonde (Nazi activist), 148
bourgeois press, 3, 9, 13–14, 131. *See also* class issues; *Hamburger Nachrichten*
Brands, H., 165–66
Bredel, Willi, 138, 198–99n28
Britain, uniforms of, 17–19
Brix, Emil Heinrich, 175–76
Browne, Samuel James, 19
Brown Shirt uniforms, 1–14, 31–55; collar liners for, 64–65; color uniformity enforced for, 102–3; Conn on early use in Hamburg, 139–40, 177–78; consumption and consumerism of, 57–68, *61–63*; cultural history approach to, 3–7, 10–11; cultural symbolism of, 54–55, 68, 85, 90; cut and characteristics of, 41–44; disagreement about inventor of, 39–41, 43, 45, 46, 53, 55; early SA uniform (1921–1923), 32–37, *37*; feedback invited about, 50–53, *51*, 102, 105; footwear, 19, 34, 35, 59, 103; and Hitler's rise to power, overview, 2, 9–10, 13; as honor garment (for social control), 68–75, 104, 144; illegality of, 65–68, 120, 123–24, 126–27, 139, 149, 167; laundering, 155–57; and *Lettow Hemden*, 38–41, *38*, 126; name-brand Brown Shirts, 11; neckties worn with, 44, 60–63;

Brown Shirt uniforms (*continued*)
as preserved artifacts, 1–2; and SA professionalization (1930–1934), 12, 95–106; SA uniform in 1926 and beyond, 31–32, 44–45, 47–50, *49*; SA uniform stages (1925–1926), 45–47; signal function of, 3, 32, 37, *37*, 55, 128, 132, 139, 159–60; sources for research, 1–2, 13; symbols (ranks, insignia) used on, 53; *Traditionsanzug* (traditional dress, 1926–1932), 12, 105; as uniforms vs. service dress, 46; white substitute shirts, 67. *See also* belts, belt buckles, and shoulder straps; caps, hats, and helmets; clash violence; consumption and consumerism; Hamburg 1921–1933; jackets and coats; symbolism; trousers and breeches; visual propaganda and image construction; Windbreakers

Brown Stores (Braune Läden), 60–63, *61–63*, 75, 139

Bruhn, Friedrich, 172

Bruhn Company, 172–73

Büttig (SA man), 171

caps, hats, and helmets: caps and feedback from SA, 50–53, *51*, 102, 106; Reichsbanner cap, 23–25, 34; RFB, 27–28; SA caps and Brown Shirt service dress, 46–53, *51*; SA caps and professionalization (1930–1934), 96, 98, 101–3, 106; SA cap with concealed helmet, 52; SA helmet prohibition, 104; SA marketing of, 60–63, *61–63*; SA Mütze (cap) of early SA, 34–37, *37*, 45–46; Stahlhelm cap and helmet, 21–23

Carl Meyer and Co., 140

Catholic Center Party, 16, 23, 33

Chemnitz police, on RFB uniform, 29

clash violence: defined, 7–8; election day (Hamburg, April 10, 1932), 165–69, 173–74; Nazi violence vs. order dichotomy, 2–3, 56–57; and SA cap with concealed helmet, 52; SA rallies and initiation of, 7–9, 29–30, 79–80, 85, 89–90, 153. *See also* Hamburg 1921–1933; mass rallies and marches

class issues: accident insurance fund, 82–83; Brown Shirts and bourgeois look, 44; Brown Shirt uniforms and cost to SA men, 47, 102, 103, 126, 144, 167–69; and food at SA rallies, 85–89, 144–45; Hamburg middle class courted by SA, 147–48, 159, 180; Hitler's exploitation of Great Depression, 135, 136, 145, 182; middle-class support for rallies, 80–83, 92, 93; of Nazi consumption and consumerism, 57–68; press as bourgeois, 3, 9, 13–14, 131; and rural-urban dichotomy, 83–84, 95, 123, 127–29; and SA rally participation, 79–85. *See also* communists and Communist party; Hamburg 1921–1933

Combat Leagues, 25

communists and Communist Party: clash violence incited by SA against, overview, 7–9; Communist Party of Germany (Kommunisitsche Partei Deutschlands [KPD]), 134; German revolution in Saxony (1924), 7; Hamburg class-based conflict in 1920s, overview, 134–36; "The Internationale," 115, 154; motorcycles used by, 79; propaganda films and depiction of, 109–18; RFB as paramilitary of, 16, 27–29; Stalinization of German Communist Party, 29. *See also* clash violence; Hamburg 1921–1933; *Hamburger Volkszeitung*; Red Front-Fighters League

Conn, Alfred: and battle of Sternschanze, 150–55, *154*; on early Brown Shirt use in Hamburg, 139–40, 177–78; first meeting with Hitler by, 140; Hamburg middle class courted by, 147–48; and Hamburg unit's marches and tactics, 89, 91, 92, 141–46, 148–50; as leader of SA brigade of Hamburg, 155–59; memoir of, as research source, 14, 132; SA joined by, 138–39

consumption and consumerism, 57–75; consumer culture and demise of democracy, 57–58; marketing and advertising by SA, 5, 11, 60–63, *61–63*, 75, 139; purchase of uniform as act of discipline, 58–59; regulated use of uniform, 63–68; revenue from uniforms, 59–63; for social control, 68–75, 104, 144
"cotton wool," 123
Cuno, Wilhelm, 135

Daily Express (British newspaper), on Brown Shirt uniforms, 167
Daluege, Kurt, 108
Dels (Truppführer), 141
Der SA Mann (publication), on Conn, 157
Dettmann (SA leader), 153
Diehl, James, 25, 26
Die SA Erobert Berlin (Bade), 108, 121–25, 127, 129
Dreckmann (Truppführer), 152

Ehrenkleid (honor garment), 68–73
Ehrhardt, Hermann, 33
election campaigns: depicted in propaganda films, 112; "Deployment of the Motor Units in Election Campaigning" (March 1932), 81; and election day clash violence (Hamburg, April 10, 1932), 165–69, 173–74; Hamburg elections (April 1932), 135, 165–69, 173–74; Hamburg rally for (May 8, 1931), 160; and Hitler Youth, 128; mass rallies and effect on voting, 77–78, 81–83, 91, 93–94; national elections (1928), 91, 95; national elections (1930), 97, 155; national elections (1933), 177–80, 182–83; as warfare, 128
Ellerhusen, Paul, 139–41, 143, 144, 150–51, 155, 179
Enneccerus (military contact of SA), 156
Erzberger, Mathias, 33
Ey, Hermann, 145, 148
Ezinger tavern (Hamburg), 161–64

Fels (SA man), 72–73
film. *See* hero-myth in literature and film
financial costs to SA men. *See* class issues
flags: early Nazi use of, 34; early swastika on, 36, *36*, 37; of Hohenzollern dynasty, 23; of Reichsbanner, 25, 26; of RFB, 28–29; Weimar Republic eagle symbol, 25, 26
Fliegerstürme (flying storm) units, 83–84
food at mass rallies, 86–89, 144–45
footwear: putties, 19, 34, 35, 59, 103; and SA professionalization, 103
Free Corps, 21, 33, 37, 39–40, 45, 139, 148
Front Line Veterans' Day (rally, 1925), 84

gender issues: female fashion of Third Reich, 4; gay men in SA, 4, 11, 40, 74; German Women's Order in Hamburg, youth group of, 156; *Kletterweste*, 48, 49, 117; masculine honor and post–World War I Weimar politics, 15, 17; masculine image at rallies, 81–82; masculinity enhanced by Brown Shirts, 42–43; Nazi women and auxiliary function, 87, 155–56; propaganda films and depiction of, 113–18
German Alpine troops, caps of, 35, 36
German Day, inception of (1921), 84
German Democratic Party, 16, 23
German Federal Archives for Documents (Bundesarchiv), 13, 34, 132
German Federal Archives for Visual Material in Koblenz (Bundesarchiv Bildarchiv Koblenz), 13
German Historical Museum in Berlin (Deutsches Historisches Museum Berlin): Brown Shirt artifact of, 41; as research source, 1–2, 13; Weimar-era uniforms in, 17, 21–23, 25, 27, 28, 29
German National Archives (Koblenz), 17
German Women's Order, youth group of, 156
Goebbels, Joseph, 107, 108, 129, 160
Göring, Hermann, 33–38, 44, 92

Grauer Rock (gray coat, Imperial Army), 68
Great Depression, 135, 136, 145, 182. *See also* class issues
Greater Hagen City News, "Do We Live in the Third Reich Already?," 98–100
Gruppe (SA groups): defined, 76; leaders of, 39, 99–100; propaganda book about, 125
Guenther, Irene, 4
Günther, Albrecht Erich, 137

Häfker (Nazi Party leader), 148, 151
Hahn, H., 165–66
Hamburg 1921–1933 (case study), 131–80; and Altona's Bloody Sunday, 169–77; and battle of Sternschanze, 150–55, *154*; City Archives of, 132; City Council elections (April 1932), 135, 166, 173–74; class-based conflict in 1920s, 134–36; Communist Party attempted revolution (1923) in, 27; Conn's SA roles in, 89, 91, 92, 132, 138–59, 177–80; geographic location and early history of, 133–34; Hamburg State Archive, 13–14; National Socialist Women's League, 155; Nazi consumption and consumerism in, 58, 60, 63–64, 71; Reichstag election violence (April 10, 1932), 165–69, 173–74; Research Center for Contemporary History, 14; SA growth in (late 1920s), 136–37; SA rallies and marches in, 77–79; and SA's dual-image construction process, 131–32, 136–37, 178–80; as traditional liberal city of Weimar Republic, 2–4, 13–14. *See also* Böckenhauer, Arthur; Conn, Alfred
Hamburger Anzeiger (newspaper): on Hamburg SA-communist clashes, 132, 162–63; as research source, 14
Hamburger Fremdenblatt (newspaper), on Hamburg SA-communist clashes, 132
Hamburger Nachrichten (newspaper): on Altona's Bloody Sunday, 169–72, 174–75; anti-communist stance of, 152, 162–63, 166; Hitler speeches covered by, 137, 141, 150; Nazi statements published in, 163; pro-Hitler stance of, 131, 132, 177; as research source, 14
Hamburger Volkszeitung (communist newspaper): on Altona's Bloody Sunday, 169–70; pro-communist stance in SA clashes, 132, 151–52, 161–62, 163–66, 167–68, 176–77; as research source, 14
Hamburgischer Correspondent (newspaper), on Hamburg SA-communist clashes, 167
Hamburg police, and SA-communist clashes, 149–53, 161–66, 169–72, 174–77
Hans Westmar, One of Many (film), 107, 109–14, 118, 121, 129
Heines, Edmund, 39–41, *43*, 45, 46, 55
Heissinger, Heinrich, 162–63
Herbst, Jürgen, 31
hero-myth in literature and film: *Die SA Erobert Berlin*, 108, 121–25, 127, 129; film of Hamburg rally (October 9, 1932), 172–73; *Hans Westmar, One of Many*, 107, 109–14, 118, 121, 129; *Hitler Youth Quex*, 107–8, 113–18, 120; as image construction, 12, 107; *Männer im Braunhemd*, 108, 125–27, 129; *SA-Mann Brand*, 107, 119–21, 129
Himmler, Heinrich, 16
Hindenburg, Paul von, 6, 126, 174
Hitler, Adolf: Brown Shirt worn by, 86; as chancellor, 174; consumption and consumerism used by, 57, 60, 64; election of (1933), 177–80, 182–83; and Hamburg SA-communist clashes, 131, 137, 140–41, 146, 150; in Imperial Army, 68; imprisonment of, 9, 33, 37–38, 44, 137, 177; male image-construction process of, 4; mass rallies and marches used as propaganda by, 11–12, 31, 56–57, 92; and material culture in fascist politics, 13; *Mein Kampf*, 9, 36; Nazi dress and opportunistic character of Nazism, 10–11, 32–33, 40–41, 44–45, 47–48, 49, 50–54, *51*; rhetoric adapted to audience by,

14; rise to power by, 2, 9–10; and SA professionalization, 95, 99–100, 104, 105; social control with uniforms by, 70. *See also* National Socialist German Worker's Party/Nazi Party
Hitler Youth: election campaign role of, 128; female branch of, 48; *Hitler Youth Quex* depiction of, 107–8, 113–18, 120; hymn of, 115; Norkus in, 107–9, 130; and SA age restrictions, 71; *SA-Mann Brand* depiction of, 119–20
Hitler Youth Quex (film), 107–8, 113–18, 120
Hoffman, Heinrich, 50
Hohenzollern dynasty, flags of, 23
Hörsing, Otto, 23
"Horst Wessel Song," 113, 121, 160–61
housing: in Hamburg, 156–59, 164–65; at mass rallies, 89–91

Ihde (SA man), 145
Illustrierter Beobachter (SA journal), 78
Imperial Army: brown fabric used in uniforms of, 10, 21, 24; and early Brown Shirt designs, 34, 38, 41–42; flags of, 23; *Grauer Rock* of, 68; jacket of, 24; and Nazi rally tactics, 92; SA officers and overlap with, 97; and SA professionalization, 97, 103; and Stahlhelm uniforms, 21
"The Internationale" (communist hymn), 115, 154

jackets and coats: *Grauer Rock* of Imperial Army, 68; *Kletterweste*, 48, *49*, 117; *Lettow Hemden* as jacket, 39; and SA professionalization (1930–1934), 96, 101–6; Stahlhelm jackets, 21–23. *See also* Brown Shirt uniforms; Windbreakers
Jagow, Dietrich von, 33
Jochmann, Werner, 14, 132
Joseph, Nathan, 68, 73

Kaiser, Susan B., 54
Kampfbinde (battle band), 36. *See also* armbands
Kampfzeit (time of struggle), 96, 107
Kasper (Communist Party member), 168
Kletterweste (climbing vest), 48, *49*, 117
Klintzsch, Hans Ulrich, 33
Koch (SA man), 171
Koch, Karl W. H., 41, 45, 108, 125–27, 129
Kosegarten (Sturmführer), 145
Krispin, Olly, 156

League of German Girls (Bund Deutscher Mädel [BDM]), 48, 113–18
lederhosen (leather shorts), 47–48, *49*
Lenin, V., 27
Lettow Hemden (Lettow Shirts), 38–41, *38*, 126
Lettow-Vorbeck, Paul von, 38, *38*
literature. *See* hero-myth in literature and film
Longerich, Peter, 2, 70, 157
Ludendorff, Erich, 6, 139
Lühr, Hans, 142, 144, 178
Lutze, Viktor, 45, 46, 66–67

Männer im Braunhemd (Men in the Brown Shirt [Koch]), 108, 125–27, 129
Marxer, Otto, 39, 40
Marxists and Marxism. *See* communists and Communist Party
mass rallies and marches, 76–94; "cotton wool," 123; food, housing, and laundry, 86–91, 144–45, 155–59, 164–65; Nuremberg national rallies, 86, 87–91, 144, 146; and rural-urban dichotomy, 83–84, 95, 123, 127–29; SA hierarchy (1926), 76–77, 80; SA hierarchy (1931), 99–100; SA mobility, 77–84; SA's growing military role, 76–77, 93–94; songs, music, and amplification tactics, 81, 84, 86, 93, 113, 121, 142–43, 145–49, 152, 160–61; spectacle of, 84–93; as visual propaganda, 11–12, 31, 56–57, 76–79, 81–85, 91–93
material culture and social control. *See* Brown Shirt uniforms; consumption and consumerism; social control

May Day (1923) celebrations, 33–35, 53, 84
McElligott, Anthony, 6–7, 132, 134, 178
Mein Kampf (Hitler), 9, 36
Meyer, Carl, 140
Mollenhauer (Truppführer), 157
Möller (Gruppenführer), 141
motorcycles: in Hamburg, 147–48, 150–52, 159; propaganda films and depiction of, 111; SA rallies and use of, 79–82, 84
motor vehicles (private), for SA rallies, 80–83, 171
Müller (retailer), 45, 47
Munich police, on Nazi professionalization, 104–5
music and songs: "Horst Wessel Song," 113, 121, 160–61; "The Internationale," 115, 154; mass rally tactics of, 81, 84, 86, 93, 142–43, 145–49, 152
Mussolini, Benito, 30

National Socialist German Worker's Party/Nazi Party (NSDAP): early image of militaristic discipline, 11–12; early SA as postwar paramilitary, 32; election depicted in propaganda film, 112; and Free Corps, 21, 33, 37, 39–40, 45, 139, 148; German Women's Order, youth group of, 156; in hiding following Beer Hall Putsch (November 9, 1923), 9, 33, 37–38, 44, 137, 177; "Horst Wessel Song" of, 113, 121, 160–61; inception of (1919), 32; May Day (1923) celebrations, 33–35, 53, 84; National Socialist Motor Vehicle Drivers' Corp (Nationalsozialistisches Kraftfahrkorps [NSKK]), 81–82, 102; National Socialist Women's League (Hamburg), 155–56; opportunistic character of, 10–11; party membership required of SA members, 97; political culture shaped by Weimar culture, 7; rebirth of (1926), 47, 50; SA absorbed by Nazi military, 106; Salzburg meeting (1926), 37, 44, 45; SS, 20, 74; violence vs. order dichotomy of, 2–3, 56–57. *See also* Brown Shirt uniforms; clash violence; election campaigns; Hamburg 1921–1933; hero-myth in literature and film; Hitler, Adolf; Stormtroopers
neckties, 44, 60–63
neo-Nazis, modern-day, 183
Nordischer Nachrichtendients (Nordic news service), on Hamburg SA-communist clashes, 161
Norkus, Herbert, 107–9, 130
NSDAP. *See* National Socialist German Worker's Party/Nazi Party
Nur beim Zeugmeister slogan, 62, 62
Nuremberg national rallies: 1927, 86; 1929, 87–91, 144, 146

Omtjes (farmer), 145, 148

Paschke (Sturmführer), 156–57
Pfeffer von Salomon, Franz: on Brown Shirt uniforms, 48–50, 49, 52–53; consumption and consumerism of SA, 60, 64, 67; and Hamburg SA-communist clashes, 141, 143; and mass rallies, 76, 80–81, 86–90, 92; SA inner strife under, 73–74; as SA leader (1926), 45, 47; and SA professionalization, 95–96, 101; social control and uniforms, 69–70
physically disabled, prohibited from SA, 70–72, 105
police: Berlin police on Nazi professionalization, 97–98; Chemnitz police on RFB uniform, 29; Hamburg police and SA tactics, 149–53, 161–66, 169–72, 174–77; Munich police on Nazi professionalization, 104–5. *See also* clash violence
professionalization of Stormtroopers: professionalization of SA under Röhm (1930–1934), 95–96; SA service dress changes, 95–105; transition to propaganda army, 95; volunteer-to-propaganda army transition, 12
propaganda: advertisement vs., 61; Nazi propaganda in literature and film, 12, 107–30, 172–73;

visual vs. verbal, 45. *See also* consumption and consumerism; Hamburg 1921–1933; hero-myth in literature and film; visual propaganda and image construction
Prussia: Brown Shirt prohibition in, 65–68, 98, 149; "Prussia's Glory" (military march), 142–43
putties, 19, 34, 35, 59, 103

Red Front-Fighters League (Roter Frontkämpferbund [RFB]): and Hamburg SA-communist clashes, 151; propaganda films and depiction of, 110, 122; Weimar-era uniforms of, 16, 17, 27–29, *30*, 32
Reich Main Security Office, 16
Reichsbanner Schwarz-Rot-Gold (Imperial Banner Black-Red-Gold): and Hamburg SA clash violence, 153; Weimar-era uniforms of, 16, 23–28, *26*, 30, 31, 34, 35, 126
Reichsparteitage (Nazi nationwide party conventions), 85
Reichswehr (German army, post–World War I), 97, 99, 105
Research Center for History (Hamburg), 132
Reserve SA, 58, 71
Röhm, Ernst: Brown Shirt cut introduced by associate of, 11; on consumption and consumerism, 60, 74; execution of, 40; and Hamburg SA-communist clashes, 167, 169; and professionalization of SA (1930–1934), 95–96, 99–106; rallies and marches, 81–82, 92; as SA chief of staff, 11, 53, 74; as SA deputy leader (1923), 37–38, 44; at Salzburg meeting (1924), 44
Rosenhaft, Eve, 7–8
Rossbach, Gerhard, 37–38, 40, 44, 95, 126–27
Rossol, Nadine, 7
RZM (SA Reichszeugmeisterei), 59–63, *63*, 65, 67

SA. *See* Stormtroopers
Saalschutz Abteilung (SA forerunner), 36
SA-Mann Brand (film), 107, 119–21, 129
Sam Browne belt, 17, 19–20, 23, 25, 28, 29, 34
SA orders (SA Befehle [SABE]): August 20, 1929, 90; August 25, 1927, 71; "Bekleidung" (July 7, 1932), 101–3; "Deployment of the Motor Units in Election Campaigning" (March 1932), 81; "Dienstanzug, Verfügung" (September 22, 1932), 103–4; "Discipline" (November 7, 1926), 69–70; "Flugwesen" (July 7, 1932), 83; "Head Protection" (August 1930), 52; June 5, 1930, 65; "Massenverpflegung-Allgemeines" (June 20, 1929), 87; "Motorstürme" (April 1, 1930), 80–81; Number One, 76, 93; Number Three ("SA and Public [Propaganda]," November 3, 1926), 44–45; Number Five (November 28, 1931), 99–100; Number Ten (November 14, 1926), 46, 47, 64, 70, 72, 73; "Reichsparteitag 1929 Massenverpflegung" (June 25, 1929), 88–89; SA inception documented by, 13
SA-Stulle (sandwich), 87
SA Verordnungsblatt (leaflet), 60
SA Wirtschaftsstelle (Economic Office), 46–47
Schill-Jugend youth organization, 39
Schirach, Baldur von, 108
Schlageter Free Corps, 148
Schlieper, Wilhelm Hans Karl, 162–63
Schrotzenberger (SA man), 144
Schumann, Dirk, 7–8
Schwerd, Friedrich, 22
Seitz, Franz, 119
Seldte, Franz, 20, 24
Severing, Carl, 68
Shoah, SA crimes of, 3
shoulder straps, 1, 17, 19–20, 46, 58–63, 126, 152
Siemens, Daniel, 3, 27
social control, Brown Shirt uniform as honor garment, 68–75, 104, 144. *See also* consumption and consumerism; visual propaganda and image construction

Social Democratic Party (*Sozialdemokratische Partei Deutschlands* [SPD]): and Hamburg SA-communist clashes, 134–35, 154; reaction to Nazi professionalization, 96–100, 104–5; secular festivals of, 84; uniforms of, 20, 23, 26
Solmitz, Luise, 55, 179
SS (Schutzstaffel), 20, 74
Stahlhelm Bund der Frontsoldaten (Steel Helmet League of Frontline Soldiers): and Hamburg SA-communist clashes, 176; and mass rallies, 84; and SA professionalization, 95, 104; Weimar-era uniforms of, 16, 17, 20–25, 24, 28, 30, 31, 34, 44
Steinhoff, Hans, 113
Stein (SA man), 144, 179
Stennes, Walter, 158
Sternschanze, battle of, 150–55, *154*
Stormtrooper Families (Wackerfuss), 3–4
Stormtroopers (Sturmabteilung [SA]): age and health restrictions, 70–72, 105; and brown uniforms of Imperial Army, 10–11; civil war threat by, 95, 98, 100, 104, 165; cultural history approach to, 3–7, 10–11; early SA as postwar paramilitary, 32; gray coats and caps of (1920–1924), 9–10; khaki shirt of (1926), 10; money management under Conn, 157–58; in Munich (1923), *37*; as paramilitary arm of Nazi Party (1933), 2; as professional army, 12, 95–106; research sources for, 13–14; RZM, 59–63, *63*, 65, 67; *SA Verordnugsblatt*, 60; SA Wirtschaftsstelle, 59. *See also* Brown Shirt uniforms; clash violence; Hamburg 1921–1933; hero-myth in literature and film; mass rallies and marches; professionalization of Stormtroopers; SA orders
Strasser, Gregor, 137, 146, 157–58
Stratigakos, Despina, 55
Stürme (SA storms): defined, 76–77, 80; propaganda films and depiction of, 110–13, 121, 124, 127
symbolism: black swastika on flags and armbands, 36; Brown Shirt as cultural symbolism, 54–55, 68, 85, 90; of Brown Shirt ranks and insignia, 53, 73; early Nazi use of armbands and flags, 34; Hamburg taverns marked as Nazi, 148; uniform insignia and SA professionalization, 100–101, 103; Weimar-era visual symbols of militarization, 16–20

Thälmann, Ernst, *30*
Thiez, Artur, 166
Third Reich: and post–World War I ideology, 15–16; Sam Browne belt of uniforms, 20
Thor Steinar (retailer), 183
ties (neckties), 44, 60–63
tobacco prohibition, 72
transportation: airplanes, 83–84; bicycles, 39, 40, 76–79, 83–84, 92–93, 125, 140, 166; motorcycles, 79–82, 84, 111, 147–48, 150–52, 159; National Socialist Motor Vehicle Drivers' Corp (Nationalsozialistisches Kraftfahrkorps, NSKK), 81–82, 102; private motor vehicles, 80–83, 171; trucks, 79–80, 82, 84, 87, 89, 92, 93
Treaty of Versailles: as emasculating, 42; German Army size restricted by, 138; and Stahlhelm, 21; travel restrictions of, 88
trousers and breeches: lederhosen allowed for Bavarians, 47–48, *49*; of Reichsbanner, 25; of RFB, 29; SA breeches and sports clothing, 36–37; and SA professionalization, 105; Weimar-era uniformity of uniforms, 18–19
Trzebiatowsky (Gruppenführer), 141

U.S. Army, on Wehrmacht uniform, 35

violence: increase in Nazi attacks after 1930, 95–97; Nazi violence vs. order dichotomy, 2–3, 56–57; and post–World War I

ideology, 15–16; SA punishment and threat of, 69–70. *See also* clash violence
visual propaganda and image construction: Brown Shirt uniform as honor garment, 68–73, 104, 144; Brown Shirt uniforms and effect on voting, 53–54; early SA uniforms and visual strategy, 32–33; hero-myth in literature and film as, 12, 107; male image-construction process, 4; Nazis' early image of militaristic discipline, 11–12; professionalization of SA as, 97–98; rallies and marches by SA, 11–12, 31, 56–57, 76–79, 81–85, 91–93; SA's age and health restrictions as, 70–72, 105; and slenderness, 5; verbal propaganda vs., 45. *See also* Brown Shirt uniform; gender issues; Hamburg 1921–1933; hero-myth in literature and film
Völkischer Beobachter (Nazi newspaper): distribution of, 78; on Hamburg SA-communist clashes, 157
Vorwärts (social democratic newspaper), "The Organization of the Killers," 96–97
Voss, Carla, 155–56
voting. *See* election campaigns

Wackerfuss, Andrew, 3–4, 131, 132, 169
Waentig, Heinrich, 65
Wagner, Winifred, 38
Wandrey (Gruppenführer), 141
Weber (Sturmführer), 58
Wehrmacht uniform, 35
Wehrwolf (paramilitary organization), 138–39
Weimar (city): mass rallies in, 47, 91, 92; and Nazi rebirth (1926), 47, 50
Weimar-era political uniforms (1918–1933), 15–30; and clash violence, 29–30; outdoor/sports clothing for, 17–19, 23; paramilitary prevalence in Weimar politics and uniformity of uniforms, 16–20; post–World War I political and cultural atmosphere, 15–16; Reichsbanner uniforms, 23–26, *26*, 30; RFB uniforms, 16, 17, 27–30, *30*, 32; Stahlhelm uniforms, 16, 17, 20–25, *24*, 28, 30, 31
Weimar Republic: Brown Shirts and fascist symbolism during (1926–1933), overview, 1–2, 11, 13, 14; clash violence, overview, 2–3, 7–9; cultural history approach to, 3–7, 10–11; eagle symbol on flag of, 25, *26*; end of, 181–83; final free national elections of, 174, 177; Hitler's rise to power, overview, 2, 9–10; as *Kampfzeit*, 96, 107; Nazis' early propaganda in literature and film during, 12; Prussia and Brown Shirt prohibitions, 66; Reichsbanner's loyalty to, 25, *26*. *See also* Brown Shirt uniforms; clash violence; class issues; Hamburg 1921–1933; Hitler, Adolf; visual propaganda and image construction; Weimar (city); Weimar-era political uniforms
Wenzler, Franz, 109
Wessel, Horst, 107, 108, 113, 121, 129, 160–61
Wessenmeier, Theodor, 157
Windbreakers: early SA use of, 34–36, *37*, 44, 47; Reichsbanner's use of, 17–18, 25; RFB's use of, 28–29; Stahlhelm's use of, 21, 23, *24*; uniformity ordered by Hitler, 64
World War I: and consumer culture, 5–6; Hitler as Bavarian soldier during, 48; postwar ideology of masculine honor, 15, 17; postwar ideology of violence, 15–16; Reichswehr (German army, postwar), 97, 99, 105; and SA cap design, 35; Treaty of Versailles, 21, 42, 88, 138

youth groups: German Women's Order, 156; League of German Girls, 48, 113–18; Schill-Jugend, 39. *See also* Hitler Youth

Zierener, Carl, 166

TORSTEN HOMBERGER was born and raised at the end of the Cold War in Hagenow, a small town in today's northern German state of Mecklenburg-Vorpommern in former East Germany. After the fall of the Iron Curtain, he attended college in the United States, eventually earning a PhD in modern European history from Washington State University. Homberger, his wife, and their two children live in Kearney, Nebraska, where he is currently employed as an assistant professor at the University of Nebraska at Kearney.